ISLANDS IN THE SKY

Borgo Press Books by Gary Westfahl

Islands in the Sky: The Space Station Theme in Science Fiction Literature
The Other Side of the Sky: An Annotated Bibliography of Space Stations in Science Fiction, 1869-1993

Other Books by Gary Westfahl

Cosmic Engineers: A Study of Hard Science Fiction
Foods of the Gods: Eating and the Eaten in Fantasy and Science Fiction (co-edited with George Slusser and Eric S. Rabkin)
The Greenwood Encyclopedia of Science Fiction and Fantasy: Themes, Works, and Wonders (edited)
Hugo Gernsback and the Century of Science Fiction
Immortal Engines: Life Extension and Immortality in Science Fiction and Fantasy (co-edited with Slusser and Rabkin)
The Mechanics of Wonder: The Creation of the Idea of Science Fiction.
No Cure for the Future: Disease and Medicine in Science Fiction and Fantasy (co-edited with Slusser)
Nursery Realms: Children in the Worlds of Science Fiction, Fantasy, and Horror (co-edited with Slusser)
Science Fiction and Market Realities (co-edited with Slusser and Rabkin)
Science Fiction and the Two Cultures: Essays on Bridging the Gap between the Sciences and the Humanities (co-edited with Slusser)
Science Fiction, Canonization, Marginalization, and the Academy (co-edited with Slusser)
Science Fiction, Children's Literature, and Popular Culture: Coming of Age in Fantasyland
Science Fiction Quotations: From the Inner Mind to the Outer Limits (edited)
Space and Beyond: The Frontier Theme in Science Fiction (edited)
Unearthly Visions: Approaches to Science Fiction and Fantasy Art (co-edited with Slusser and Kathleen Church Plummer)
World Weavers: Globalization, Science Fiction, and the Cybernetic Revolution (co-edited with Wong Kin Yuen and Amy Chan Kit Sze)
Worlds Enough and Time: Explorations of Time in Science Fiction and Fantasy (co-edited with Slusser and David Leiby)

ISLANDS IN THE SKY

THE SPACE STATION THEME IN SCIENCE FICTION LITERATURE

Second Edition, Revised and Updated

by

Gary Westfahl

THE BORGO PRESS

An Imprint of Wildside Press LLC

MMIX

*I.O. Evans Studies in the Philosophy
and Criticism of Literature*
ISSN 0271-9061

Number Fifteen

CONTENTS

To my children,

ALLISON AND JEREMY,

who I hope will someday
accompany me on a
visit to a space station;

and to my wife,

LYNNE,

who will probably prefer
to stay home.

Introduction to the Second Edition

My research into space stations began in 1986, for reasons discussed below, and soon generated a 1988 article published in a critical anthology and, in 1989, a first version of this book, rejected by one publisher on the grounds that its subject matter was too narrowly focused to merit publication. In response, I lengthened the manuscript to incorporate additional research and added a "Polemical Introduction" designed in part to argue against the attitude that had inspired its rejection; this version was accepted by Borgo Press in 1991 and updated one final time in 1994. After the risible editing work of another individual was rejected, Robert Reginald personally prepared the manuscript for publication; his principal modification was to replace my parenthetical page references with full-scale endnotes, adding twelve pages to the book. In April, 1996, the volume finally appeared; however, due to the increasing difficulties being experienced by Borgo Press, the book received relatively little notice and distribution, and it fell out of print when Borgo Press ceased operations in 1998.

Still, despite ongoing work on other projects, space stations remained an important aspect of my career. In 1997, I was approached by Gregory Benford and George Zebrowski, editors of a forthcoming anthology to be entitled *Skylife: Space Habitats in Story and Science*, to compile an annotated bibliography of works involving space stations for that anthology, eventually published in 2000. Working more closely with Zebrowski, and adjusting myself to his broader concept of habitations in space, I reacquainted myself with old texts and learned about some new ones while preparing the bibliography, which appeared as the anthology's final section, "Space Stations and Space Habitats: A Selective Bibliography."

Then, in 1999, I was contacted by PBS producer Diana Dresser, who was working with Stephen Lyons on a forthcoming episode of *Nova*, "Stationed in the Stars," which would analyze the difficult process of building the international space station; she wanted to find a copy of my book and get some advice on finding classic illustrations of space stations to use on the program and its website. After several discussions, I was also commissioned to write an essay on space stations, "Inspired by Science Fiction," for the Nova Online website about the episode; as of 2009, it remains available at:

www.pbs.org/wgbh/nova/station/inspired.html

Finally, in 2000, I received an e-mail message from Patrick Gyger of the Maison d'Ailleurs, who had just received a grant from the European Space Agency to hire researchers to examine science fiction as a source of new ideas for scientific projects—precisely the sort of practical use of science fiction that I had long advocated. With my background, I naturally agreed to write a report on space stations for the project, entitled Innovative Technologies from Science Fiction, and a few ideas presented in that report were later posted on the ITSF website (www.itsf.org). I also agreed to anonymously contribute a brief overview of space stations in science fiction to the European Space Agency brochure BR-176, Innovative Technologies from Science Fiction for Space Applications, which appeared in June 2001 (a downloadable version is available at the website).

All in all, contemplating all this evidence of continuing interest in the subject, and having also received occasional inquiries from individuals hoping to find copies of the book, I eventually resolved to seek a publisher for a Second Edition of *Islands in the Sky*. Originally, I envisioned a thoroughgoing revision that would significantly expand and update the main text and remove the "Polemical Introduction," since it seemed to irritate some reviewers and draw their attention away from the materials presented thereafter. However, after a graduate student read the book and remarked that she had especially appreciated the first chapter, I have resolved to retain it. This is not, by the way, the first time that a piece of writing irksome to my colleagues has been warmly welcomed by those outside their circle. Then, after rereading the book, I decided to leave the text basically as it was, for two reasons. First, with two massive projects on my agenda, I would have found it difficult to undertake and complete a massive revision in a timely manner. More importantly, beyond adding scattered references to works that appeared after 1994, or to works originally overlooked in my research, I could think of nothing significantly new or different to add to my original research and analysis.

Still, to provide purchasers of the original edition with an incentive to purchase the Second Edition as well, I did make some significant additions to Chapter 13, discussing a number of newer works. And to further expand the book, I added my article for Nova Online, retitled and based upon my original text instead of the edited version now online, as well as my previously unpublished report to the ITSF and the brief overview I anonymously contributed to its brochure, as three new chapters. In some respects, to be sure, they only reiterate material that the book has already covered, though there are differences in organization and emphasis; for example, while I am generally inclined to accept Edward Everett Hale's "The Brick Moon" as the first story about a space station, the assignment to focus on the interaction of science and science fiction for Nova Online made it expedient to downplay Hale and instead begin with Konstantin Tsiolkovsky. The new chapters also include references to sixteen additional works not mentioned in the first edition, and if nothing else, their presence means that I am no longer publishing a book with an inauspicious thirteen chapters, which may make the Second Edition luckier than the first.

The manuscript of this book has been prepared from the original files sent to Borgo Press, thus reinstating the concise system of parenthetical page references to works listed in a concluding bibliography. I have reviewed the entire text and made minor adjustments in the language, principally to eliminate references to "recent" science fiction stories that can no longer be so described. However, with the noted exceptions of the expanded chapter and the added chapters, the book is more or less identical to the one originally published in 1996. The only other difference worth mentioning is that my book-length annotated bibliography, *The Other Side of the Sky: An Annotated Bibliography of Space Stations in Science Fiction, 1869-1993*, originally envisioned as an accompaniment to the volume but indefinitely delayed, will now be appearing in print, also from Wildside Press. Its principal value is that it discusses hundreds of relevant works which this book did not have the space to discuss.

—Gary Westfahl
Riverside, California
May, 2009

Preface

by Gregory Benford

About 370 million years ago, a mere eye-blink on the scale of planetary time, a little-understood catastrophe profoundly disturbed life in the sea.

Some believe immense meteors struck the oceans, sending great tsunamis crashing into the reefs around the continents. We do know that after the disruptions, the first scaly creatures began to waddle through the steamy swamps of Greenland. They looked like oddly shaped fishes on legs, fleshy fins adapted for walking. They fed on insects and their first expeditions were tentative. Like the first land plants, they still used the seas for breeding, and so returned to their ancient home regularly.

They ventured into an alien environment by carrying as much of the ocean with them as they could. Though they learned to breathe the rich, warm air, they developed methods for holding fluids inside for bodily regulation.

Today our own blood still sings with the same salinity as the sea. Our hearts knock with an ancient rhythm. Bony defenses have become more subtle supports for our swollen heads. We echo many of the defenses those early amphibians used to seal themselves against the threat of dehydration on land.

Now the recent disruption of technology has pushed our species out into a raw, threatening environment. We seek to slip free of gravity's cruel grip and live in the aching vacuum of space. And we use similar strategies of enclosure, bringing much of our world and our selves with us.

Yet here I must agree with Gary Westfahl that analogies are a trap when discussing stations in space. Nautical terminology haunts space travel fiction generally; I've used it often myself. Harking back to the previous great age of exploration seems natural, with a silky inevitability.

But the space station is an awkward subject for such graceful, sweeping terms. It holds elements of both land and sea, of openness and closure—just as the early struggling amphibians evolved by using what they could of the sea-learned regulatory ways, but deforming themselves to use the fresh freedoms of land.

Perhaps this bivalence is central to the intermediate quality of space stations in fiction, why they so often combine masculine technology, "right-angled in all its particulars," with feminine curves, so that Kubrick's station in *2001: A Space Odyssey* is "a cold engineering triumph which evokes dainty beauty."

Such unexpected insights abound in this first study of the subject. I was particularly struck by his detailed treatment of Louis Charbonneau's neglected *Down to Earth* (1967). It stresses the abandonment of hologram projected images of earth's field and stream, which are used to comfort the station inhabitants, for the hard reality of life in a hollowed-out asteroid. Much space station fiction is strikingly pastoral—a fact Westfahl underlines to devastating effect. Confrontation of unwavering facts is conspicuously lacking in much science fiction, not merely that dealing with space stations.

Westfahl hammers out many cogent and striking observations: on the sources of conflict in such fiction; on their own studied, domestic rejection of the cold vacuum only meters away; on their conspicuous lack of imagination (especially considering the great freedom minimal gravity allows); on the "truly incredible...claims that such habitats will in fact function as the perfect environment for the rebirth of old cultures"; on clear signs that sf writers fear space stations and everything they might represent; on signs that the genre "is covertly committed to the exploration of the phony unknown."

There are serious charges, amply backed up. They could only be made through deep scholarship, such as is seldom seen these days.

I echo his observation here: the understanding of science fiction requires not new theories, but new data. The field is vast and complex, and best rewards detailed study. His analogy with the sciences is striking: "Just as Darwin both studied barnacles in excruciating detail and provided a grand and comprehensive theory of evolution, true literary scholars must be both bibliographers and critics." So I was pleased to see the companion bibliography, *The Other Side of the Sky*, a thorough look at the surprising broadly use of space stations in sf.

Dr. Westfahl has proved here that less can well be more. Taking a small area, he has discerned major themes and evasions in the whole genre. His discoveries are sobering. Yet the successes he finds also amplify into a vision of what this field can do well—and that is, finally, the more telling observation.

—Gregory Benford
November 24, 1990

Acknowledgments

I must first thank Dr. T. Lindsay Moore, formerly of Claremont Graduate University, who, as discussed below, inspired me to begin work on this project. I appreciated the capable assistance of Clifford Wurfel, Karen Mokohoro, Kristy Layton, Gladys Murphy, and the other staff at the J. Lloyd Eaton Collection of Science Fiction and Fantasy in the Rivera Library of the University of California, Riverside, in tracking down the numerous science fiction novels and stories discussed here; I single out for special thanks the indefatigable Daryl F. Mallett, formerly of the Eaton Collection, who was particularly helpful in solving various research problems. (More information on how I researched this project is provided in the introduction to *The Other Side of the Sky*.)

In completing this study, numerous friends and colleagues provided assistance or encouragement. Bradford Lyau and Karen Anderson drew upon their formidable knowledge of science fiction to suggest some relevant texts; a conversation with Gregory Benford at the Ninth Annual Eaton Conference on Science Fiction and Fantasy provided a key insight; and at the same gathering I spoke with a gentleman whose name I cannot recall who told me about the unique space station in Michael Moorcock's *The Fireclown*. Suzan Rutledge at UMI Research Press presented some helpful suggestions and Brett Cooke of Texas A&M University offered some encouraging words; and while he made no direct contributions to this book, I must also thank William Spengemann, now Professor Emeritus of English at Dartmouth College, for serving as my adviser at Claremont Graduate University and contributing greatly to my ability to study science fiction and organize and write a book on that subject.

Thanks are due to George Slusser and Eric S. Rabkin who, as conference coordinators, allowed me to present a paper about my early research into space stations at the aforementioned Eaton Conference, and who, as editors of the critical anthology, *Mindscapes: The Geographies of Imagined Worlds*, accepted a later version of that paper, "Islands in the Sky: Space Stations in the Universe of Science Fiction," for inclusion in that volume; and George Slusser, who has long served as Curator of the Eaton Collection, must be additionally acknowledged as a continuing inspiration in all my work in science fiction. I also thank Edward James, editor of *Foundation: The International Review of Science Fiction*, for agreeing to publish a version of Chapters 10 and 11 in that journal under the title "Small Worlds and Strange Tomorrows: The Icon of the Space Station in Science Fiction," and for his generous support for my other research projects. And the letters that came to *Foundation* in response to that article—particularly one by David Gillon in No. 53—were helpful in preparing a final version of this manuscript. I also thank Robert Reginald of Borgo Press for agreeing to publish the first edition of this book, and for his labors in preparing the original manuscript, including the correction of several errors.

Finally, I owe a great deal of thanks to Patrick J. Moran and other friendly and supportive co-workers at the Learning Center of the University of California, Riverside; David Werner and the other faculty of the University of La Verne's Educational Programs in Corrections, also for friendship and support; and to my wife Lynne and children Allison and Jeremy, who were obliged to endure my absences from home and occasional distracted expressions as I researched and wrote this book.

—Gary Westfahl
Riverside, California
December, 1994

For the Second Edition:

First, I gratefully acknowledge permission from the European Space Agency and its Innovative Technologies from Science Fiction project, as conveyed by Patrick Gyger, to republish my ITSF report on space stations as the fifteenth chapter of this edition. Persons interested in ITSF should visit its website, www.itsf.org, for further information and a downloadable brochure which includes my anonymous contribution, "Space Stations and Space Colonies." I should also thank Gregory Benford, George Zebrowski, Diana Dresser, and Patrick Gyger, for their noted assistance in helping to maintain my interest in space stations during the last decade with their assignments.

For ongoing support and friendship, numerous colleagues should be thanked; those not already mentioned in the previous section include Ivan Adamovic, Richard Bleiler, George F. Butler, Amy Chan, John Clute, Martin Coleman, Melissa Conway, Arthur B. Evans, Joan Gordon, John Grant, Donald M. Hassler, Veronica Hollinger, Fiona Kelleghan, Mark R. Kelly, David Langford, Rob Latham, Farah Mendlesohn, Kathleen Church Plummer, David Pringle, Andy Sawyer, Darrell Schweitzer, David Seed, Fred Shapiro, and Wong Kin Yuen. Thanks are due to John Betancourt and the others at Wildside Press who assisted in the preparation of this volume. And as always, my co-workers at the Learning Center and Educational Programs in Corrections, my wife Lynne Westfahl, my children Jeremy Westfahl and Allison Westfahl Kong, and my son-in-law Steven Kong, merit grateful recognition.

—Gary Westfahl
Riverside, California
May, 2009

PART ONE

PARAMETERS

1. *Beyond the Planet Earth*:
A Polemical Introduction

I am tempted to introduce this book with a single sentence: I have examined over 500 novels, stories, films and television programs about space stations, and I have some interesting things to say about them. Many people, I know, would be happy to read a book with such an introduction, and those readers should feel free to skip this chapter and begin with the next one. However, I also hope to attract at least two other kinds of readers: first, the scientists, engineers, and policymakers who have worked on the international space station and may work on similar projects in the future, and second, literary critics. To persuade those particular readers, I am obliged to be more loquacious.

Perhaps I should begin by explaining exactly why I initially chose this subject. As everyone should know, the United States, along with the European Space Agency, Japan, Canada, and Russia, has been working on building and occupying what can claim to be the world's first space station—since the previous efforts, America's Skylab and the Soviet Union's Salyut and Mir, were little more than modified space vehicles. In 1985, a friend of mine, T. Lindsay Moore, then a government professor at Claremont Graduate University, was working as a consultant to the Jet Propulsion Laboratory and the National Aeronautics and Space Administration, advising them during the four-party negotiations that would decide on the management structure—that is, the government—of the proposed space station. Anxious to pursue every conceivable line of inquiry, he asked me to look at space stations in science fiction to see if these stories could provide useful ideas and insights.

As I must hasten to add, I never received any money from these agencies for my efforts, although I worked hard as part of Dr. Moore's project and contributed several suggestions; and it is probably just as well, for if word had leaked out that I was in any way on the government payroll, I might have been the recipient of a

"Golden Fleece" award. One can easily imagine former Senator Proxmire's righteous indignation: imagine spending taxpayers' money to pay someone to read science fiction! And yet, the concept is not as absurd as it might seem.

Building a space station, after all, is not a simple or inexpensive proposition. Before a space station can be successful, a number of problems must be confronted: the continuing need to justify the expense of the project to a skeptical Congress and an indifferent public; the search for the most efficient design and method of construction; the task of ensuring the station's safety against natural disaster and armed attack; and the difficulty of planning and implementing a fair and workable management structure for a multinational endeavor. As a matter of prudence, any possible source of information that might help resolve some of these problems should be consulted—even, I would argue, discussions of space stations in science fiction.

The authors of science fiction usually, though not always, have a good scientific background and an interest in scientific matters. They constitute a close-knit community who read each other's stories, frequently correspond, and regularly meet at science fiction conventions and informal gatherings. As a result, science fiction writers are regularly borrowing, criticizing, or modifying each other's ideas. As John W. Campbell, Jr., said about rocketry in "The Science of Science-Fiction," "Genuine engineering minds have considered the problems [of rocket spaceships], mulled them over, argued them back and forth in stories, and worked out the basic principles that will most certainly appear in the first ships built" (5-6).

Suppose that a scientist or administrator working on the space station were told that an intelligent and knowledgeable group of people had been regularly meeting to discuss the possible designs and functions of a space station, and that records had been kept of those meetings. That person might well be interested in looking at those records, since they might contain some valuable concepts and suggestions. And this is exactly one way, I submit, that the modern genre of science fiction can be construed: as a continuing brainstorming session on scientific ideas and possibilities. For that reason, it is perfectly logical to consult science fiction if someone is preparing a new scientific project.

Literary critics may protest at this point that this approach to works of fiction is reductionist and demeaning; with all the important and meaningful purposes that literature can achieve, how can one look at these works as nothing more than depositories of practical ideas and useful suggestions? However, this attitude is first absurd by its very nature: however much critics of certain schools would care to deny it, literary texts are, inescapably, products of a particular time and situation and provide valuable information about the contexts that produced them. And looking at literature from a utilitarian perspective in no way prevents or denigrates other examinations of a strictly literary nature; in fact, a scholar preparing a history of nineteenth-century whaling could—and should—consult *Moby Dick* without in any way compromising or lessening its literary stature. Finally, this attitude is particularly absurd in the case of science fiction, because from its beginning as a genre, *critics and writers have repeatedly celebrated science fiction as, among other things, a valuable source of scientific information and ideas.*

Two of the major critical voices who developed and shaped the tradition of modern science fiction—Hugo Gernsback and John W. Campbell, Jr.—explicitly endorsed this function of the genre. Gernsback firmly believed that science fiction stories were worthwhile because they might offer useful ideas to working scientists: as he wrote in one editorial, "Imagination and Reality," "An author may not know how to build or make his invention of a certain apparatus or instrument, but he may know how to predict, and often does predict, the use of such a one. The professional inventor or scientist then comes along, gets the stimulus from the story and promptly responds with the material invention" (579). Campbell broadened this perspective by arguing that science fiction could consider not only new inventions but how they might affect an imagined future society, useful information for policy makers considering the introduction of those inventions; he stated his position in an essay, "The Place of Science Fiction":

> For a long time, through all history, if men tried a new idea, and it proved to be an exceedingly sour one, the result was disastrous to a relatively small group. Unfortunately, a small group, today, may be able to try out some interesting idea that happens to involve the annihilation of the planet Earth. The old method of trial and error comes to a point where it is no longer usable—the point where one more error means no more trials....
>
> Science fiction can provide for a science-based culture...a means of practicing anything in imagination—suicide, murder, anything whatever....
>
> [Some] errors of detail in prophecy are inevitable; the important aspect of imaginative exploration

of areas of no practice is that the basic outlines of the consequences of a particular course of action can be worked out. (16)

In addition to these critical voices, major authors of science fiction have also testified that such practical purposes influenced their own writing. Two examples specifically involve space stations: in "I Remember Babylon," Arthur C. Clarke wrote, "Back in 1945, while a radar officer in the Royal Air Force, I had the only original idea of my life...it occurred to me that an artificial satellite would be a wonderful place for a television transmitter...I kept plugging [the idea] in my books" (2). And David Brin described his story, "Tank Farm Dynamo," as a "propaganda piece," designed primarily to publicize his idea for a new type of economical, energy-producing space station. Here are two noteworthy authors freely admitting that they were employing their fiction to present and promote their own scientific ideas. Thus, if we read these authors' works looking for valuable suggestions, they could hardly become indignant, since providing such suggestions was actually one of their goals.

However, even though many of the writers of science fiction are indeed well qualified to discuss the future, the medium they choose for their speculations may not seem to merit serious attention. After all, these people are in the business of providing entertainment; if there is value in researching books about space stations, surely, it might be argued, one should look at nonfiction. There, one would expect the thoughtful explorations of serious scholars, while fiction would offer only the wild ideas of dreamy visionaries.

In fact, I maintain that exactly the opposite is true.

I support my position by considering the fictional and nonfictional treatments of space habitats. In the novels and stories I read about space habitats, as discussed in Chapter 8, such structures repeatedly emerged as highly questionable concepts, based on overly optimistic projections and subject to a host of significant problems; given the present state of technological and social progress, they simply do not seem realistic. Thus, there is a great deal of wisdom in Chet Kinsman's response to a dreamy advocate of space habitats in Ben Bova's *Kinsman*:

> "It would be wonderful if we could leave all the greed and anger and suspicion of our fellow men back on Earth and come out here fresh and clean and newborn."
>
> "I got news for you, fellas...It ain't gonna happen

that way!" (210-211)

After this delightfully pointed exchange, it is surprising to turn to Bova's nonfiction book about humanity's future in space, *The High Road*, and find a far less critical attitude toward space habitats:

> [The space colony] is a dream, a good dream, one that is needed to keep the long-range possibilities of space technology before our eyes. Humans will live in space permanently, raise families there, and expand through the Solar System....
> Space colonization will be a reality. Our children will build one after another and use the colonies not merely to house themselves halfway between the Earth and the Moon but to sail outward to the asteroids and beyond. (231, 233)

Other books about space habitats, like G. Harry Stine's *The Space Enterprise* and O'Neill's *The High Frontier*, rhapsodize even more about the utopias in space that might be built; one of them, T. A. Heppenheimer's *Colonies in Space*, is reduced to gibbering about Saturday night in a space habitat: "Water fights will be great fun.... Each of the three towns in the colony can have a couple of movie theaters...[restaurants] no doubt will feature a big salad bar along with baskets of fruits...of course, people will have their stereos, their tape decks, and TV's" (211, 215-216).

Why is there such a contrast between the insight of *Kinsman* and other novels and the giddy optimism of *The High Road* and other works of nonfiction? The answer, I would argue, lies in the nature of the two media. Desperate to persuade people to support activities in space, writers of nonfiction are driven to become shrill in their advocacy, unconvincing in their rosy depictions of space life, and blind to potential problems and hazards. But writers of fiction face a different and more demanding task: since narrative requires conflict, they must soberly consider what sorts of problems or difficulties might arise in a space settlement and how these might be resolved. It is by means of this thought process, I maintain, that a true critical examination of the space habitat idea emerged; and while skeptics questioned the virtues of these structures in other forums—many quoted in Mack Reynolds and Dean Ing's *Trojan Orbit*—it was in science fiction that the true, inherent difficulties in building and maintaining a space habitat came out, even in novels by authors like Ben Bova and Lee Correy [G. Harry Stine] who offer no such criticisms in their nonfictional treatments of the idea.

I eventually lost contact with Dr. Moore, the Jet Propulsion Laboratory, and NASA, and the practical perspective that I initially brought to my research became less and less important, so much so that most of my possibly valuable insights and suggestions were ultimately banished to a twelfth chapter here that is basically unrelated to the rest of the study. Still, a concern for the practical sometimes surfaces in the main text, as in Chapter 4, where I explain why building a space station is a very good idea, and in Chapter 8, where, as noted, I explain why building a space habitat is a very bad idea. Overall, the use of science fiction for such purposes seems completely defensible and provides one argument for research of this type.

Although this reasoning may persuade those with a practical interest in constructing and maintaining a space station to read this book, literary critics—the other special audience I seek—will remain unconvinced. One problem is the discipline's general attitude toward science fiction: despite its multitudes of relevant texts, despite its exponential growth as a genre in the twentieth century, and despite its increasing quality and prominence in the literary marketplace, science fiction is still regarded today as a rather small and insignificant field in literary circles. So it is that the critic whose entire published output concerns Shakespeare's history plays is accepted as a veritable Renaissance man, while the critic who studies scores of science fiction texts is said to be overly specialized. And in regards to the subject of this book, the common assumption, which I have repeatedly encountered, is that space stations occur only in a tiny number of science fiction works, and that even in those they most frequently figure as unimportant background elements. In response to this belief, it seems that I must defend at some length my decision to study a minor topic in an already minor field.

One possible answer would simply be to point to my bibliography, separately published as *The Other Side of the Sky: An Annotated Bibliography of Space Stations in Science Fiction 1869-1993*, which describes a total of 948 relevant works. Any subject that appears in so many narratives, I might argue, cannot be considered a "minor" one. Still, I would readily concede that space stations remain a relatively infrequent theme in science fiction, and, I might add, one rarely addressed in its most famous titles; so why should a critic bother to read a lengthy discussion of an obscure topic largely found in unknown works?

The fact that I must respond to this question is an indictment of the field of literary criticism in general, and science fiction criticism in particular.

Let me offer a few facts and figures concerning science fiction. The world's largest institutional collection of science fiction, the J. Lloyd Eaton Collection of the University of California, Riverside, now houses almost 100,000 items—most of them novels, anthologies, and magazines of science fiction—and my own research suggests that the collection is far from complete. Granted that the Eaton Collection includes numerous duplicate editions of books, frequently reprinted stories, and works of marginal interest, one still emerges with the conservative estimate that there must be at the very least about 150,000 novels and stories that could reasonably be classified as science fiction. When I feel like showing off, I can impress others with my apparently vast knowledge of the field, but I estimate that I could claim true familiarity with only about 5,000 of those works and could pretend to be familiar with perhaps 5,000 more. And most critics in the field, I suspect, know far less than I do. Yet this does not prevent science fiction critics—and I include myself here—from presenting grand theories, general observations, and profound commentaries about the nature and purpose of science fiction—all based on their knowledge of only a very small fraction of the genre. These critics, it seems, literally do not know what they are talking about. How, then, can they justify their work?

One safe and easy answer is that this appalling ignorance of their own subject does not really matter; most of the unexamined texts of science fiction are simply junk, and literary critics properly ignore them to focus their attention on the few works that really merit close examination. In other words, critics should feel free to talk about "science fiction" when they really mean "superior science fiction."

But there is first one problem: *how do you know it is junk if you have not read it?* I look over my annotated bibliography and see, for example, Konstantin Tsiolkovsky's *Beyond the Planet Earth*, a visionary if somewhat stodgy novel which encapsulates and anticipates almost all of the ideas and themes of later space station novels; James Gunn's *Station in Space*, a grim assessment of humanity's future in space of a kind that is almost unique in the genre; Arthur C. Clarke's *Islands in the Sky*, an apparently simple novel that nevertheless manages to simultaneously emulate and deconstruct the genre of juvenile space adventure; and Richard A. Lupoff's *The Forever City*, a bizarre juvenile novel which incorporates a unique and haunting vision of the life and death of a space habitat. These stories may not be literary masterpieces, but they aren't junk either; they are genuinely interesting texts that warrant and would richly reward detailed analysis. And yet, even though their authors are hardly unknown, these works, and many others like them, are never discussed, and rarely even mentioned, in examinations of science fiction; and who knows how many more worthwhile texts have so far escaped critical attention?

Even in the face of such evidence, one might still argue that there are no undiscovered masterpieces, no significant works beyond those which have already been examined, in the genre of science fiction, and therefore no need to extend one's vision beyond the currently accepted "canon." However, there is then a second problem: to fully understand a text, one must know something about the circumstances which produced it. Consider, for example, Walter M. Miller, Jr.'s *A Canticle for Leibowitz*. A critic who knows little about science fiction might conclude that Miller is being remarkably innovative in abandoning the typical historical model of the genre— upward linear movement by means of scientific progress—to offer instead two distinct and atypical models: Viconian historical cycles, and Christian teleology. And if *A Canticle for Leibowitz* is the only novel we are reading from its period, that might remain our conclusion. However, what if it turns out that there are a number of other science fiction stories which also employ Viconian and teleological structures? What if it turns out—as I can demonstrate—that there are earlier texts which specifically apply such structures to the specter of nuclear holocaust and to the promise and perils of life in space? In that case, Miller's novel is not diminished, but enriched, as it emerges as a commentary not only on earlier assumptions about linear progress but on earlier uses of alternative models as well. In short, if critics do not know what sorts of works surround their selected masterpieces, they cannot fully understand them.

Another answer to my question would acknowledge that there may be some surprises, some unexpected pockets of quality, in the vast and unexplored universe of science fiction, and would further accept that some knowledge of the entire field may be necessary and interesting even if all of its works are not superior literature; nevertheless, a detailed awareness of lesser texts is not important if one obtains a thorough knowledge of the genre's masterpieces, which in themselves will enable the critic to fully understand and appreciate the entire range of possibilities in the genre. This assumption, implicit in most treatments of science fiction, is offered explicitly in Darko Suvin's *Metamorphoses of Science Fiction*: "If one may speculate on some fundamental features or indeed axioms of [science fiction] criticism, the *first* might be that the genre has to be and can be evaluated proceeding from its heights down, applying the standards gained by the analysis of its masterpieces" (36). But the attitude that superior examples must precede and inform any discussion of an entire field is found nowhere else in academic research. Does the study of a horse enable us to better understand a planarium? Does the structure of a multinational corporation explain the functioning of a liquor store? Can we ignore any study of coal and draw conclusions about it simply by examining diamonds? Surely, biologists, economists, and geologists would laugh at the notion that the characteristics of their field's best and brightest representatives can be fruitfully employed as a means to understand all of its many forms and features; and similarly, critics should laugh at the notion that a novel like *A Canticle for Leibowitz* contains and explicates all of its lesser counterparts.

Critics are thus driven to two conclusions: that even if their sole concern is to interpret the genre's masterpieces, they still require some knowledge of the entire range of science fiction literature; and that if they acknowledge that all science fiction might be of some interest, then they cannot rely on a few selected works to learn about that literature. Thus, science fiction critics worthy of that name must be committed to a thorough—and detailed—study of science fiction.

I do not wish to imply that science fiction has not been the subject of thorough examination; in fact, the extent and enthusiasm of science fiction research in most ways have been remarkable. Yet we observe a curious division of labor. On the one hand, there are "bibliographers" who ferret out and present bulks of undigested information, typically in a format that is ideal for ready reference but which fails to provide any overview of or insight into its subject. On the other hand, there are "critics" who offer theories and commentary—sometimes worthwhile, sometimes less than worthwhile—which are typically based on a close reading of a handful of works. In other words, the people who are doing extensive research are not drawing conclusions, and the people who are drawing conclusions are not doing extensive research.

This strikes me as bizarre.

In search of a better model for literary research, I turn to the late Stephen Jay Gould, the well-known scientist and writer; surely, one might suppose, such an intelligent and capable biologist would have devoted all of his energies to the major theories and the large issues in his field. However, while Gould wrote on many of these, the one area where he was an acknowledged expert, the area in which he spent most of his time, was the study of an obscure species of land snail found in the Bahamas. He defended this work in his essay "Opus 100":

Why, indeed, spend so much time on any detailed particular when all the giddy generalities of evolutionary theory beg for study in a lifetime too short to manage but a few? Iconoclast that I am, I would not abandon the central wisdom of natural history from its inception—that concepts without percepts are empty (as Kant said) and that no scientist can develop an adequate "feel" for nature (that undefinable prerequisite of true understanding) without probing deeply into minute empirical details of some well-chosen group of organisms. Thus, Aristotle dissected squids and proclaimed the world's eternity, while Darwin wrote four volumes on barnacles and one on the origin of species. America's greatest evolutionists and natural historians, G. G. Simpson, T. Dobzhansky, and E. Mayr, began their careers as, respectively, leading experts on Mesozoic mammals, ladybird beetles, and the birds of New Guinea. (168)

And in a specific slap at his colleagues who are literary critics, Gould exclaimed, "Fieldwork is not like the one-hundred-thousandth essay on Shakespeare's sonnets; it always presents something truly new, not a gloss on previous commentaries" (183). With this comment, Gould pinpointed a central paradox in literary studies.

None of his colleagues accused Gould of wasting his time on a trivial subject; for biologists understand that the detailed examination of even tiny subjects can yield rich rewards, and that such painstaking work is in fact a necessary prelude to grand theories and conclusions. However, in literary criticism we frequently separate the activities of research and analysis, denigrating those who discover and present new data as mere "bibliographers" while celebrating those who analyze what has already been analyzed as true "critics." And the problem with this attitude is simple: as many other fields demonstrate, it is only by means of and in response to the discovery of new data that new theories, new ideas, emerge. For example, during most of the twentieth century, planetary science was a moribund field because astronomers could obtain no additional information with optical telescopes, so they focused instead on stars and galaxies where observations were still incomplete. Today, with mounds of new data from radio astronomy, satellites, and space probes, planetary science is one of the most exciting fields of astronomy, as scientists are busy crafting new theories of planetary development and evolution in order to account for the wonders they have now observed.

Literary criticism may be the only field where critics who offer new data are ignored, or forced to fight for the privilege of presenting their findings, or relegated to the low status of "bibliographer"; and this is patently ridiculous. Imagine an astronomer who refuses to examine *Voyager* photographs of Neptune because he prefers continued scrutiny of tiny, fuzzy images and you have a picture of the English professor who condemns all literature outside of the time-honored canons as "junk" unworthy of consideration. Truly, if critics really wish to improve their understanding of literature, they require not new *theories*, but new *data*; and in literature, new data mean new texts. In reference to science fiction in particular, we badly delude ourselves if we believe that brilliant new insights can emerge from rereading after rereading of Stanislaw Lem, Ursula K. Le Guin, or William Gibson, no matter how admirable those authors are; rather, we risk becoming like those nineteenth-century astronomers who stared so hard at Mars through inadequate telescopes that they began to believe they were seeing canals. Criticism of science fiction simply cannot progress without continuing, thorough research in the field; and "critics" of science fiction cannot, as it were, farm out such labor to lesser creatures called "bibliographers"— instead, they must get their hands dirty and do this work themselves. Just as Charles Darwin both studied barnacles in excruciating detail and provided a grand and comprehensive theory of evolution, true literary scholars must be both bibliographers and critics.

Therefore, although I will be providing as my primary goal information and, I hope, insight into the subject of space stations in science fiction, I also offer the approach of my work as a critical statement in itself and as a model for further research. Bluntly, those who wish to be known as literary critics must break down the stupid division between bibliographers who uncover data and critics who analyze it and instead understand that the two activities can and must go together, that bibliography is a necessary prelude to criticism, and criticism is the natural consequence of bibliography. And I propose that science fiction criticism be the vanguard of this new attitude. That is, each science fiction critic should first acknowledge full and complete understanding of every single work in the field as her ultimate objective; each critic must abandon the cozy and lazy comfort of shared knowledge of a few "canonical" works and instead commit herself to an intense examination of some particular area of the field; and each critic must learn to depend on her own detailed studies, and those of others, in constructing her all-encompassing theories and grand judgments about science fiction. With a continuing influx of new information, critics can expect their ideas concerning science fiction to continually improve, as happens in virtually all other disciplines committed to preferentially examining new data; and they can do their work while looking down with condescension at their colleagues in other fields who are still wasting their time re-interpreting what has already been repeatedly interpreted.

Some may fear that science fiction critics will invite the ridicule of their colleagues if they are seen to be examining works which are admittedly in many cases not of the highest quality—but such fears are groundless. Most other critics ridicule us anyway, even when we slavishly ape their snobbish posturings and elitist attitudes. Science fiction critics have nothing to lose, and everything to gain, by approaching their subject honestly and completely and demonstrating the true value of that approach. In sum, they must stop imitating the failed and futile limitations of conventional critics and offer instead a new methodology which those other critics can imitate.

The two projects which I present provide a written record of the methodology I propose. Confronted with the topic of space stations in science fiction, my first impulse was to compile an annotated bibliography; and over several years that bibliography grew, as I indicated, to 948 works, which I summarized and often discussed in some detail in *The Other Side of the Sky*. In the text of this critical study, I can be observed cautiously moving from bibliography to criticism, beginning with an historical overview, moving into discussions which blend together bibliography and criticism, and concluding with two critical essays.

While one might follow this kind of methodology with virtually any topic in science fiction, careful analyses of various subjects will necessarily have various results, just as some snails are more interesting than other snails; according to Gould, the greatest insights will come from studying "some well-chosen group of organisms." Therefore, to convincingly present a study of space stations as a model for further research, I must finally demonstrate that my topic is not only properly researched but also "well-chosen." And in fact, although I paradoxically did not really choose this topic, I have serendipitously found the roles played by space stations in science fiction to be unusually problematic—and unusually illuminating.

By all rights, one could readily argue, space stations should be a central and crucial element in the genre. While many themes in science fiction, like aliens, space exploration, robots, and time travel, have analogues in old travelers' tales, myths, and legends, the concept of moving into the middle of nowhere and building a home there is only about a century old; true, there have been tales of "flying cities," from Aristophanes's Cloudcuckooland to Jonathan Swift's Laputa, but these have always remained close to Earth, physically and spiritually, and project a feeling of familiarity, while the space station is necessarily a strange place in a strange location. Thus, in a genre theoretically dedicated to novelty, there should be a natural attractiveness about the truly novel idea of space stations. And surely, there is something inherently exciting about designing, building, and occupying an entire new world in the midst of outer space; the possibilities for new environments and lifestyles are literally endless. In addition, plans and proposals for space stations have repeatedly gained wide publicity and have inspired outbursts of interest in the genre. Yet always, after these brief periods of prominence, space stations have tended to fade away like a passing fad. Even today, with some lingering excitement about grandiose space habitats and the emergence of a true space station in Earth orbit, science fiction writers often seem strangely indifferent to the subject. For these reasons, then, what might be cited as a weakness in my research—that space stations are a relatively uncommon topic in science fiction—is actually its most fascinating aspect: given everything that should make the subject appealing to writers, why have they frequently chosen to ignore space stations, or push them into the background?

Seeking an answer to this question leads to the problems at the heart of science fiction.

To examine those problems, one must first look at the general process of writing a narrative which employs a particular object or setting in the manner of an icon; when an author does this, certain decisions must be reached, certain issues must be resolved. I list them without implying that these decisions must be reached in any particular order or that they must be reached as a matter of conscious intent.

First, no object can exist in a vacuum—although in a book about space stations, I should instead say "in a conceptual vacuum"; therefore, the author must provide some overall context or environment for the chosen object or setting. Next, the author must develop both a practical and a literary justification for including the object; that is, the object must perform some function in the story, and the object must project some theme or resonance that is relevant to the story.

In many genres, a number of objects or settings have well-established contexts, functions, and characteristic themes and can therefore be readily employed without difficulty. To use an example found in Vivian Sobchack's *Screening Space* (a work I will discuss more thoroughly in Chapter 10), consider the railroad in the genre of westerns. The nineteenth-century American frontier offers both a familiar general context and a number of specific contexts. The typical narrative functions of the railroad are not troublesome: it can be seen simply as a tool of commerce, a means of transporting people and materials and making profits for its builders, and for some individuals, it can serve as a passport to adventure, a way to explore unknown places and peoples. Finally, the railroad is traditionally associated with various themes, most notably the growth of civilization and the death of the natural world. Therefore, while there is room for individual initiative and creativity, the railroad of the American West is a clearly defined icon which creates no special problems for writers.

In science fiction, the situation can be more complex.

First, like all forms of non-mimetic narrative, science fiction involves objects and settings which do not exist and are thus by nature unfamiliar. While in theory this feature offers the writer of non-mimetic fiction virtually unlimited possibilities, in practice one often finds surprisingly limited possibilities; in modern fantasy, for example, objects and conventions from ancient myths, legends, and literature may be employed again and again with amazing rigidity and lack of creativity. This suggests that the "freedom" of non-mimetic fiction may in fact have a paralyzing effect on writers who, intimidated by vast new prospects, instead timidly rely on well-worn devices.

In addition, there are particular problems created by the peculiar critical tradition of science fiction. As indicated, Hugo Gernsback demanded that science fiction incorporate accurate scientific information and carefully develop all of its predictions from that information; while John W. Campbell, Jr., further demanded that science fiction be firmly based on a process of logical, scientific thought. For these reasons, authors may find that the objects or devices they wish to employ may be precluded by strict application of scientific fact and scientific logic.

Finally, modern science fiction has functioned, also as already indicated, as a closely connected community whose members eventually achieve some sense of consensus not only on particular scientific matters, as described by Campbell, but on the general outlines of future history, as explained by Donald A. Wollheim in *The Universe Makers*; and while this consensus may be helpful to writers as a guideline in their explorations of unknown territory, it can also serve as another bothersome constraint on those explorations.

All of these problems can be seen in the ways that space stations have appeared in science fiction.

In the first place, space stations force writers to confront one of the genre's central environments—outer space—a realm that remains, despite some tentative forays, largely unknown and unfamiliar to human experience. For that reason, writers have traditionally fallen back on metaphor, particularly the metaphor of space as a vast new ocean. However, space stations by their very nature challenge that metaphor, and as they grew larger and more common in science fiction, a new metaphor forcibly emerged—space as a new frontier, a vast expanse of territory—although this image is also unsatisfactory.

In defining narrative functions for the space stations, writers can devise any number of businesses for them to engage in, although not all of them seem reasonable or conducive to extended narrative. Excitable writers can transport to space stations many of the conventional menaces of the genre, to make them serve as places for adventure, although more sober-minded writers have examined these escapades and concluded that they are illogical and unlikely, and that persons in search of adventure would be well advised to travel elsewhere. And overly optimistic writers can picture space stations as perfect, utopian communities, although more skeptical writers carefully note that a space community can be successful only under certain conditions and only for certain types of people.

To deal with such problems, science fiction writers then attempt to transform the space station: into a spaceship, to make it better suited for adventure; into a space habitat, to make it a better home; and into a space elevator, to make it better for business. However, the transformation into a spaceship simply avoids the problems of life in space, while the transformations into space habitats and space elevators literally and figuratively magnify those problems.

Finally, writers have discovered a number of characteristic themes to be evoked by a space stations—cycles in human history, transition, frustration and madness, and withdrawal and inward movement—and putting these all together, an apparently consistent and satisfying picture of the icon of the space station appears to emerge. Nevertheless, lurking behind this consensus are a number of unraised issues, unresolved problems, unrealized and disturbing possibilities; and one must conclude that science fiction writers have largely ignored the true implications of the space station and have failed to examine the concept in the thorough and logical way demanded by their genre.

All in all, I believe it is a quite interesting story.

And it is a story that I could not have told with a detailed look at ten or twenty "representative" works, or even with a survey of fifty or 100 works—as I know from my own experience; for several times during my research I paused to write down my conclusions, and at least twice I believed that my project was finished. But each time, as I reconsidered the works that I had examined, and as I looked at a number of additional works, I found that there were new elements to incorporate, new mysteries to ponder, new matters to discuss; and only after a complete examination of over 500 works was I willing to declare that the puzzle was at least in part solved—although there are no doubt a number of missing pieces awaiting the attention of other scholars.

In short, while this introduction has argued for the value of thorough and comprehensive bibliographical work as a necessary prelude to critical study, the rest of this book will demonstrate its value; for just as "Aristotle dissected squids and proclaimed the world's eternity," I have examined what may appear to be a grain of sand in the genre and I have seen the entire universe of science fiction.

2. *Into the Sea of Stars*:
Definitions and History of the
Space Station in Fiction

Believing reports that the literature of space stations was rather limited, I began my bibliographical research with a cluttered list of possibly relevant works, tales of generation starships and long space voyages, artificial worlds and flying cities, isolated planetary outposts and underground colonies; however, as I became aware of the wealth of material actually available, my task instead became to establish meaningful parameters.

Accordingly, I defined a space station as "an artificial structure designed to remain permanently in the vacuum of outer space, either in a fixed position or a fixed orbit, and designed for permanent human habitation." The most familiar type of space station, of course, is the large spinning wheel or torus built out of metal, ranging in size from an office building to a city block, although such facilities come in many shapes and sizes; however, I also included in my research these related types of structures:

1) *Spaceships* which are parked in a permanent position or orbit to serve as space stations, like the S. S. Randolph in Robert A. Heinlein's *Space Cadet* or the "Dead Star Station" in Jack Williamson's story of that name;

2) *Space stations which are transformed into spaceships*, a development seen in works like Ben Bova's *Exiled from Earth* and Thomas N. Scortia's *Earthwreck!*;

3) *Inhabited asteroids*, when those asteroids have been hollowed out, tunneled through, or otherwise built on or modified to the point where they may be considered artificial structures, like the asteroid in

Robert A. Heinlein's "Misfit" which is "converted" into a space station; and

4) *Space habitats*, large enclosed spheres or cylinders which have terrestrial fields and structures on their interiors.

I excluded from my research stories like Michael McCollum's "A Greater Infinity" which refer to previous or existing space stations—Skylab, Salyut, Mir—without adding any speculative material about them. I also decided to exclude from my research the following types of structures, for these reasons:

1) *Generation starships*, vessels which take hundreds of years, and several generations, to reach another star, first seen in Don Wilcox's "The Voyage That Lasted 600 Years"—because, despite the fact that most of their residents will spend their entire lives in space, these enclosures still maintain a sense of traveling and have as their goal an eventual landing on a planet, not permanent life in space;

2) *Flying cities*, large inhabited platforms within a planet's atmosphere, like the "vacation city" visited in Hugo Gernsback's *Ralph 124C 41+*—because, despite their similarities to space stations, these communities are not truly isolated from the planet's surface and lack contact with the environment of space; and

3) *Artificial worlds*, huge artificial constructs of planetary dimensions like Larry Niven's *Ringworld*—because these places offer no sense of living in space and completely mimic a natural world in the environment and the problems they present.

For the record, I distinguished a space habitat from an artificial world by this criterion: a person who suddenly found herself in a space habitat would immediately realize that she was in an artificial structure in space—by seeing landscapes curving up into the sky, or large windows filled with stars; but a person who suddenly found herself on an artificial world would have no immediate way of knowing that it was not a natural world.

Needless to say, all these guidelines were not without gray areas and ambiguities—at what point does an inhabited asteroid become a space station? at what point does a space habitat become an artificial world?—and I tended to incorporate the borderline works I located. I also strayed from my own criteria in a few cases to include a few prominent works whose structures have consistently been, or could logically be, regarded as "space stations": the "space station" in Stanislaw Lem's *Solaris*, although that structure—in the novel, unlike the film—would be better described as a flying city; the Death Stars of George Lucas's *Star Wars* and *Return of the Jedi*, although I would classify them simply as large armed spaceships; the "Ship" of Alexei Panshin's *Rite of Passage*, which remains permanently in space although its residents continue, paradoxically, to think and act like starship passengers; and the "Cities in Flight" of James Blish's four novels, which look like cities in space but actually function as spaceships, occasionally landing on planetary surfaces. Many readers would expect a study of space stations to mention these works; so, despite some misgivings, I decided to include them to meet those expectations.

To discuss the history of space stations in science fiction, I must first confront and refute the common notion that science fiction writers somehow failed to predict or realize the importance of space stations. One finds even people like Ben Bova and Isaac Asimov, writers who should know the field well, repeatedly parroting this incorrect perception. Consider this passage from Bova's *The High Road*:

> the concept of building mammoth colonies in space, where nothing but emptiness exists today, never originated in a science fiction story. Science fiction writers (myself included) always assumed that the first permanent human settlements would be on or beneath the surface of another world: the Moon, Mars, Venus, for example. Plenty of stories were written about space stations in orbit around the Earth. George O. Smith wrote a famous series about a station placed along the orbit of Venus. But they were always seen as way-stations, outposts, not permanent colonies.
>
> "Planetary chauvinism" is the way a rueful Isaac Asimov described the writers' failure to imagine colonies built in empty space....
>
> In the autumn of 1969... [Gerard O'Neill and his students] literally invented what has come to be called the L-5 space colony concept: gigantic space habitats built between the Earth and the Moon, big

enough to house thousands or even millions of permanent residents in a completely Earthlike environment. (227)

Here, Bova is absolutely and completely wrong.

First, one cannot ignore the large utopian community accidentally established in an artificial satellite circling the Earth in Edward Everett Hale's "The Brick Moon" (1869), however unscientific the story is; and John Munro's *A Trip to Venus* (1897) unambiguously predicts "artificial planets":

> "Independent, free of rent and taxes, these hollow planetoids would serve for schools, hotels, dwelling-houses—"
> "And lunatic asylums."
> "They would relieve the surplus population of the globe...." (61)

And in Russia at the same time, Konstantin Tsiolkovsky was boldly predicting, in "Changes in Relative Weight" (1894) and *Dreams of Earth and Sky* (1895), that there would be communities in space with millions of inhabitants.

Moving further ahead, J. M. Walsh's *Vandals of the Void* (1930) and Murray Leinster's "The Power Planet" (1931) both depict space stations which are large and impressive, each housing hundreds of inhabitants, and each devoted to different purposes—respectively, a space fortress and a space power station. Jack Williamson's "The Prince of Space" (1931) depicts a perfectly realized space habitat:

> They were, Bill saw, at the center of an enormous cylinder. The sides, half a mile away, above and below them were covered with buildings, along neat, tree-bordered streets, scattered with green lawns, tiny gardens, and bits of wooded park...As they stepped out, it gave Bill a curious dizzy feeling to look up and see busy streets, inverted, a mile above his head. The road before them curved smoothly up on either hand, bordered with beautiful trees, until its ends met again above his head. (877-878)

So much for the claim that O'Neill and his students "literally invented" the idea! And Everett C. Smith and R. F. Starzl's "The Metal Moon" (1932) features a similar idea, a huge inhabited globe with an upper half enclosed in crystal with beautiful, Earthlike scenery. A large flying city in space figures in H. Thompson Rich's "The Flying City" (1930). Basil E. Wells's "Factory in the Sky" (1941) is a gigantic sphere in the asteroid belt which is home to over a million people. C. L. Moore's *Judgment Night* (1942) features a massive, artificial "pleasure world" offering a variety of diverse environments. Even Smith's *Venus Equilateral* stories, lumped together by Bova with all the other "way-stations" and "outposts," actually was a functioning community of 500 people, with a broad range of facilities and amenities, described as "so much like a town on Terra" (407). And in the next decade, there are the Space Terminal seen in Robert A. Heinlein's "Space Jockey" (1947), said to resemble an Earth city, the "artificial moon" in Arthur C. Clarke's "The Lion of Comarre" (1949), the twenty-two large resort satellites of Jack Vance's "Abercrombie Station" (1952), and the happy community in space seen in E. C. Eliott's Kemlo novels (1954). To be sure, the attitude that Bova speaks of is true of *most* earlier science fiction writers; but it is simply outrageous for him to assert that "Science fiction writers...*always* assumed that the first permanent human settlements would be on or beneath the surface of another world," and that space stations in science fiction prior to the 1960s were "*always* seen as way-stations, outposts, not permanent colonies."

As for the late Isaac Asimov, he must be accused in one instance of deliberately ignoring the historical record in order to celebrate his own originality. In its introduction to Asimov's "Reason" (1941), *Isaac Asimov Presents the Best Science Fiction Firsts* claims that the story "first suggested using satellites to collect solar power and beam corrected forms to earth" (207). Yet a decade earlier, Murray Leinster's "The Power Planet" (1931) described a space station which generated electric power from the convection between its sun-heated side and its cold side and beamed that energy to Earth— exactly what Asimov alleges that he "first suggested." And that story is hardly obscure: in his introduction to George O. Smith's *The Complete Venus Equilateral*, Arthur C. Clarke called it a "classic" (6). Furthermore, beyond the legalistic language of Asimov's claim, the whole idea of solar power from space stations might be traced further back to Otto Gail's *The Stone from the Moon* (1926), where large mirrors attached to a station were envisioned as a means of sending concentrated sunlight to Earth—as also seen in Edmond Hamilton's "Space Mirror" (1937); and even earlier, Tsiolkovsky's works contained numerous suggestions for generating solar power in space communities—although with a primary interest in colonizing outer space, Tsiolkovsky never thought about beaming the power to Earth. Overall, in the context of these earlier works, it is difficult indeed to regard Asimov's "Reason" as any type of significant "first."

Thus, there is indeed a history of space stations in science fiction—a rather extensive one, in fact. The puzzle, as I have observed, is how this history became invisible. To be precise, there are four times during the development of the genre when space stations emerged as important factors—and four times when they faded from view.

First, before the time when science fiction emerged as a recognized genre, individual writers in different countries independently came up with the idea of space stations. In America, Hale's "The Brick Moon" described an artificial satellite intended to serve only as an aid to navigation which is instead launched with people on board. In Germany, Kurt Lasswitz's *Two Planets* (1897) featured two Martian space stations above the Earth's poles and anticipated the use of such stations as spaceports, observation posts, and military bases. In England, Munro's *A Trip to Venus*, as noted, discussed the concept of "artificial planets" in space, though none appear in the novel. And a bit later, another English work—J. D. Bernal's *The World, the Flesh, and the Devil* (1929)—proposed building gigantic spheres in space which would provide earthlike interiors—the space habitats of later science fiction.

One of these pioneering figures must be singled out for special attention: the Russian visionary Konstantin Tsiolkovsky, who repeatedly speculated about, and advocated, human habitations in outer space. He first developed the idea of artificial "rings" built around asteroids in "Changes in Relative Weight" (1894); a year later, in *Dreams of Earth and Sky and the Effects of Universal Gravitation*, he considered inhabitants destroying their asteroids so the rings could unwind as free-floating "necklaces" in deep space; and in *Beyond the Planet Earth* (1920), he discussed building huge "greenhouses" in orbit around Earth. This last work must be regarded as the major prophetic work on the permanent habitation of outer space, presenting innumerable ideas that later surfaced in stories of space stations and space habitats: the benefits of life in zero gravity, "especially for the weak and ailing" (251), the ideal cylindrical shape of a space dwelling, the prospects of mining asteroids for needed materials and constructing "factories and workshops" (304) to process them, "flying" in zero gravity with artificial wings, proposals for using solar energy, and a projected lifestyle of nudity and complete freedom in outer space. And Tsiolkovsky had at least one admirer in Russia, writer Aleksandr Beliayev, whose *The Struggle in Space* (1928) described an "airship" that can "navigate in airless space" where people can "last an indefinitely long time away from the planet" (114).

More detailed and realistic work on the design and function of space stations occurred in the 1920s, when members of the German Rocket Society like Hermann Oberth and Wernher von Braun thoroughly developed the concept; indeed, Oberth is usually credited with originating the term "space station" (Alexander 53). And we can detect the influence of Oberth and the German Rocket Society in at least one contemporary German novel, Gail's *The Stone from the Moon* (1926).

Germany also produced a major nonfictional discussion of the subject, *The Problems of Space Flying*, written by a Society member named Hermann von Noordung. When American editor Hugo Gernsback had that work translated and published it in his magazine *Science Wonder Stories* in 1929, von Noordung immediately inspired a few stories about space stations. One novel of that time, J. M. Walsh's *Vandals from the Void* (1930), even mentioned him by name: "The plans for the Gaudien [space station] were actually based on designs drawn up so long ago as the year 1929 by Captain Hermann Noordung, a German engineer and authority on mechanics, who was perhaps the first of all Earth-men to deal with the problem of space navigation seriously" (482). And Gernsback further promoted the idea in an editorial for the April, 1930 issue of *Air Wonder Stories* called "Stations in Space."

Oddly enough, what may qualify as the first magazine story about an inhabited space structure appeared in a magazine Gernsback was not associated with—*Astounding Stories of Super-Science*, whose August, 1930 issue featured H. Thompson Rich's "The Flying City." The story tells of an alien race which constructs an immense disk when their home planet was doomed by an approaching star; for a long time, they had been "voyaging through space on their marvelous disc...content to drift on and on in the interstellar void, breathing an atmosphere produced artificially" (264). However, since "some of its mighty engines were nearing the exhaustion point" (264), they decide to invade and occupy the Earth, and the story focuses not on the city but on a scientist's efforts to defeat them.

What is striking about the other stories of the 1930s and early 1940s is their creativity in placing space stations throughout—and beyond—the Solar System: they are found near the Sun in Jack Williamson's "Crucible of Power" (1939); in the orbit of Venus (forming an equilateral triangle with Earth and Venus) in Smith's *Venus Equilateral*; between Earth and Mars in Robert A. Heinlein's "Misfit" (1939); orbiting Mars in Walsh's *Vandals of the Void*; in the orbit of Mars, but on the opposite side of the Sun, in Manly Wade Wellman's "Space Station No. 1" (1934); in the asteroid belt in Basil E. Wells's "Factory in the Sky" (1941); and out in interstellar space in Jack Williamson's "Dead Star Station" (1934) and Wilson Tucker's "Interstellar Way-Station" (1941). In finding a need for space stations in virtually every part of the universe, these authors in a way outdid their successors, who tended to focus more on Earth-orbiting stations. The 1930s also had its Earth-orbiting stations, but these seemed designed mainly as source of energy, as in Leinster's "The Power Planet," Hamilton's "Space Mirror," and Robert A. Heinlein's "Blowups Happen" (1940). Overall, though, these early space station stories are undistinguished even by the standards of their time, generally offering little more than vignettes and routine adventures against the novel backdrop of the station and not really considering the unique problems of building and maintaining such a station; for example, both Williamson's "The Prince of Space" and Hamilton's "Space Mirror" employ their novel structures in space only as backdrops for contrived adventures of alien invasion involving, respectively, Martian vampire plants and miniaturized Mercurians armed with poison needles.

After World War II, the United States started its own space program, and major figures in it like the transplanted von Braun vigorously promoted in nonfiction books and articles the building of a space station as an early step in space exploration; the new prominence of the idea led to innumerable stories, often aimed at younger readers, describing the construction of the first space station in Earth orbit. These include Robert A. Heinlein's "Delilah and the Space Rigger" (1948), Rafe Bernard's *The Wheel in the Sky* (1953), J. Lloyd Castle's *Satellite E-One* (1954), Lester del Rey's *Step to the Stars* (1955), Murray Leinster's *Space Platform* (1956), and Arthur C. Clarke's "The Other Side of the Sky" (1958). While earlier stories had depicted a first flight to the Moon which was launched from Earth, the typical pattern now was to build a space station first and go to the Moon from there, as seen in Robert Marsten's *Rocket to Luna* (1952), del Rey's *Mission to the Moon* (1956), Leinster's *Space Tug* (1957), and the film *Project Moonbase* (1953). This is also the time when space stations began to appear as minor elements in various stories, now accepted as familiar objects in the future landscape which could be briefly noted and visited without elaborate explanation. Given the important role envisioned for the space station in various plans for America's space program, it is surprising to find them so often relegated to the background or to the ghetto-within-a-ghetto of children's science fiction.

In the 1960s, President Kennedy canceled plans for an early space station to concentrate on a manned mission to the Moon; thus, space stations now lacked a role in the space program to provoke interest, and indeed the entire mood of the genre during this "New Wave" period shifted away from space in general, and from space stations in particular. It was not until 1969 that Gerard O'Neill brought space stations to prominence yet again, this time in a new guise—or rather, the revived old guise—of space habitats. This concept was enthusiastically embraced by science fiction writers of the 1970s, who presented many of these large earthlike constructs in works like Joe Haldeman's "Tricentennial" (1976), Ben Bova's *Colony* (1978), Charles Sheffield's "Transition Team" (1978), Juanita Coulson's *Tomorrow's Heritage* (1981), and Sam Nicholson's "He Who Fights and Runs Away" (1982). However, space habitats soon became less prominent in science fiction, although there were noteworthy exceptions like William John Watkins's *Going to See the End of the Sky* (1986), Richard A. Lupoff's *The Forever City* (1987), and Isaac Asimov's *Nemesis* (1989).

The late 1970s also brought into science fiction the new idea of a "space elevator," a space station physically connected to the Earth's surface by strong wire, featured in stories like Arthur C. Clarke's *The Fountains of Paradise* (1979) and Charles Sheffield's *The Web between the Worlds* (1979). These mammoth structures appeared—and virtually disappeared—with remarkable speed.

Thus, the pattern emerges again and again: a sudden new interest in the subject of space stations and a burst of related stories—around the turn of the century and in the 1930s, the 1950s, and the 1970s—and then a prolonged period of relative silence.

In a sense, the rest of this book will be devoted to exploring why space stations have repeatedly failed to assume a major role in science fiction, and what minor roles they have assumed; but there is one issue in science fiction which is notably affected by space stations, as can be seen with special clarity when these stories are considered in chronological order: namely, the image of outer space itself. To put it simply, the presence of space stations tends to challenge and confuse the way we conceptualize space.

Since ancient times, when the first space traveler—in Lucian's *True History*—literally *sailed* to the Moon and Sun in a ship driven off course, the dominant metaphor for space has been the sea. We can first see the continuing power of this image in science fiction in the titles of novels like Gregory Benford's *Across the Sea of Suns* and William Forstchen's *Into the Sea of Stars*, and in numerous comments in space station stories: Walsh's *Vandals from the Void* notes that "It was odd how the old sea-jargon still linger in speech; one would have thought the interplanetary service would have developed its own terms" (443); a station commander asserts in Fletcher Pratt's "Project Excelsior" that "I am the captain of a ship at a distance from land" (90); a space station scientist in Jack C. Haldeman II's *Vector Analysis* feels as if he was on "the deck of the *Marie Celeste*" (95); and the commander of a space station in Ben Bova's *Peacekeepers* likens himself to "the captain of an ocean vessel" (87) and his station to a submarine (88). And, in the reality of the American space program, the title of the official NASA history of Project Mercury, by Loyd S. Swenson Jr., James M. Grimwood, and Charles A. Alexander, was *This New Ocean*, and accepted NASA terminology includes words like "astronaut" (literally, "star sailor") and "docking." This metaphor defines space travel as sailing through the ocean of space to get to other planets; thus, in *Conquest of Space*, that title refers not to the space station of the opening scenes, but to the expedition to and coming habitation of Mars (and in the film's planning stages, other planets in the Solar System as well).

In the beginning, the idea of space stations did little to disturb the image of a space sea, since early stations were usually small and isolated, like little lighthouses in space. A common expression for space stations which embodied nautical thinking was "islands"— seen in the title of Arthur C. Clarke's space station novel, *Islands in the Sky*, and in the name chosen by O'Neill for the first space habitat, Island One.

However, even while O'Neill was paying homage to the picture of space-as-sea he was also undermining it, because implicit in his advocacy of space habitats—also called space colonies—is a new image of space as a place to *inhabit*, to *colonize*, as something resembling *land*. John F. Kennedy's memorable phrase, "the New Frontier," embodied this new idea perfectly, and the term was adopted by space habitat enthusiasts, although many preferred to speak of "the High Frontier." So, while voyagers in earlier science fiction traveled through empty space from planet to planet, the space in modern stories is cluttered with space habitats, space stations, power satellites, space factories, and other structures—so much so that in Lee Correy's *Manna*, the simple act of flying from Earth to a space colony is a nightmarish exercise in avoiding collisions with innumerable objects in space. A vivid picture of the "ever more crowded" region around Earth is presented in Paul Preuss's *Breaking Strain*:

> little Earth was ringed like giant Saturn—with machines and vehicles, not with innocent snowballs. There were bright power stations collecting sunlight and beaming microwaves to antenna farms in Arabia and Mongolia and Angola and Brazil. There were refineries, using sunlight to smelt metal from moon sand and captured asteroids, distilling hydrocarbons from carbonaceous chondrites and mining diamonds from meteoroids. There were factories that used these materials to cast the perfect ball bearing, to brew the perfect antibiotic, to extrude the perfect polymer. There were luxury terminals to serve the great interplanetary liners and entertain their wealthy passengers, and there were orbiting dockyards for the working freighters. There were a dozen shipyards, two dozen scientific stations, a hundred weather satellites, five hundred communications satellites, a thousand spy-eyes.... (57)

Now the "conquest of space" meant just that—claiming, occupying and utilizing regions of space, not other planets.

Despite the power of this new image of space-as-land, though, it has not replaced the image of space-as-sea; rather, nautical terminology continues to exist as an awkward accompaniment to terrestrial terminology. Thus, describing a space station often creates severe metaphoric confusion. Thus, while introducing the space station orbiting Venus in *Breaking Strain*, Preuss says it is "part harbor, part trainyard, part truckstop" (203). Another apt example is David Brin's story, "Tank Farm Dynamo"; on the one hand, space vehicles in the story come in for "landings"—the narrator comments that "A few purists still refused to call the docking a 'landing'" (192)—implying a space station is like a piece of land; yet the station has a "Captain's Cabin" to give the place "the flavor of a Caribbean cruise" (199-200), and at the end of the story Brin's character says the station is "anchored" to Earth (204), reaffirming the image of a space station as something on an ocean. There is even a curious mixture of nautical and terrestrial imagery in the title's description of Brin's space station—a "tank [water] farm [land]".

Because widely accepted metaphors often constitute one of the few safe grounds in the uncertain arena of futuristic projections, authors clearly have at least one motive for ignoring space stations in their fiction: their absence enables them to continuing employing the comfortable old image of space as a vast empty ocean. When structures begin to fill those regions, creating the sort of urban sprawl seen in Correy's *Manna* and Preuss's *Breaking Strain*, there is a need for a new image of space as a vast expanse of land, which does not accord with the conventional perspective. Furthermore, the continuing power of the oceanic metaphor does not simply represent the persistence of old terminology; it also suggests some resistance to the idea that the cold dark regions of space are in fact the proper place for humans to settle. These conflicting impulses appear even when considering what appears to be a matter of little importance— the design and appearance of space stations.

3. *The Wheel in the Sky*:
Space Station Design and Appearance

From the beginning, those who envisioned space stations realized that such structures in space would need to rotate in order to maintain some semblance of gravity; this naturally led to proposed designs of a rounded shape. The most familiar configuration, of course, is the torus, described in George Kinley [Edmund Cooper]'s *Ferry Rocket* as "a large silvery car tyre, or a heavy wheel, joined by a spherical hub by two tubular spokes" (55), celebrated in the title of Rafe Bernard's *The Wheel in the Sky*, featured in most popular illustrations, and seen in landmark films like *Conquest of Space* and *2001: A Space Odyssey*. Yet this is not the only possible rounded design; other works have presented space stations in the shape of spheres (Edward Everett Hale, "The Brick Moon"), immense rings around worlds (Tsiolkovsky, "Changes in Relative Weight"), dumbbells (Otto Gail, *The Stone from the Moon*), cylinders (Robert A. Heinlein, "Delilah and the Space Rigger"), tops (Spacedock in the film *Star Trek VI: The Undiscovered Country*), discs (the film *Project Moonbase*), cones (Frank Belknap Long, *Space Station #1*), and even helices (Arthur Byron Cover, *Stationfall*). In keeping with this tendency, space habitats also feature rounded designs, usually spheres or cylinders, so the interior landscape is curved and earthlike.

However, the modern space station designer now understands that in space there is no need for a streamlined or circular configuration; a space station can simply be a random collection of gridwork and modules and still rotate if necessary. This is the sort of station seen in modern films like *Earth II* and *Moonraker* and in stories like Steven Gould's "Rory," where the station is "a bewildering construct of struts, tubular passages, and spherical chambers" (99); and the current structure of the international space station is similar in design and spirit. Still, rounded images, and particularly the image of the space wheel, remain persistent and powerful; I recall seeing, for example, a children's magazine with a cover featuring a cross-word puzzle in the shape of such a standard space station. Surely, the "wheel in the sky" is one of the most prominent and powerful images ever promulgated by science fiction.

This specific design endures as a visual icon, I believe, in part because of the peculiar contradiction it represents. On the one hand, the space station is a structure of metal frames and panels bolted together, right-angled in all its particulars—eminently technological and masculine in spirit. On the other hand, the overall shape is circular and rounded, suggesting the human form and a literal and figurative evocation of the feminine. It was exactly this sort of contrast, I suspect, which inspired Stanley Kubrick to combine his revolving space station in *2001: A Space Odyssey* with the music of *The Blue Danube Waltz*—it is a cold engineering triumph which evokes dainty beauty. These spinning structures therefore provide a peculiar mixed image: the traditional linearity of space travel combined with the cyclical motion of the space station both in its rotation and its orbit—a striking combination which also seems related to the simultaneous imagery of land and sea associated with the space station.

These contrasts also inform the noticeably different depictions of space station interiors. Their nature as metal configurations suggests an appearance that should be spartan, unadorned, strictly functional. When exaggerated, this criterion can develop into an appearance that is bizarre, alien, inhuman. But when seen as human habitations, space stations can move in the opposite direction and have an appearance that is comforting and familiar.

The stark and unattractive space station is no doubt the most common: metallic walls, bulkheads, narrow corridors and tiny quarters. David Brin's "Tank Farm Dynamo" refers to the station's "Spartan lifestyle" (199), and Ted White's *Secret of the Marauder Satellite* says, "The Station is engineered as a cross between a submarine and a house trailer" (53). These stations are often not described in detail because there is little to describe; hence, one finds, for instance, Lee Correy's abrupt dismissal of the subject in *Manna*: "When you've seen one space station you've seen them all" (66). The ultimate extension of this bland image of space station appearance is seen in Sector Twelve General Hospital in James White's stories and Basil E. Wells's "Factory in the Sky": despite their immense size and special features, they otherwise seem much like, respectively, a terrestrial hospital and factory.

In contrast to this functional approach, a few works argue that as a new and different type of environment, a space station should have a unique look. In Curt Siodmak's *Skyport*, the architect of a space station says, "After all, people are in space and not at the corner of Broadway and Ninth" (80) and proposes extravagant futuristic decor for the space hotel. In Richard Louis Newman's *Siege of Orbitor*, a station provides a "space-oriented interior" (61), and Robert A. Heinlein's "Waldo" suggests an innovative approach to designing and furnishing a space station:

> Waldo's home had been constructed without any consideration being given to up-and-down. Furniture and apparatus were affixed to any wall; there was no "floor"...the furniture and equipment was all odd in design and frequently odd in purpose...The lack of need for the rugged strength necessary to all terrestrial equipment resulted in a fairylike grace in much of the equipment in Waldo's house. (311)

The station in the film *Project Moonbase*, with a script co-authored by Heinlein, also offered some unusual touches in its design: going into the space station, the protagonists pass someone apparently walking upside down, and they confer with station residents who seem to be sitting on the wall. Here also there is also no "consideration being given to up-and-down," with disorienting results. And James P. Hogan's *Endgame Enigma* argues that some deliberate touches of the bizarre might be helpful to inhabitants of a space habitat:

> The strangest thing was the geometry, or lack of it—for everywhere and on all levels, walls met at odd, asymmetrical angles, passages branched between buildings, roadways curved beneath underpasses to emerge in a different direction, and nothing seemed to run square to anything else, anywhere. Presumably the intention was to break up the underlying continuity and dissolve the sense of living inside a tube. If so, it worked. (19)

Finally, and on a grander scale, one finds strangeness in a station's decor celebrated in C. L. Moore's *Judgment Night*, where there is a deliberate attempt to create a large number of unusual and unearthly environments within her vast "pleasure world."

The third option in space station appearance is to strive to make the station, in the words of Murray Leinster in *Space Tug*, "as normal and Earthlike as possible. The total absence of weight...needed to be countered, as a way of staying sane, by the effect of normal-seeming chairs and normal-seeming food" (51). In the space station complex of Larry Niven and Stephen Barnes's *The Descent of Anansi*, "the niceties of gracious living were creeping aboard...oil paintings, sculpture, an achingly beautiful tinsel and brown glass mobile...many moonscapes" (34). And in Thomas N. Scortia's *Earthwreck!* it was decided that

> the stark utilitarianism of previous space vehicles would be a bad morale factor for men confined to space for extended periods...designers had met the challenge in a number of remarkable ways, including the use of recessed skylights above the working areas, colorful folding tables that disappeared into walls, bright coveralls and tunics, light carpeting with an intricate pleasing design on all the surfaces. (28)

In films, a contrast with *Project Moonbase* is provided by *Conquest of Space*, where residents enjoy normal gravity and a conventional-looking environment; indeed, the scene where the crew is watching a television program from Earth makes the station look very comfortable and homelike. This desire for the familiar finds its ultimate expression in James Blish's Cities in Flight—which retain the appearance of Earth cities—and, of course, in the attractive and very terrestrial landscapes of the space habitat.

Still, despite what Leinster's *Space Tug* calls the "sound psychology" (51) of such homey decor, some react negatively to the effort to make the station seem too comfortable, too commonplace and everyday in appearance; a visitor to a space station in Melinda Snodgrass's *Circuit* "found she was faintly disappointed that everything was so homelike. She wished something would indicate to her that she was in space" (30). And a resident of the Golden Rule space habitat in Heinlein's *The Cat Who Walks through Walls* disliked the use of common street names that were designed to give the place an aura of familiarity.

In fact, an attitude arises that these attempts to mimic terrestrial designs in a space station are not only undesirable, but dangerous as well. This is the message of Louis Charbonneau's *Down to Earth*; here, the actual appearance of a hollowed-out asteroid serving as an "emergency landing outpost" is continually concealed by a series of realistic holographic projections of ordinary Earth scenes, so that a resident walking from one part of the station to another would appear to be traveling down a crowded street in an Earth city. These images are designed to make the family living there feel at home, but they also enable an evil intruder to travel around the station without being detected; he can effortlessly blend in with the other figures they see walking about. Thus, the comforting illusions are also threatening; and the station head finally resolves to turn off the projections, both to more easily locate the interloper and to confront the harsh reality of their true environment.

The novel, by the way, provides a perfect example of how the intrinsic nature of science fiction can distort conventional narratives: as the story progresses, the holograms, intended as an ornamental backdrop to the action, increasingly become the focus of the story and the decision to eliminate them emerges as the story's true climax, while the melodramatic adventure of stopping the intruder diminishes to a minor issue; the protagonists' actual triumph comes when they face the reality of space, and capturing their opponent becomes little more than a mopping-up operation. Clearly, Charbonneau discovered in writing that the scientifically imagined background of his novel was more interesting than his story, and he correspondingly shifted his attention to deal with it.

Charbonneau's novel is also interesting because it ultimately asserts that a space station by definition cannot be earthlike, and the best course is to accept and confront its alien nature. This issue will become particularly relevant, as discussed below, in considerations of space habitats: by design, they are supposed to provide the look of a planetary landscape, to serve as a new Earth; but as even the stories created by their proponents indicate, space habitats in truth can never be like planets, and the belief that they can becomes a misleading and dangerous illusion.

Overall, then, there are three basic ways to consider the basic nature of space stations. One view is that the space station is simply a place to do business, neither frightening or comforting; here, the complete remark in Correy's *Manna* is illuminating: "When you've seen one space station you've seen them all, military or civilian. Is there much difference between a military office building and a civilian office building?" (66) Correy thus likens a space station to an office building, with all that implies; and the appropriate appearance here is bland and functional.

A second argument is that the space station is a fundamentally alien place, cold and threatening, like a haunted house filled with hidden horrors. This outlook suggests an appearance that is bizarre and disorienting.

Finally, the space station can be regarded as one's home, an ordinary and comforting place, a true human community in space.

With this view in mind, the station's appearance should be domestic and familiar.

These three images can be seen as consequences of the two basic metaphors for space suggested by the space station—ocean and land. From the beginning of time, men have gone to sea for business, not pleasure, and their voyages have involved long periods of routine activity and boredom combined with occasional crises; thus either a neutral appearance—like a "submarine," as White's novel significantly suggested—or a strange appearance can accord with the image of space as a vast new sea. In contrast, land is a place where people settle, live, and feel comfortable; thus, a homey and domestic appearance can accord with the image of space as the New Frontier.

Interestingly, these three attitudes can also be detected in the various names which authors develop for their space stations. Reinforcing the image of the businesslike and prosaic are numerical names, like "Space Station One," the official name of the station visited in the novel and film *2001: A Space Odyssey*, and by far the single most common space station designation, found in numerous works including Robert A. Heinlein's "Delilah and the Space Rigger," Judith Merril's "Survival Ship," Frank Belknap Long's *Space Station #1*, and Manly Wade Wellman's "Space Station No. 1." And there are also space stations numbered Three (Frederik Pohl, *Man Plus*), Four (Isaac Asimov, *Nemesis*), Five (Asimov, "Reason"), Six (Bob Buckley, "The Star Hole"), Seven (Gill Hunt, *Station 7*), Eight (*Queen of Outer Space*), Eleven (George Bishop, *The Shuttle People*), Fourteen (Berl Cameron, *Solar Gravita*), and Forty-Two (C. E. Fritch, "Many Dreams of Earth"). Greek letters are another popular designation, with Space Station Alpha (Ben Bova, *Kinsman*), Gamma (Fritz Leiber, "Kindergarten" and *The Wild, Wild Planet*), Delta (Jack Haldeman II, *Vector Analysis*), and Omega (Alfred Slote, *Omega Station*); while the High Pentagon of Frederik Pohl's *Heechee Rendezvous* is made up of five space stations called Alpha, Beta, Gamma, Delta, and Epsilon. Similar in spirit are more recent names derived from the station's location, like "Low Earth Orbit" station, or "LEO," and the "L1 Sat" in W. T. Quick's "High Hotel," LEO-2 and LEO-3 in Arthur C. Clarke and Gentry Lee's *Rama II*, and Geosynch in Juanita Coulson's *Tomorrow's Heritage*. One can hardly imagine less imaginative or interesting names—it is like the settlers of Jamestown deciding to name their settlement "City Number One" or "Latitude 38 Degrees"—and they clearly indicate the fact that inhabitants regard the station as little more than a base of operations, not a home or settlement.

There are also names which suggest the unusual or transcendent, including poetic created names like Astropol (Otto Gail, *The Stone from the Moon*), Stellopolis (Kenneth Bulmer, *Star City*), Cyrille (C. L. Moore, *Judgment Night*), the Crystal Moon (Poul Anderson, *Hunters of the Sky Cave*), and Molidor (Frank Belknap Long, *This Strange Tomorrow*). Names from ancient myths, legends, and literature are sometimes found: the orbital city Laputa, in Alexis A. Gilliland's *Long Shot for Rosinante*; Heimdall, the "rainbow bridge to the stars," in Jerry Pournelle's "High Justice" and "Consort"; Daedalus, in John Stith's *Memory Blank*; the Pleiades, in Martin Caidin's *Four Came Back*; Prometheus One, in Harry Harrison's *Skyfall*; Cerberus Star Ring, in George R. R. Martin's "The Second Kind of Loneliness"; Olympus Station, in Allan Steele's *Orbital Decay*; Athena, in Tom Maddox's "Snake-Eyes"; and Atlantis, the official name in Charles Sheffield's *The Web between the Worlds* and the nickname for Einstein Station in Vonda N. McIntyre's *Barbary*. Here, the station names evoke the faraway and exotic, the feeling that one is truly venturing into and living in a strange new world.

Lastly, there are names that hearken back to Earth environments by borrowing and building upon the name of a city or country on Earth, such as Supra-New York in several Heinlein stories, including "Space Jockey," New New York in Joe Haldeman's *Worlds*, New America in Victor Appleton's *The City in the Stars*, New Hanford in Thomas R. Dulski's "My Christmas at New Hanford," and Toledo Cylinder in Michael Swanwick's "Ginungagap." People from Earth's past are also honored in space station names, typically rocket pioneers, scientists, or astronauts: Konstantin Tsiolkovsky (Stan and Fred Goldstein, *Star Trek Spaceflight Chronology*, Haldeman, *Worlds*, and others), Albert Einstein (McIntyre, *Barbary*), Robert Goddard (William MacBride Allen, *Farside Cannon*, Juanita Coulson, *Tomorrow's Heritage*, and others), Stephen Hawking (Richard A. Lupoff, *The Forever City*), Yuri Gagarin (Chris Claremont, *FirstFlight*), Gus Grissom (William Earls, "Jump," and Mack Reynolds, *Chaos in Lagrangia*), and Neil Armstrong (Dale Brown, *Silver Tower*). And in Michael Swanwick's "Ginungagap" and Allan Steele's *Clarke County, Space*, a space station is named for a science fiction writer, Arthur C. Clarke. In such names, the space station pays tribute to dreams and activities started on Earth and reaffirms its connection to the home planet. Lastly, stations given affectionate nicknames based on their resemblance to familiar objects—the Doughnut and the Wheel are found in innumerable works—also seem to function as a comforting reminder of life on

Earth.

As I discuss these three images in the next chapters, however, I should note that there is rarely a clear correlation between the described appearance of the station, its overall mood, and its name. The space station in E. C. Eliott's Kemlo novels is described in familiar terms and characterized as a comfortable domestic community; why, then, was it given the cold and prosaic name of Satellite Belt K? Why was the bland factory station with a severe system of punishment in Jerry Pournelle's "High Justice" given an exotic name from Norse mythology? And why was the station with the most terrestrial appearance, the hollowed-out asteroid of Louis Charbonneau's *Down to Earth*, imbued with such an atmosphere of tension and mystery? One could argue that science fiction authors typically lack either the skill or desire to carefully coordinate their names and descriptions with the moods of their stories; or, more charitably, one might find in these incongruities a deliberate attempt to make use of the dichotomy between the station's appearance and the story's atmosphere—which I believe became one of Charbonneau's purposes in *Down to Earth*, to contrast the reassuringly familiar environment with the threat of the mysterious intruder. However, these conflicting images, names, and auras may also reflect a true ambivalence about the space station itself—something that is neither like the sea nor the land, something that is not quite a neutral place of business, not quite an arena for thrilling adventure, and not quite a happy home.

PART TWO

FUNCTIONS

4. "Factory in the Sky":
Space Stations as Businesses

One can speak of the romance and adventure of sea travel, but throughout history, people have ventured into uncharted oceans primarily as a practical matter of business, expecting to earn back their investments from their efforts. Certainly, that is what motivated Columbus and Magellan. Similarly, science fiction writers, as well as NASA scientists and administrators, can wax eloquent about humanity's basic desire to "go where no man has gone before," but they must justify the cost of building a space station by describing the useful and profitable functions that such a facility would perform.

While creating their most extravagant visions, science fiction writers have always realized that a building a space station would be an expensive proposition, and as part of the projection of a plausible and internally consistent fictional world—as is usually demanded in science fiction—they have been obliged to offer sound reasons for such expense. Thus, even in a work as juvenile as Victor Appleton II's *Tom Swift, Jr., and His Outpost in Space*, one finds a surprising note of adult economic reality: in planning his station, Tom calculates that "The total cost of the project on paper was staggering—far above his wildest estimates" (112). Similarly, a teenage boy in Robert S. Richardson's *Second Satellite* estimates the cost of building a station as "Ten billion maybe" (125). In a novel equally juvenile—though in this case not specifically aimed at a juvenile audience—the space station in Frank Belknap Long's *This Strange Tomorrow* was "a fifty billion dollar project"—in 1966 dollars (14); and amidst the melodrama of Martin Caidin's *Killer Station* (1984) one learns that the station cost "forty-five billion dollars" (258). Even to an unsophisticated audience, such literally astronomical costs must be justified. And beyond maintaining the logic of the background, authors have an additional aesthetic rationale for explaining the need for a space station; surely it would be difficult to build an atmosphere of drama and excitement while describing a completely purposeless facility.

In discussing at some length what science fiction writers have posited as the practical and spiritual benefits of space stations, I can both demonstrate both the vitality of the field and refute to some extent the standard argument against construction of the international space station: namely, that such a space station can serve no useful purpose. For example, an editorial entitled "Another Shuttle? Not Now," in the *Los Angeles Times* of August 12, 1986, urged postponement or abandonment of the space station project, complaining, "No one has yet said what the space station is going to be used for" (II, 4). Science fiction works, however, suggests that such views are short-sighted, and that space stations will in fact serve a variety of important purposes in humanity's near and far future.

In the imagined early stages of space travel, science fiction writers find two logical and exciting reasons to build a space station. One of these—to achieve military superiority over the Earth—they almost unanimously condemn; the other—to assist in the further exploration and exploitation of space—they almost unanimously endorse.

The first major role for an Earth-orbiting space station is essentially to serve as a space fortress: an armed facility, usually equipped with nuclear missiles aimed at Earth, designed to maintain peace on—and not incidentally, American hegemony over—the entire planet. The logic behind such stations is the old military principle of seizing the high ground—in this case, the sky above the ground. A slightly mad professor in Slater Brown's *Spaceward Bound* exclaims, "What was it Archimedes said about the lever? Give me a lever and a point to rest it on and I will move the world. Well, give me a space station and an orbit for it to move in and I will rule...the world" (82). And as stated in Robert Smith's novelization of the film *Riders to the Stars*, an armed space station would mean "A *pax Americana*" because "The ambition to destroy would be a hopeless ambition in a world with a new swiftly-moving man-made moon" (65, 159). Similarly, George Kinley's *Ferry Rocket* states that "the two space stations kept the peace of the world by virtue of the terrible destruction that, from the two-hour orbit, could be unleashed anywhere upon the defenceless earth" (55). A general occupying a space station in Michael Yamin's "The Dreamers" puts matters more bluntly: "We can command all Earth with this Station" (79).

Although critics like H. Bruce Franklin occasionally picture science fiction as militaristic and "technocratic" (as in his *Future Perfect* 394), it is remarkable to note that in the late 1940s and 1950s, which such plans were most widely promulgated, one finds a general consensus in the genre opposing such military space stations. There is first of all a purely idealistic argument against them, presented in one early work, Michael Yamin's "The Dreamers" (1947). "The builders of this Station had looked up, not down" (79), the protagonist says, and he argues that space should be an arena of international cooperation and peaceful exploration; using such a station for killing and conquest simply perpetuates patterns from humanity's primitive past. The story's hero is so determined to prevent his station, once an international project to peacefully conquer space, from being converted into a space fortress that he arranges an atomic explosion to blow up the entire facility, including himself, and hopes that someday in the future more enlightened people may reenter space with better plans. And plans to use a space station to establish "orbital dictatorship" (68) are forcefully resisted by the idealistic denizens of Astropolis in Brown's *Spaceward Bound*.

In addition, both stories which oppose, and those which appear to endorse, such military stations also express a number of entirely practical objections to the plan. First, while the high ground on Earth is difficult to reach and assault, an object in space is completely exposed to numerous forms of attack; as Albert Saari stated in his story of that name, a military space station is a "Sitting Duck"—"practically defenseless and vulnerable" (128). Getting down to specifics, science fiction writers have thoroughly documented the various ways that a hostile nation might attack a military space station. Enemies might try to sabotage the station even before it gets off the ground, as in David Duncan's *Dark Dominion*, Leinster's *Space Platform*, and C. M. Kornbluth's *Not This August*, in which the military satellite was completed "troubled though the progress of its construction was by sabotage" (82); they can launch missiles at the station, as in Leinster's *Space Tug*, or even an atomic bomb, the method used to destroy the massive Death Star in *Star Wars*; they can try to run into the station with a spaceship, as is planned in the film *Project Moonbase*, or they can hurl any large object at it—Kris Neville's "Earth Alert!" ingeniously suggests the Washington Monument; they can send a saboteur to surreptitiously enter the station and damage it, as in Hal Clement's "Fireproof"; they can slip an impostor aboard the station, as occurs in *Project Moonbase*; they can send a small band to enter and seize control of a space station, as occurs in Robert A. Heinlein's *Between Planets* and Ben Bova's *Millennium*; or they can persuade a loyal crewman to turn traitor, as in Caidin's *Killer Station*. And although one story of space combat, Irving W. Lande's "Slingshot," posits that American and Russian space stations will be protected by a sort of gentleman's agreement while their spaceships fight with each other, such an informal arrangement clearly provides no sound defense.

It is little wonder, then, that the commander of the military station in *Space Tug* is literally going crazy as he must deal with one destructive attack after another; and more generally, dangerous insanity caused by the tension of manning a space fortress represents another problem with the military space station. Kris Neville's "Cold War" and "Satellite Secret," Laurence M. Janifer and J. L. Treibich's *Target: Terra*, and James Gunn's *Station in Space* all describe or illustrate this peril. A peculiar temporary solution to the problem is suggested in Gunn's novel: because, as the station commander observes, it is simply the threat of nuclear attack, not the attack itself, that makes a military space station effective, he has removed all the missiles from the silos, so the station no longer poses any danger. But of course, this information would surely be revealed someday, requiring that the station be rearmed and offering no permanent answer to the problem—which is exactly what is about to happen in Neville's "Satellite Secret," although the news that the American stations have been disarmed is fortuitously not revealed to the Russians when the informant happens to speak first to an American spy.

Not only does a military space station literally invite armed attack, but there is also an additional problem with the concept of space as the "high ground": while the high ground on Earth is limited in size and easy to completely occupy, space is by nature vast and limitless, so that any nation with the means and motive can neutralize the power of the space fortress by orbiting its own armed facility; and this is exactly the situation seen in Fletcher Pratt's "Project Excelsior" and Theodore L. Thomas's "Satellite Passage," although the tensions between the American and Soviet space stations in those stories are mitigated by friendly contact between their crews.

For all these reasons, military space stations only serve to increase tension and make war more likely—another argument against their construction; as del Rey states in *Mission to the Moon*, "With two stations, things would be worse than ever...the war couldn't be prevented" (17). In Edmund Cooper's *Seed of Light*, for example, a nuclear war occurs because of the launching of an armed station— "an outpost that might have been a springboard for the stars, but wasn't. An outpost that humanity had turned into a loaded pistol, pointing at the great head of the world" (43); and in the final section of *A Canticle for Leibowitz*, by Walter M. Miller, Jr., one factor mentioned as part of the atmosphere of increased tension that eventually leads to the climactic nuclear war is a military space station: "the space forces of the Atlantic Confederacy...totally destroyed one enemy space station known to be involved in a guidance system for space-to-earth missiles" (229).

There are two novels I can think of where a military station achieves a desirable end—C. M. Kornbluth's *Not This August* and Ben Bova's *Millennium*—but each ends ambiguously. In Kornbluth's novel, the launch of a military satellite does bring about the removal of Russian troops occupying America, but in the final chapter the hero explicitly warns that the militarization of space can only lead to endless cycles of escalation: "It isn't over and it'll never be over. What happens next is the Reds build a bombardment satellite of their own.... We use those years to build a better satellite that'll shoot them out of the sky" (189). So the story ends with the hero renouncing military action to join in a pacifistic prayer for peace. And in Bova's *Millennium*, the lunar colonists' seizure of the American and Russian anti-ballistic systems will apparently force those countries to recognize the Moon's independence and eventually join in a world government—but the instigator of the revolt, Chet Kinsman, dies in a strange atonement for his murder of a Russian cosmonaut years ago. Thus, conflict casts a shadow over its optimistic conclusion, and a later sequel, *Colony*, depicted humanity as still embroiled in disputes even after world government is established. The message seems to be that a military space station *might* be useful if it is employed quickly to achieve a particular end; but in the long run it will always be counterproductive.

Thus, we find that the scientifically knowledgeable writers of science fiction effectively carried on an extended debate on the virtues of military space stations in the 1950s and found the idea fundamentally flawed; and since the 1960s saw no efforts to militarize space, one might argue that their message was taken to heart. However, in the 1980s, with those stories and their conclusions long forgotten, the Reagan administration presented and pursued a new proposal for military space stations, with the modern wrinkle of nuclear-powered lasers instead of nuclear bombs and an announced focus strictly on defense. And after years of lavish expense and research on the Strategic Defense Initiative, or "Star Wars," some of the same arguments found in the science fiction of the 1950s have surfaced to call the whole project into question: namely that space-based stations would be highly vulnerable to Soviet attack, that there is nothing to prevent the Soviets from building similar stations, and that the whole enterprise seems likely to increase tensions and the possibility of nuclear war.

These old lessons also emerge in a number of more recent novels about military space stations, notably including James P. Hogan's *Endgame Enigma*, George Bishop's *The Shuttle People*, Ben Bova's *Peacekeepers*, Dale Brown's *Silver Tower*, and Frederik Pohl's *Heechee Rendezvous*. In Hogan's novel, an armed Russian space station is perceived as so vulnerable to attack that the Soviet government devises an elaborate ruse involving a mock-up of a space station in a huge underground chamber, designed to persuade American visitors held captive there that they are actually in a space station and that the station has no military equipment. But even this remarkable strategy fails, as the truth comes out and a successful American threat prevents any attack. In *The Shuttle People*, Bishop offers the standard argument—"As we now know, space stations command the world" (82)—but his story undermines it: a group of deranged astronauts find it relatively easy to take over a space station, bring an H-bomb to it, and pose a credible threat to the United States government. A similar problem emerges in Bova's *Peacekeepers*, where a military facility in space designed to monitor the world and prevent war is almost seized by some renegade officers who wish to take over the world; and as the commander struggles to defend his station, he employs the analogy first presented by Saari: "We're like a sitting duck up here" (101). In Brown's *Silver Tower*, although the author tries to demonstrate the usefulness of a military facility in space for observation and defense, his Armstrong Space Station is soon being attacked by two Soviet space shuttles, and its heroine, like Kornbluth's hero in *Not This August*, ends the novel with a bleak prognosis of continuing military escalation in space: "too much success, like Skybolt has had now, can breed a need for more and more...I wanted to develop it for defensive reasons only. But now...." (379; author's ellipses). And while giving some background on the High Pentagon, a complex of five space stations visited in *Heechee Rendezvous*, Frederik Pohl explains how the military station almost immediately provoked imitation and conflict:

> At one time, they said, [the High Pentagon] had been the very latest in defense. Its huge nuke-fueled missiles were supposed to be able to zap any enemy missile from fifty thousand miles away. Probably they indeed could—when they were built—and maybe three months after that, until the other fellows began using the same pulse-hardening and radar-decoy tricks and everybody was back to Go. Unfortunately they all "went," but that's a whole other

story. (234)

In all these works, then, armed space stations are once again presented as open to attack, easy to imitate, and likely to increase world tensions and the possibility of armed conflict—the conclusions already reached in the science fiction of the 1950s.

Finally, while both old and new stories indicate that military space stations will not be helpful in a war on Earth, a few works suggest that space stations might be useful in defending Earth against an attack from space, serving as sentinels or fortresses. In Theodore Sturgeon's "Unite and Conquer," unmanned defense satellites will eventually be joined by a manned space station as a way to protect Earth from space invaders—even though those invaders are ultimately revealed to be a hoax. In Gordon R. Dickson's "Steel Brother," lonely commanders on asteroid stations keep a constant vigil to see and fend off the assaults of mysterious hostile aliens; in Mark McNeil's "Scratches in the Dark," stations are set up in the asteroids to look for the alien invaders that have already infiltrated the Earth; in Orson Scott Card's *Ender's Game*, a space station is the base where the hero directs his battles against the aliens; in Arthur C. Clarke and Gentry Lee's *Rama II*, Excalibur Station is constructed to watch for the coming of a second spaceship from the mysterious—and possible hostile—Ramans; and in Frederik Pohl's *The Annals of the Heechee*, humans and aliens build the Watch Wheel near the home of the mysterious Assassins to detect any activity on their part. On a grander scale, *Star Trek VI: The Undiscovered Country* reveals that the Federation of Planets guards against Klingon invasion with "space stations and star bases along the Neutral Zone." An unusual variation on this idea is found in Horace B. Fyfe's "Sinecure 6," where space stations are built by a future Earth devastated by plagues and radiation in order to warn an expedition returning from Alpha Centauri to stay away and avoid contamination; here, space stations serve to keep away *friendly* visitors to ensure "the future of the human race" (64).

The other popular role for a space station—the one celebrated and not criticized—is epitomized in the title of Lester del Rey's *Step to the Stars*: the space station serves as a place where humans can adjust to life in space and prepare for and launch expeditions to the Moon and other worlds; Robert S. Richardson's *Second Satellite* calls a proposed space station "our stepping stone to the planets. Our springboard into deep space" (125). The first novel to offer such a justification for a space station was Otto Gail's *The Stone from the Moon* (1926), where the builder of the station explains:

[the space station] for the first time makes at all possible future advances into the realm of the planets...a space ship for interplanetary travel doesn't need the first and last of these loads [leaving and returning to Earth] if it starts the trip right from the station in space, where it's built. And saving fuel is everything. (333)

Occasionally, these stations are seen as strictly transitional structures: in Murray Leinster's *Men into Space*, based on the television series of that name, the hero speculates that the space station he is building "will eventually be junked" (67), as a hazard to future space navigation; and obsolete, cannibalized space stations in Jack C. Haldeman II's *Vector Analysis* are described as "expensive junk" (50).

However, the most common scenario is that the space station, once travel to other planets is achieved, remains in position to become what Richard Elam, Jr., in "The Ghost Ship of Space" called a "space service station" (132): a place where spaceships from Earth can dock and transfer travelers to deep-space vehicles that take them further, a place also offering services like refueling, restaurants, and shops. Robert A. Heinlein in "Space Jockey" describes one of these stations as "hardly more than a fueling point and restaurant-waiting room" (25); Robert and Barbara Silverberg's "Deadlock" calls such facilities "halfway-houses for space travelers" (98); and a similar station seen more recently is the Customs Satellite orbiting Earth in Joe Haldeman and Jack C. Haldeman II's *There Is No Darkness*.

Space stations which assume this sort of role—as a stopover on the way to and from further destinations—are dramatic and important when space travel is just beginning, and trivial and insignificant once such travel becomes commonplace. This transformation occurs in a remarkably parallel fashion in two juvenile trilogies of the 1950s, del Rey's Jim Stanley/Fred Halpern trilogy—*Step to the Stars, Mission to the Moon,* and *Moon of Mutiny*—and Murray Leinster's Joe Kenmore trilogy—*Space Platform, Space Tug,* and *City on the Moon*. In each series, the first novel concerns the building of the first space station, which is naturally the focus of the book; the second novel pays less attention to the station to concentrate on the launch from the station of a mission to the Moon; and in the third novel, the space station, barely noticed, is just a place where the protagonist stops while going from Earth to the Moon.

In stories that do not deal with the initial construction of the space station, stopover facilities from the beginning become almost invisible background elements. The works of Robert A. Heinlein provide apt illustrations here. Regular readers of Heinlein will no doubt recall the space habitat in his novel, *The Cat Who Walks through Walls*, the specially-equipped satellite home of "Waldo," the asteroid converted into a space station by Heinlein's "Misfit," or even the Space Station No. 1 being built by "Delilah and the Space Rigger." However, there are many other space stations in his works that are usually not noticed or forgotten: Supra-New York, the earth-orbiting station seen or talked of in "Space Jockey," "It's Great to be Back," and "The Green Hills of Earth"; Space Terminal, orbiting the Moon, visited or mentioned in the first two stories above and "Ordeal in Space"; Terra Station, where Heinlein's *Space Cadet* and his friends enjoy a brief vacation; Circum-Terra Station, occupied and destroyed by Venusian rebels in *Between Planets*; the station that the emergency rescue mission takes off from in "Sky Lift"; the station containing a nuclear power plant launched in "Blowups Happen" and destroyed in *To Sail beyond the Sunset*; the space stations that beam laser messages to the Moon in "Searchlight"; and the space habitat at the L-5 point referred to in *Friday*. These stations are hard to remember because they are not memorable; typically they function in these stories simply as interludes, touches of local color, or as background elements in some larger adventure occurring in space or on the surface of a planet.

The invisible space station is also a feature of the first six *Star Trek* feature films. Every one of them begins or ends with the *Enterprise* docked at, approaching or leaving a space station in Earth orbit, but these facilities are never focused on as significant environments. Indeed, the creators of these movies, so concerned about continuity in other areas, more than once change the name or appearance of this station.

To argue against space stations as places to launch space missions, or to stop and rest during such missions, given the inherent logic of such stations, one must argue against space travel itself; and that is the singular perspective ultimately offered in Gunn's *Station in Space*. After establishing in the earlier sections that space stations are not useful in a military way, Gunn finally depicts a manned mission to Mars that fails for the same reasons that all previous missions failed: men on long space journeys inevitably go mad. This story, which at first seems a tacked-on addition to a novel otherwise concerned with space stations, instead constitutes its final argument against them: if man cannot travel into deep space, then there is indeed no reason at all to build a space station. Gunn's bold conclusion is that "The exploration of the unknown is always a fraud" (109).

Since few if any other authors maintain this bleak perspective, their space stations survive the test of utility; and moving further into the future, they establish space stations with a number of other roles, in Earth orbit and beyond, based on the obvious advantages stations in space offer for certain activities. In addition to serving as spaceports, space stations can also take a more active role in controlling and regulating traffic in space; since they can be located in any region of space, they can be ready to assist any space traveler in danger; because they can offer the experience of space without many of the hazards of space, they are an excellent place to train young spacemen; stations in space have ready access to solar energy which can be profitably harnessed; they can easily obtain and process mineral resources in space and provide a base for other forms of industry; they are well positioned for communication services—telephone, radio, and television—connecting different regions of Earth and space; with variable gravity, controllable environments, and the vantage point of deep space, they are uniquely well equipped for scientific research, especially in meteorology and astronomy, and also offer new possibilities in advanced medical care; their isolation can make space stations ideal for retreat or hermetic existence; far away from conventional or confining locations, they can serve as places for strangers and organizations to meet; they promise new possibilities in entertainment—and confinement; they might preserve the human race in case of disaster on Earth; and space stations can serve as an inspiration and symbol of human progress to the people on Earth.

As space travel becomes more common, some regions may become dangerously crowded at times, and a space station would be a logical facility to maintain order. In Eliott's *Kemlo and the Zones of Silence*, one main function of the space station is traffic control—it "sent out the controlling waves to keep the giant space and rocket ships on their true course" (7); Stewart Cowley's *Starliners* describes one common type of future space facility called the "Traffic Control Station...which monitors and directs all movement in the busiest of spacelanes"—their "wheel-like forms are familiar to anyone who has boarded a liner" (90); and in the *Doctor Who* serial "Revenge of the Cybermen," the Doctor and his friends visit a manned space station designed to be "a beacon to guide and service space freighters" (as described in Terrance Dicks's novelization, *Doctor Who and the Revenge of the Cybermen* [4]).

Although almost all space stations might be able to offer emergency assistance to threatened space travelers, some stories envision networks of stations standing by especially for such rescue operations. This is the main purpose of Robert A. Heinlein's Space Station E-M3, constructed in the story "Misfit"; Fritch's "Many Dreams of Earth" imagines a network of "living space stations" set up to aid distressed spacemen in the Solar System; and Charbonneau's *Down to Earth* envisions a number of "emergency landing outposts" scattered throughout the Galaxy. Stations may also be established for particular needs, like Jack Williamson's "Dead Star Station," "established as an aid to navigation" through a dangerous passageway in the Orion Nebula and "to go to the aid of any endangered vessels" (180).

Space stations as schools for future youngsters have been seen in three children's television programs: the 1956 BBC series *Space School*, the 1977-79 CBS series *Space Academy*, and the 1987-89 CBS cartoon series *Galaxy High School*, described in the book by that name by Ann Hodgman. In written science fiction, Heinlein's *Space Cadet* learns about life in space on the S.S. Randolph, an old spaceship now left in permanent Earth orbit as a station for cadet education; but the more common pattern is for a stopover station to also serve as a training area for advanced space students, a pattern seen in countless stories, including Richard Elam Jr.'s "The Iron Moon," Robert Marsten's *Rocket to Luna*, Blake Savage's *Rip Foster in Ride the Gray Planet*, and the anonymous "generic novel" simply entitled *Science Fiction*.

As already noted, space stations which will harness solar power and beam it to Earth are an old idea, presented in Gail's *The Stone from the Moon* (1926), Murray Leinster's "The Power Planet" (1931), Edmond Hamilton's "Space Mirror" (1937), and Isaac Asimov's "Reason" (1941); and in Pelham Groom's *The Purple Twilight*, there are plans to build a number of "Terminals in Space" to beam concentrated sunlight to barren regions of Earth and make them habitable. However, it seems that doubts about the feasibility of such stations soon emerged, as seen in the way the proposal is abruptly dismissed in Asimov's *The Caves of Steel* (1953), and such stations did not become prominent again until the oil embargoes of the 1970s brought a new urgency to the search for new sources of energy. Now, such stations, called "powersats," are regularly featured in modern novels like Harry Harrison's *Skyfall* and Lee Correy's *Manna* and *Space Doctor*.

Space stations are sometimes seen as ideal places to process raw materials from space and manufacture goods; one early and spectacular example is Basil E. Wells's "Factory in the Sky," an immense metal sphere in the asteroid belt which builds spacecraft and other devices. Mining and processing are also two of the main businesses of the flying cities in James Blish's Cities in Flight novels. More modest space factories appear or are mentioned in more recent stories like Jerry Pournelle's "High Justice," John Brunner's *The Shock Wave Rider*, Joseph Green's "Three-Tour Man," Joe Haldeman's "More Than the Sum of His Parts," Spider and Jeanne Robinson's *Stardance*, and Lee Correy's "Industrial Accident"; Arthur C. Clarke's *Imperial Earth* mentions "the zero-gravity orbiting factories" (242); Charles Sheffield's *Between the Strokes of Night* features Salter Station, primarily devoted to capturing and mining asteroids—"they also extracted enough platinum, gold, iridium, chromium, and nickel to make up almost half of the world's supply" (54); and the rebellious space colony in Larry Niven and Stephen Barnes's *The Descent of Anansi* is trying to support itself by making and selling a new super-strong cable. An especially grandiose—and grim—example of a huge factory in space is Vulcan in Allan Cole and Chris Bunch's novel, *Sten*, where workers live their lives as virtual slaves in various industrial compounds. One particularly intriguing possibility often raised in these stories is employing the vacuum of space to grow gigantic crystals, and the most memorable aspect of the ride Horizons at the Walt Disney Epcot Center is a visit to the space station Bravo Centauri, where one can see a huge crystal being formed.

Another possible type of industry in space is briefly mentioned in Stan and Fred Goldstein's *Star Trek Starflight Chronology*, which describes the development of "spacefarms," described as "huge orbiting windmill-shaped constructions" (51)—essentially expanded versions of the space "greenhouses" built in Tsiolkovsky's *Beyond the Planet Earth*; and large-scale agriculture is often depicted as one function of enormous space habitats. Dan Simmons's *The Fall of Hyperion* extravagantly envisions space-dwellers tending "massive comet farms" with their "hard vacuum crops" (435). Farming on a more modest scale takes place in the space station of David Brin's "Tank Farm Dynamo." More unusual facilities in space which produce food include the automated, and rather irrational, food-processing station in Robert Sheckley's "Paradise II," and the Food Factory, a huge construct in Frederik Pohl's *Beyond the Blue Event Horizon* which collects elements from the Solar System's Oort Cloud and transforms them into food.

Finally, while the term "industry" can conjure up images of smokestacks and smelters, there is one other form of industry that might fruitfully be developed in space: the entertainment industry.

Specifically, what better location could there be for the filming of science fiction movies? Thus, the space station in Clarke's *Islands in the Sky* becomes home to a company doing location shooting for a space adventure, and in Richard A. Lupoff's *The Forever City*, space habitat Yukawa obtains considerable income from a studio producing holographic films based on old science fiction stories.

Manned space stations which relay communications to and from various parts of Earth and space are also frequently seen, most prominently in George O. Smith's *Venus Equilateral*, a station in Venus's orbit forming a perfect triangle with that planet and Earth, designed to maintain constant communication between the two planets. Arthur C. Clarke featured such satellites in several works, most prominently in *Islands in the Sky* and "The Other Side of the Sky," and communications networks sponsor the building of a space station in *Tom Swift, Jr., and His Outpost in Space* by Victor Appleton II. Although it was not designed as a space station, a mission to Mars aborted by a nuclear war stays in Earth orbit and becomes a valuable communication link between, and an inspiration to, scattered communities struggling to rebuild their lives in Philip K. Dick's *Dr. Bloodmoney; or, How We Got Along after the Bomb*. Other examples of space stations employed for communication include Geosynch, the space station headquarters of a major communications network in Juanita Coulson's *Tomorrow's Heritage*, and the illegal radio station broadcasting from a space station in the film *Thunderbirds in Outer Space*; while Rick Raphael's "The Mailman Cometh" depicts a space station as a different sort of communications center—a post office in deep space receiving and dispatching mail.

Clearly, a space station is an ideal place for some types of scientific research. Two of these functions involve observation, either of Earth—meteorology—or of outer space—astronomy. Douglas R. Mason's *Satellite 54-Zero* depicts a station devoted to meteorological study, and the station in Lester del Rey's *Mission to the Moon* "was obviously valuable for weather predictions" (80). And Arthur C. Clarke's *The Fountains of Paradise* describes converted military stations that do more than watch the weather:

> It had not been easy to persuade the surviving superpowers to relinquish their orbital fortresses and hand them over to the Global Weather Authority...Now the lasers that had once threatened mankind directed their beams into carefully selected portions of the atmosphere, or onto heat-absorbing target areas

in remote regions of the earth. (139)

Similarly, Ben Bova's "The Weathermakers" mentions lasers beamed from space stations as one way to stop hurricanes; Gill Hunt's *Station 7* mentions space stations in Earth orbit used "for weather observation and control" (25); and the station in Ellen MacGregor and Dora Pantell's *Miss Pickerell and the Weather Satellite* relays weather predictions to Earth and conducts meteorological research.

As for astronomy, the benefits of an observatory in space were described as early as 1897 in John Munro's *A Trip to Venus*: a space vehicle "would be a novel observatory, quite free from atmospheric troubles. They might be able to make some astronomical discoveries...One of these days, I suppose, we astronomers will be packed in bullets and fired into the ether to observe eclipses and comets' tails" (36, 43). In addition, Hugh Walters's *Terror by Satellite* takes place in a space observatory; Clarke's *Rendezvous with Rama* mentions "the orbiting observatories" (6); a manned space telescope figures in John Alfred Taylor's "Grave-11"; "the new satellite observatory" (43) helps locate a missing lunar miner in Roger Kuykendall's "All Day September"; and Theodore Kubaska's "Univan and the Wheelies" takes place in the Hans W. Blumish Station for Planetary Observation. Another space station—"Stag Head detector station" (111) in William F. Powers's "Meteor"—exists specifically to look for and announce the approach of dangerous large meteorites.

Beyond observation of the Earth and the stars, space stations in later stories, reflecting a new awareness that space may be filled with strange, inexplicable objects, are set up to monitor and investigate these phenomena. Examples include the station built for close study of the bizarre Jansky Singularity in Brian N. Ball's *Singularity Station*; the stationary spaceship near *The Black Hole* in the film of that name; the Star Rings built around "Nullspace" in George R. R. Martin's stories "The Second Kind of Loneliness" and "Nor the Many-Colored Fires of a Star Ring"; the space station built near a black hole in Bill Johnson's "Meet Me at Apogee"; and Heaven, the space habitat near the singularity or "Highway" to other worlds in William Gibson's "Hinterlands."

In addition to studying alien phenomena, a space station can also serve as a place to study alien life forms or artifacts. The most prominent example is the space station established especially to study the mysterious living ocean in Stanislaw Lem's *Solaris*; but there is also the station which investigates alien beings returned by space probes in Jack C. Haldeman II's *Vector Analysis*, the station used to study an alien spacecraft in Joseph P. Martino's "Persistence," and Gulf City, in Charles Sheffield's *Between the Strokes of Night*, which is attempting to study strange creatures in space, far away from the radiation of any star.

Another common premise in science fiction is that space stations might be an ideal place to study strange phenomena inside the human brain—to investigate and develop people's psychic powers. The idea is mentioned in George Bishop's novel of the near future, *The Shuttle People*, where "the antispiritualistic, materialism-oriented Russians had been conducting experiments...trying to establish whether the space environment somehow altered the physical laws governing thought transmission on earth" (159-160). Farther in the future, Terry Greenhough's *Thoughtworld* is a hollow artificial planetoid set up to prove Tynar's Hypothesis: that people's mental powers will increase in the absence of gravity. Finally, Gordon R. Dickson's *The Pritcher Mass* envisions a space platform beyond Pluto as the best location for a huge construct of psychic force, jointly created and manipulated by crewmen with paranormal powers, which will be used to search for other planets where Earth's threatened populace might migrate to.

Other space stations are devoted to special types of research which require zero gravity or isolation. The space station in Horace B. Fyfe's "Thinking Machine" carries on unique scientific research: miniature planets are built, orbited, and sometimes destroyed in an effort to gain a better understanding of actual planetary systems. In Hal Clement's "Answer," a space station houses a gigantic computer used for scientific research which cannot function near radio waves. Murray Leinster's *City on the Moon* discusses the need to use space stations for especially hazardous research: "That was the reason for the Space Laboratory.... They did research too dangerous to attempt on Earth, or even the moon" (21)—specifically, research involving atomic energy. Similarly, the Spacelab orbiting Regulus 1 in the film *Star Trek II: The Wrath of Khan* is designed to complete Project Genesis far from any planet where it might produce disastrous consequences, and a distant space station in Thomas R. Dulski's "My Christmas on New Hanford" is developing a hazardous and devastating anti-matter bomb. Other scientific research facilities in space include the unseen Science Wheel in Mack Reynolds's *Satellite City*; "The Moon of Advanced Learning," a six-man research center in Earth orbit, seen in Robert F. Young's story of that name; the Penrose Institute orbiting Mars in Charles Sheffield's "All the Colors of the Vacuum"; and the "Lagrange One zero-gravity research satellite" mentioned in Clarke's *The Songs of Distant Earth*.

Inevitably, there will be a need for medical treatment in space, and a hospital in orbit might also have advantages in that flexible gravity and environmental conditions could facilitate certain types of medical treatment. The most advanced space station of this type seen in science fiction is James White's Sector Twelve General Hospital, described in several of his novels, an immense structure said to resemble a gigantic Christmas tree where various sections duplicate the environments of the sixty-eight known species of intelligent life; White also refers to "smaller multi-environment hospitals" scattered throughout the Galaxy (*Hospital Station* 114). In the near future, there are several more modest facilities of this type, including the "Louis Pasteur satellite hospital" (35) mentioned in Clarke's *The Songs of Distant Earth*, the Hospital Wheel of Mack Reynolds's *Satellite City*, the "Satellite Hospital Outpost" (441) of Sharon Webb's "Itch on the Bull Run," and the "satellite hospital" (135) planned in Richard Elam, Jr.'s "The Ghost Ship of Space." And smaller medical facilities based on space stations devoted to other purposes are seen in numerous stories, including Lee Correy's *Space Doctor* and Elizabeth Moon's "ABCs in Zero G."

In addition to medical treatment, psychological treatment might also be provided in a space station, although this approach seems less likely to yield good results. Certainly, no reader would be impressed by space station Molidor in Frank Belknap Long's *This Strange Tomorrow*, where people with mental problems are forcibly sent to undergo what has to be the most bizarre form of psychological treatment ever seen in fiction—"space therapy," consisting of brutal beatings by sadistic guards, long hours endured doing nothing but staring out into space, and outlandish "entertainments" featuring ballet dancers and clowns, designed somehow to recapture the spirit of childhood. It is little wonder that, as one character admits, most patients confined at Molidor end up worse off than they were at the start. The therapy offered at New Horizon, a space station mental hospital in Patricia A. McKillip's *Fool's Run*, seems a bit more logical, although the "Dream Machine" they develop to look into the minds of patients offers no discernible benefits in the novel, and in fact only provokes a chain of events culminating in a disturbed prisoner's daring escape.

Aside from doctors and psychologists, dedicated professionals of a quite different kind—monks and nuns—might find the isolation and spartan environment of a space station a perfect place for a monastery or retreat, and one such facility is described in Michael Moorcock's *The Fireclown*: "the space station monastery circling in space, away from the things of Earth...had a detached air of calm about it" (98). However, this particular monastery is a science fiction in-joke: the monks are striving to become "clear" according to the precepts of Scientology, and their home is called the Monastery of St. Rene Lafayette (an old pseudonym of L. Ron Hubbard). A similar station, representing a more conventional religion, is mentioned in Joe Haldeman's *Worlds*: Jacob's Ladder, "a huge and beautiful space structure that combined the functions of church, monastery, and hotel" (22), which is maintained by the World of Christ evangelical organization until it plunges into the Earth's atmosphere.

A space station would be an ideal place for humans and aliens to meet—neutral ground, as it were—and one small facility specifically designed for contact with an alien is Damon Knight's "Stranger Station." Space colonies are the regular meeting places for humans and alien Investors in Bruce Sterling's *Schismatrix*, and in Thomas Wylde's "Space Shuttle Crashes!" there is a proposal "to build a space port at L4 to lure UFOs down to solve Earth's problems" (244). A grander version of this purpose is seen in Construct, the huge "artificial planet" (191) in Haldeman and Haldeman's *There Is No Darkness*, built by aliens to provide suitable environments and meeting places for all sentient races. And the chance to meet—and have sexual encounters with—aliens is the main attraction of the Big Junction in James Tiptree, Jr.'s "And I Awoke and Found Me Here on the Cold Hill's Side," although that is not, it seems, the station's main purpose.

In addition, space stations frequently figure as environments where traditional enemies can meet without animosity or hostility. Thus, Americans and Russians converse in a friendly manner at the space station in *2001: A Space Odyssey*; humans and Klingons intermingle uneasily but peacefully at Space Station K-7 in the *Star Trek* episode, "The Trouble with Tribbles"; and representatives of two warring alien races meet under truce conditions at the space station in John Brunner's *Sanctuary in the Sky*.

For similar reasons, an organization might choose a space station as its headquarters, since it is a place which offers no special advantage to particular individuals or groups. One example is seen in Clarke's "The Lion of Comarre," where the officials of the world government meet on an "artificial moon" orbiting the Earth, a means to provide a global perspective and ensure that "no narrow parochial viewpoint" interferes with their decision making (12, 13). In Michael P. Kube-McDowell's "Menace," the Planetary Survey Service has its headquarters in a space station near Earth, and the interstellar agents of Ron Goulart's *Star Hawks: Empire 99* are based in a space station orbiting the planet Esmeralda. And in the *Doctor Who* episode "The Trial of a Time Lord," the Time Lords choose to assemble on a massive space station as an appropriate place to pass judgment on the apparent crimes of the Doctor.

Perhaps the most beautiful and memorable space stations in science fiction are the pleasure stations, designed to attract visitors in search of various amusements. Two extravagant visualizations of such facilities are the Pleasure Bubble, seen in Everett Smith and R. F. Starzl's "The Metal Moon," a gigantic sphere whose upper half is a magnificent city enclosed in crystal, and the Crystal Moon, visited by Ensign Flandry in Poul Anderson's *Hunters of the Sky Cave*, which features "clear-glass walls...curving and tumbling like water" and massive "synthetic jewels, ruby, emerald, diamond, [and] topaz" (125). And for interior beauty, no space station can match the multiplicity of dreamlike environments available in the immense "pleasure world" of Cyrille in C. L. Moore's *Judgment Night*.

Other spectacular creations in science fiction include Somtow Sucharitkul's *Mallworld*, a huge cylindrical shopping center with over 20,000 "shops, hotels, department stores, holopalaces, brothels, psychiatric concessions, suicide parlours, and churches" (24)—not to mention the scandalous amusement park, Copuland—and Cosmos's, the huge "spa/casino/nightclub/hotel satellite" (cover blurb) visited by Ron Goulart's Exchameleon in *Everybody Comes to Cosmo's*. In addition, Jack Vance's "Abercrombie Station" mentions twenty-two "resort satellites" in orbit around Earth (20); Earth-orbiting space stations in Gill Hunt's *Station 7* are used "even as entertainment centres" (25); Robert Silverberg's *Regan's Planet* and *World's Fair 1992* envision the 1992 Columbian Exposition being held in a space station, offering not only innumerable exhibits and shops but also exhibits of living creatures from Mars and Pluto; Curt Siodmak's *Skyport* describes the construction of Sky Wharton, a glamorous orbiting hotel; the unsold television series pilot *Starstruck* features a restaurant in space; Mack Reynolds's *Satellite City* is a station which features gambling casinos and other entertainments; and Kenneth Bulmer's Hook, "star-spanning man of the future," visits the pleasure city in space, Stellopolis, in *Star City*. Then there are the stations built and designed to serve as space brothels, notable examples being the 5000 Doors Moments of Bliss satellite in Philip K. Dick's *The Crack in Space* and the Velvet Comet described in four novels by Mike Resnick. Finally, for pleasures of a more family-oriented nature, Alfred Slote's juvenile *Omega Station* appropriately suggests transforming a mad scientist's space station into "a summer camp" (143).

There are obviously exciting possibilities for the arts in a space station, with a perfect vacuum and zero gravity available, but these are rarely mentioned. The most prominent exception is the orbiting dance studio in Spider and Jeanne Robinson's *Stardance*, which dancers use to invent and perfect the art of zero-gravity dance. Bob Buckley's "The Star Hole" describes one noteworthy advance in the plastic arts: "a sculpted ice dream floating just outside the celebrated zero-G studio port of Sky Station Six" (72). Dan Simmons' *Hyperion* refers to space-dwellers who have "explored new dimensions of aesthetics and ethics and biosciences and art and all the things that must change and grow to reflect the human soul," but offers no specifics (468). And Fritz Leiber's "The Beat Cluster," describing "activities suitable for freefall," mentions "dancing, artistic creation in numerous media and the production of sweet sound" (199), "freefall yoga" (201), "space diving," and "water sculpture" (202).

Oddly enough, there are few space stations set up specifically for physical activity or as gymnasiums; space stations almost always have places to exercise, but these are typically described as large storage chambers or empty compartments converted into, and used by the crew as, recreational areas. As one indication of the unique possibilities in zero-gravity athletics, Chris Claremont's *FirstFlight* mentions a new sport—"SkyBall" (24).

In stark contrast to these facilities for entertainment, the arts, or athletics, there are large numbers of space prisons, grim constructs typically reserved for the most despised and dangerous of Earth's outcasts and criminals. Some of these have a unique clientele: Harlan Ellison's "The Discarded" describes an endlessly orbiting spaceship which houses malformed mutants, the grim effect of nuclear war, who are despised and unwanted by the remaining "normal" people of Earth; and Ben Bova's *Exiled from Earth* envisions the world's genetic engineers being rounded up and sent to a space station by the world government, which worries that their work might upset the delicate political balance on Earth.

Other prisons in orbit are reserved for those criminals, especially terrorists and revolutionaries, which authorities are likely to regard as most dangerous to Earth. Examples of such facilities include the space prison which orbits around Curt Siodmak's *City in the Sky*; the space habitat in William Forstchen's *Into the Sea of Stars* used as a prison for "political unreliables, conscientious objectors, and disarmament activists" (172); the large orbiting prison known as the Underground in Patricia A. McKillip's *Fool's Run*; the endlessly flying prison spaceships of Clifford D. Simak's *Empire*, including "the Vulcan Fleet, the hell-ships of the prison fleet" reserved for "the most vicious and most depraved of the Solar System's criminals" (91); the "prison workships" (110) in the asteroids feared by the hero of Stanley Mullen's "Fool Killer"; the orbiting prison cells maintained in M. Max Maxwell's "Prisoner 794"; the space prison near Venus in Charles Sheffield's "Dinsdale Dissents"; and the prison satellite Pris-Sat Z9 in the anonymous story "Rough Justice."

Long ago, Konstantin Tsiolkovsky's "The Aim of Astronautics" suggested that habitations in space would be necessary in order to preserve the human race should disaster strike the planet Earth: "Man must at all costs overcome the Earth's gravity and have, in reserve, the space of at least the Solar System. All kinds of danger lie in wait for him on the Earth" (370). In John Brunner's *The Crucible of Time*, a race of aliens is strongly motivated throughout its history by exactly such a concern, as they gradually realize that their planet lies in a turbulent region of space, which has brought disastrous climatic changes and meteorites, and which will eventually destroy their planet. They therefore develop the racial goal of moving into and living in space as a way to maintain their species and finally succeed in building a "vast artificial globe" (5) to inhabit just before their planet is devastated. And in Jack Williamson's poetic but nonsensical "Born of the Sun," humans are driven to build an "ark" to live in space when they learn that the Earth and other planets are simply gigantic eggs, about to hatch and produce gigantic children of the sun.

More plausible stories involving human beings have also featured space stations designed to preserve the race, although the methods may involve the transportation of eggs and embryos, not actual people. This is the specific function of the space station in Thomas Wylde's "The Nanny": in the event of devastating war on Earth, the crew was instructed to launch and fly a starship to Alpha Centauri containing frozen human eggs which could later be grown to keep the human race alive; and in Vernor Vinge's "Long Shot," a space station is used to monitor and instruct an intelligent spaceship, Ilse, which is also sent to Alpha Centauri with a supply of human embryos. Another space facility designed to preserve humanity, though by means of a different plan, is seen in a *Doctor Who* serial, "The Ark in Space," where the entire population of Earth is placed in suspended animation in a space station so that they can survive while solar flares temporarily make their planet's surface uninhabitable.

Finally, there are stories describing space stations built for other purposes that are forced into the role of humanity's last hope when a devastating war breaks out on Earth: Tyrone C. Barr's *The Last Fourteen*, Thomas N. Scortia's *Earthwreck!* (both discussed in Chapter 7 below), and Charles Sheffield's *Between the Strokes of Night*; in addition, while Earth is not completely destroyed in Joe Haldeman's *Worlds*, the knowledge and technology of the orbiting space habitats prove to be essential elements in humanity's gradual recovery. When these planetary disasters occur unexpectedly, the plans for survival must be desperately improvised and, at least in the case of Barr's novel, do not seem to turn out successfully— suggesting the need for space stations specifically prepared for such an eventuality.

All of these proposed roles for space stations, grand or trivial, prosaic or exotic, nevertheless have some kind of practical angle, emphasizing the financial, scientific, or humanitarian benefits of a space station for such things as manufacturing, research, and space rescue. However, there is an undercurrent in several stories suggesting that a space station might also serve as an inspiration, a source of pride, for the inhabitants of Earth—a role that sometimes comes to the forefront in those stories which take place before the space station gets off the ground. To be sure, in some of these stories the goal of a space station simply serves as a device to provoke routine adventure on Earth: in John Weir Cross's *The Stolen Sphere*, heroic young acrobats must recover a small working model of a space station which has been stolen by a villain; an underground research lab working on building a space station is menaced by malfunctioning robots in the film *Gog*; and in Frank Belknap Long's *The Martian Visitors*, the engineer who is in charge of completing a new space station finds himself distracted by a Martian who has teleported to Earth. However, other stories of this type imbue the dream of a space station with genuine spiritual meaning: there is real sense of excitement about human possibilities in the discussion of "artificial planets" in John Munro's *A Trip to Venus*, and in David Duncan's *Dark Dominion*, the builder of a space station hopes that "by lifting men's eyes to the stars he will lead them to forget their differences on earth" (10). There is also Slater Brown's *Spaceward Bound*, where the Young Astropolitans' desire for space travel, including the construction of a space station to be used as "a fuel dump in space" (66), manifests itself as an almost religious fervor. In such stories, beyond any utilitarian value, a space station can function as a significant and inspirational symbol of both scientific and social progress.

Even stories which describe operational space stations sometimes focus on their spiritual importance to all people everywhere.

Thus, although their interiors and residents are never seen and their purposes left vague, the space stations seen in the film *Gorath* clearly function as emblems of scientific progress and achievement, especially in the closing scenes, where pictures of the stations accompany the narrator's optimistic speech about human development continuing on, even in the wake of disaster. In a similar spirit, Curt Siodmak's *City in the Sky* and Mack Reynolds and Dean Ing's *Trojan Orbit* describe the people of Earth as concerned about and supportive of the success of a space community in Earth orbit.

I can finally mention one other "spiritual" purpose for a space station, although the idea is far removed from the scientific spirit which permeates almost all of these stories. This unique proposal is also found in Siodmak's *City in the Sky*: "Astrological papers earnestly discussed the influence of artificial satellites on human fate. If such an influence could ever be scientifically examined, the astrologers reasoned, then satellites could be sent aloft to create certain destinies" (72). Indeed, while something as tiny as Sputnik could be logically discounted as astrologically insignificant, those space stations which attain large size and population might well merit a place in horoscopes. If one grants the validity of astrology, this idea would make space stations strangely important facilities—new factors influencing the destiny of the human race.

Besides the value of a space station as an inspirational symbol, many of the other purposes listed above may also seem a bit visionary, especially in regards to a station to be built in the 1990s; yet even in the near future, many of these functions could become realities. It would be cheaper and easier to launch unmanned probes like *Galileo* and *Magellan* from a space station than from the space shuttle; a space station might well provide needed assistance to a space mission which experiences catastrophic failure on the edges of Earth's atmosphere; proposals for networks of solar power stations will be feasible when oil becomes expensive and difficult to obtain—which might happen sooner than predicted, given the ongoing crises in the Persian Gulf—and a functioning space station in place would be the logical base for their construction; NASA already plans various types of scientific research in fields like medicine and metallurgy; and the problems of the Hubble Space Telescope demonstrate that there might be some advantage in a manned orbital observatory. Even apparently long-range proposals for space hotels, space churches, and space film studios may be realized in the near future: with thousands already on airline waiting lists ready to pay dearly to get a ticket for the first flight into space, the argument of Ben Bova's "Isolation Area"—that a space hotel and resort would generate huge profits almost immediately—seems logical; with major charismatic religious groups continuing to attract large sums of money, the described development of Jacob's Ladder in Haldeman's *Worlds* does not seem completely outlandish; and with science fiction filmmakers like George Lucas and Steven Spielberg awash in funds from their latest hits, the filming of a space epic near a space station as in Clarke's *Islands in the Sky* seems a real possibility. The list of things a space station might "be used for" is in fact almost unlimited, given a long-term perspective; and given the lapses in science fiction prophecy concerning other areas of scientific progress, we can also be sure that there are purposes for space stations that have not yet been anticipated.

To be sure, many of these ideas have already been aired by NASA publicists—as seen, for example, in a booklet by Walter Froehlich called *Space Station: The Next Logical Step*—without having much of an impact; and there is in fact one logical way to debunk such suggestions. Advocates of a space station invariably depict a number of other simultaneous initiatives in space, and indeed, in the context of a vigorous program of space exploration and activity, a space station repeatedly emerges as useful, even necessary. It is as a solitary object in an otherwise uninhabited universe that the space station can seem useless. Thus, if someone wants to argue that there is no particular need to explore or exploit outer space in the near future, it then becomes possible to argue that there is no particular need for a space station.

Anticipating exactly this kind of resistance to the construction of a space station, science fiction writers have seized upon a particular sort of character as an essential element in the process—an extremely wealthy person obsessed with the idea of space travel. Von Gorf, in Otto Gail's *The Stone from the Moon*, is the prototype of this figure, a businessman who admits to beguiling his stockholders and colleagues with fanciful tales of huge profits when his actual and sole interest lies in the conquest of space. Later figures in this tradition include: the hard-driving businessman Regan who builds the space station for the 1992 Columbian Exposition in *Regan's Planet* and *World's Fair 1992*, virtually as a matter of personal pride; Laura Hansen, who wants to use her space station as a base for further space exploration in Jerry Pournelle's "High Justice" and "Consort"; and Salter, who maintains a space station in Charles Sheffield's *Between the Strokes of Night* as part of his individual crusade to improve the human race through various types of research. Determined tycoons investing in and building space stations also figure in Curt Siodmak's *Skyport*, Spider and Jeanne Robinson's *Stardance*, and Lee Correy's *Space Doctor*. In this common scenario, then, there emerges one final purpose for a space station: as the ultimate toy for bored billionaires, one project which is capable of fully occupying all of their energy and intelligence in ways that no earthy endeavor can match.

Of course, even the most obsessed businessman must be concerned about the issue of safety: a space station which is attacked, blown up, or occupied, a space station where residents go mad or refuse to stay, can obviously make no profits and serve no useful purpose. In an entirely different manner, science fiction writers of a certain kind must also be concerned about the safety of a space station—be concerned, that is, that the space station is not too safe, not too comfortable, that it can be a suitable setting for action and adventure. Therefore, before accepting the image of a space station as a place for routine business, one must first ask: is there anything here to be afraid of?

5. *Killer Station*:
Space Stations as Haunted Houses

Despite long hours of boredom and inactivity, sea travelers may suddenly experience terrible and unexpected danger; and for that reason, no doubt, seamen are notoriously superstitious, and tales of nautical ghosts, haunted ships like the *Flying Dutchman*, and mysterious curses fill the folklore and literature of the sea. And since the modern genre of science fiction is rooted in melodrama, as I have demonstrated in "Man against Man, Brain against Brain," writers who deal with space stations seem driven to provide strange menaces and thrilling adventures, which often provide the station with the atmosphere of a haunted house. Still, writers in the genre of science fiction—the good ones, at least—cannot simply employ old stratagems of heroes and villains, dangers and rescues, in new contexts; charged with the responsibility of presenting accurate scientific information and reasonable scientific predictions, they are obliged to consider the actual likelihood of such events in their futuristic worlds, and amidst all the action and adventure, we do find authors who carefully weigh the probability of these dangers and conclude that it is low indeed—reassuring news, no doubt, for the designers of the international space station, but distressing news, perhaps, for some writers of science fiction.

In almost any type of fiction, of course, an atmosphere of impending doom is a useful dramatic device, even if nothing threatening actually occurs; and numerous stories provide subtle signs to indicate that space stations might indeed be quite dangerous places. For one thing, stations are often under military or quasi-military command, the type of discipline necessary in times of crisis; in several early stories like Murray Leinster's "The Power Planet," women are not allowed to serve on space stations, suggesting an environment not suitable for members of the weaker sex; and there are frequently only a few men in a space station crew, implying a desire to limit possible loss of life. In many depictions of space stations in science fiction, however, there is no need to merely hint of danger; rather, danger explodes upon the scene.

Science fiction stories repeatedly emphasize the overall vulnerability of space stations. The station in Jack Williamson's "Crucible of Power" is called "frail as a bubble" (29); a character in Curt Siodmak's *City in the Sky* wonders, "How can the [International Space City] be made less vulnerable?" (9); the commander of George O. Smith's *Venus Equilateral* says the station is "as vulnerable as a half pound of butter at a banquet for starving Armenians" (290); residents of the station in Melinda Snodgrass's *Circuit* are called "sitting ducks" (121) and the heroine later "realized how fragile and tenuous man's hold in space was" (219); and Lee Correy's *Manna* asserts that "A powersat is a terribly vulnerable thing" (104). Specifically, the hazards which threaten space station residents fall into three categories: natural disasters—meteors and malfunctions; alien invasions—monsters and microbes; and manned attack—marauders and madmen.

Earlier novels like Bernard's *The Wheel in the Sky* and Appleton's *Tom Swift, Jr., and His Outpost in Space* express considerable fear of meteors striking the station, though we now know the chance of such an encounter is very low; still, the possibility of such a disaster remains, and even a more recent work like Douglas Mason's *Satellite 54-Zero* mentions that "All around the clock there was one man in space gear, ready to go out and deal with any emergency like major meteorite penetration" (62). The station in Anne Mason's *The Dancing Meteorite* is at one point threatened by a large meteorite magnetically manipulated by aliens trying to damage the station, and the space station in the *Doctor Who* serial, "The Wheel in Space," is at one point threatened by a meteorite shower. Another problem, stressed in Martin Caidin's *Killer Station*, is increased radiation from solar flares, which would require crewmen to retreat behind thick shielding; someone wryly comments in Lee Correy's *Space Doctor* that "If God had meant people to live in space, He would have coated them with lead" (160-161). Michael Flynn's "The Washer at the Ford" describes how several cosmonauts in Mir space station died of radiation sickness because of an intense solar flare. Radiation threatens a space station in a different way in Appleton's *Tom Swift, Jr., and the Cosmic Astronauts*: as Tom's Outpost in Space begins "twirling at a deadly rate," he explains that "Cosmic radiation...affects all our instruments...it must have triggered off our station's stabilizing mechanism" (83-85).

Even if such natural dangers can be handled, manmade objects in space could easily pose a hazard: the spaceman in Clarke's "The

Haunted Spacesuit" is working to avoid a collision between a space station and a defunct satellite, and a missile sent by Tom's "space friends" accidentally "plowed into the space wheel with a sickening jolt" in *Tom Swift, Jr., and the Cosmic Astronauts* (130). Similar accidents are described in Richard Louis Newman's *Siege of Orbitor*—"the ship he was stationed on collided with a middle-sized space station" (11); Richard Elam, Jr.'s "Mercy Flight to Luna"— "While they were coming into dock on the giant revolving wheel which was the space station, something had happened to the braking rockets and the ship had collided with the hangar" (83-84); and Steven Gould's "Rory"—"The shuttle from Ceres blew up. It took the docking pad with it" (104). And any sort of equipment failure or mechanical problem in a space station could be disastrous; Thomas N. Scortia's *Earthwreck!* comments that "In space it took only a small miscalculation to bring you quickly into a dangerous situation" (117) and the solar power satellite in Harry Harrison's *Skyfall* never becomes operational, and ultimately crashes to Earth, because of a series of accidents and malfunctions.

Not surprisingly, the makers of visual science fiction—films and television programs—have repeatedly employed the more colorful theme of alien invasion. In films, an energy beam from Venus blows up a space station in *Queen of Outer Space*; virulent ambulatory behemoths infest a space station in *The Green Slime*; gaseous energy beings from Mars invade one space station and teleport others to the surface of Mars in *War of the Planets*; and a strange "space fungus" menaces space station residents in *Mutiny in Outer Space*. On television, poisonous flowers from outer space attack a space station in the *Outer Limits* episode, "Specimen: Unknown"; adorable but ravenous "tribbles" cause problems in Space Station K-7 in the *Star Trek* episode, "The Trouble with Tribbles"; and aliens disguised as human beings infiltrate a space station in the *Buck Rogers in the Twenty-Fifth Century* episode, "Mark of the Saurian." In the British television series *Doctor Who*, the space stations visited by the Doctor and his friends are regularly invaded by one alien race or another: in "The Wheel in Space," rats infesting a space station turn out to be Cybermats, created by the evil robots called Cybermen as part of their plan to invade Earth; in "The Ark in Space," wasp-like beings called the Wirrn invade a space station containing Earth's population in suspended animation so they can infest the human bodies, absorb their knowledge, and conquer the universe; and in "Revenge of the Cybermen," a strange space plague afflicting Space Beacon Nerva turns out to be caused by poison injected by surreptitious Cybermats, now being employed as part of the Cybermen's plot to destroy the planet Voga.

Slightly more plausible are the alien menaces depicted in written science fiction. These include the "space sharks" living in the vacuum of space which attack Tucker's "Interstellar Way-Station"; the miniaturized Mercurians who inject humans with a fatal poison in Edmond Hamilton's "Space Mirror"; the Mercurian "silly dillies," the silicon creatures "who could drill through the shell of a space station" (166), mentioned in Blake Savage's *Rip Foster in Ride the Gray Planet*; the berserker-like alien warship that threatens to destroy the space station in Ted White's *Secret of the Marauder Satellite*; the humanoid Martians that occupy the space station in Lester del Rey's *Siege Perilous*; the aliens who plant a robot impersonator on a space station in Theodore Kubaska's "Univan and the Wheelies"; the mysterious "space plague" that kills four out of eight space station crewmen in Martin Caidin's *Four Came Back*; and the "dream plague" transmitted from a captured flying alien which threatens the crew of space station Delta III in Jack C. Haldeman II's *Vector Analysis*. And while they are not alien life forms, a character in Arthur C. Clarke's *Islands in the Sky* describes two other forms of biological infestation: "do you know what our biggest trouble used to be?...*Mice*...do you know how we [got rid of them]?...We used *owls*!...the problem then, of course, was to get rid of the *owls*" (40-41). The story turns out to be a tall tale, but the problem remains possible, and an actual infestation of rats is mentioned in Vonda N. McIntyre's *Barbary*.

A more common danger to a space station, however, is other human beings seeking to destroy it. I have already listed many of the methods available in discussing the drawbacks of military space stations; but it should be pointed out that even space stations devoted to peaceful purposes often fear—or experience—an armed attack. Thus, C. L. Moore's *Judgment Night*, strictly a "pleasure world," is eventually assaulted by missiles—the heroine dreads "bombs cracking through this twilight sphere in which she floated" (22); Smith's *Venus Equilateral*, a communications satellite, is placed under siege by a band of space pirates; Mike Resnick's space brothel, the Velvet Comet, is threatened by a fanatic with a nuclear bomb in *Eros Descending*; and the artificial planetoid Theeo in Terry Greenhough's *Thoughtworld*, devoted to peaceful mental research, is sabotaged again and again. Although no problems occur, the peaceful World's Fair satellite of Silverberg's *Regan's Planet* and *World's Fair 1992* is haunted by the possibility of sabotage: a character in the latter novel notes that "two or three really determined saboteurs could come here containing the components of a small disassembled fission bomb in their luggage" (101). The sole resident of the orbiting satellite in Dick's *Dr. Bloodmoney*, benignly serving as a "disc jockey" for his devastated planet, is uniquely menaced by a mutant on Earth who keeps "squeezing" the astronaut's heart with long-range psychic powers. The danger of sabotage or attack of some kind is also mentioned in Lee Correy's *Space Doctor* (56), Fritz Leiber's *A Specter Is Haunting Texas* (164), Basil E. Wells's "Factory in the Sky" (72), and Douglas R. Mason's *Satellite 54-Zero* (167)—all works involving non-military space stations.

Even if an actual assault does not occur, financial scheming can also become a way to attack a station: in Smith's *Venus Equilateral*, a scheming investor at one point manipulates the stock market in an effort to *buy* the communications satellite and thus remove its residents; in Resnick's *Eros Ascending*, an accountant is sent to the Velvet Comet to doctor its books and create fictional huge losses, which would force the space brothel to close down; and in Horace B. Fyfe's "Thinking Machine," an evil Arcturan purchases a space station in order to exploit tiny aliens.

In addition to outsiders determined to destroy space stations, the residents of such stations display an alarming tendency to go mad; as already noted, one contributing factor can be the tension of manning an atomic space fortress, but even in other types of stations, various forms of madness can emerge and pose yet another hazard to a station. Such insanity may simply be a reaction to the real and imagined hazards of space station life, or, as suggested in Terry Greenhough's *Thoughtworld,* a result of the absence of gravity: "Vitch's corollary" to Tynar's Hypothesis is "That the failings of cellular brains, such as delusions, madness, neuroses, obsessions and hatred, must also increase in potency in no-grav" (79).

To be sure, it is hardly surprising that men who are alone in an isolated space station might become unbalanced, as in C. E. Fritch's "Many Dreams of Earth," George R. R. Martin's "The Second Kind of Loneliness," and J. T. McIntosh's "Hallucination Orbit"; indeed, in the latter story the fact that any solitary person in space will quickly go insane is universally and calmly accepted. However, even when conditions are more amenable, there is concern about possible or actual insanity in many stories, including Murray Leinster's "The Power Planet" (202), George Bishop's *The Shuttle People*, Ben Bova's *Exiled from Earth* (181-182, 198), Melinda Snodgrass's *Circuit* (188), Leinster's *City on the Moon* (160-162), Josephine Rector Stone's *Green Is for Galanx* (32, 65), Larry Niven and Stephen Barnes's *The Descent of Anansi* (87), Robert A. Heinlein's "Space Jockey" (28), and Lester del Rey's *Siege Perilous*

(8).

In addition, almost every conceivable type of specific mental problem has afflicted at least one station inhabitant in science fiction: paranoia (Ted White, *Secret of the Marauder Satellite* 22, 126, and Edmund Cooper, *Seed of Light* 17, 38), "cabin fever" (Dick, *Dr. Bloodmoney* 260), being "island happy" (Sam Merwin, Jr. "Star Tracks" 146), claustrophobia (Lester del Rey, *Siege Perilous* 54), agoraphobia (Greenhough, *Thoughtworld* 29, and Leiber, *A Specter Is Haunting Texas* 17), schizophrenia, psychosis (both in Laurence M. Janifer and J. L. Treibich, *Target: Terra* 62, 90), suicidal tendencies (J. M. Walsh, *Vandals of the Void* 460), sadism, homicidal mania (both in James Gunn, *Station in Space* 89), neurosis (Murray Leinster, *Space Tug* 53), religious mania (the film *Conquest of Space*), xenophobia (James White, *Star Healer* 21), acrophobia (Hal Clement, "Answer" 161), catatonia (Frank Belknap Long, *This Strange Tomorrow* 55), and psychosomatic illnesses (Lee Correy, *Space Doctor* 64). Even a robot succumbs to space station insanity in Isaac Asimov's "Reason," where a new robot assembled in a station promptly develops the delusion that he is the prophet for some robotic god and that the humans around him are only inferior creatures.

As if all these problems were not enough, some authors have posited unique new types of psychological disorders which will arise as a result of life in space. These include "genetic fever" in Bernard's *The Wheel in the Sky* (73, 74, 88), "space shock" in Frank Belknap Long's *Space Station No. 1* (28), "space madness" in Curt Siodmak's *Skyport* (67), the "space jitters" in Basil E. Wells's "Factory in the Sky" (73), "satellite nerves" in Sam Merwin, Jr.'s "Star Tracks" (147), "space craziness" in del Rey's *Step to the Stars* (25, 33, 58, 86), "space fatigue" in the film *Conquest of Space*, the "Space Platform Blues" in John Norment's "Space Platform Xz204c Does Not Answer" (88), "solitosis" in McIntosh's "Hallucination Orbit," and being "space happy," mentioned in the film *Project Moonbase* and Appleton's *Tom Swift, Jr., and His Outpost in Space* (207).

The whole situation threatening the sanity of space station residents is aptly summed up in one statement from del Rey's *Siege Perilous*: "space gnawed at men's minds" (6). And people with space gnawing at their minds can become a real danger to themselves and their crewmen, like the man who "suddenly announced that he was going outside with a butterfly net to catch meteors" in Arthur C. Clarke's "The Other Side of the Sky" (39), the megalomaniac commander of an orbiting observatory who takes over the station and attempts to conquer Earth in Hugh Walters's *Terror by Satellite*, and the deranged astronauts who form a conspiracy to kill opponents and dominate the world in Bishop's *The Shuttle People*. Such problems have apparently become routine in the future world of Paul Preuss's *Breaking Strain*, where the author speaks of policemen prepared to cope with the "drunkenness and homicidal rage and other forms of insanity that commonly afflict the human residents of space stations" (230). This sort of space-induced madness is benign and harmless, it seems, only when the entire crew goes mad—a development better examined in the next chapter on space stations as residences.

Given all these possible dangers—meteors, radiation, collisions, attack, sabotage, and madmen—it is little wonder that a feeling sometimes emerges that life on a space station is truly frightening, a never-ending series of threats and potential dangers: Niven and Barnes's *The Descent of Anansi* speaks of "death waiting outside every wall" (101) and Thomas N. Scortia's *Earthwreck!* describes "the menace of violent death a few millimeters of steel or mesh-reinforced plastic away" (23). The space station begins to seem like a den of horrors, a haunted house. In some stories, the atmosphere of fear and foreboding becomes overwhelmingly powerful: the residents of the space stations in Damon Knight's "Stranger Station" and Stanislaw Lem's *Solaris*, for example, become almost paralyzed with terror as they confront the mysterious, huge alien they are assigned to study.

A few space station stories consciously employ horrific and supernatural imagery in presenting the hazards of space: in Clarke's "The Haunted Spacesuit," a space station crewman goes out into space to intercept a dangerously close satellite and starts to hear noises in his suit. Soon, he is scared out of his wits:

> Even now, I do not like to recall those next few moments, as panic slowly flooded my mind like a rising tide, overwhelming the dikes of reason and logic which every man must erect against the mystery of the universe. I knew then what it was like to face insanity; no other explanation fitted the facts...though I was in utter isolation...I was not alone. The soundless void was bringing to my ears the faint, but unmistakable, stirrings of life. (64)

Here is Clarke uncharacteristically imitating the prose of H. P. Lovecraft! Similarly, in Mark McNeil's "Scratches in the Dark," a crewman in an asteroid station is maddened by mysterious noises:

> And, as the lights and instruments failed, the scratching returned, growing louder, more predatory.
> It seemed to sense his vulnerability. Jason began seeing apparitions in every shadow. He told himself that it was his fear, but his heart pounded nevertheless. Something was warning him. Each new transit of the corridor brought him closer to hysteria, a plateau of fear he was unwilling to face...His hand hovered over the controls for the exterior camera, but he could not bring himself to touch the controls, to view the horror that awaited him. (115, 116)

And in Janifer and Treibich's *Target: Terra*, a station resident trying to account for a number of mysterious accidents is driven to fanciful supernatural explanations:

> Perhaps, he told himself, one of the Station personnel had a background that included Transylvanian relatives...And perhaps the relatives—vampires, they might be, or carelessly sewn monsters, or small fluttery impossibilities that laughed—had come to visit the Station. If the stories about such beings were even halfway true, they wouldn't require suits, or even ships...He told himself he was being foolish. But an almost weightless walk down a black and lonely corridor was not terribly conducive to rational thought. (9-10)

While these evocations of the supernatural are clearly frightening to space station residents, a more whimsical approach to the subject of haunted space stations is provided in Don Sakers's unique anthology *Carmen Miranda's Ghost Is Haunting Space Station Three*, based on Leslie Fish's "filk song," "Carmen Miranda's Ghost." Here, actual ghosts are seen as regular visitors to space stations, although they are generally not presented as menacing; only one story, Amanda Allen's "Rolling Down the Floor," depicts Carmen Miranda's ghost as ghoulish and menacing. In the other stories, the spirits are friendly: all authors note that Carmen Miranda's ghost leaves behind fresh fruit for the crewmen to eat; in B. W. Clough's "Provisional Solution," Carmen and other ghosts actually want to assist in the conquest of space (Julia Child's ghost appears to help improve the quality of space food); and in Leslie Fish's "Bertocci's Proof," Carmen helps a crewman locate and reunite with his deceased lover.

In more typical science fiction stories where a space station starts to seem like a haunted house, there are a number of possible resolutions. Some people simply flee from the horror; for example, in Correy's *Space Doctor*, it is said that "The strangeness of the environment, the constant awareness of death near them or around them, the invisible specter of ionizing radiation, and the relative isolation of GEO Base got to a few of them...[They were] frenetic, disturbed people" (165). And shortly thereafter, a nurse suddenly announces that she is returning to Earth, saying that she "can't take another day of living in these cans with death outside their walls" (173). For these people, the true nature of life in a space station remains unresolved, as they abandon the problem without further investigation.

Second, the space station residents who stay and confront the situation may discover that the terror and mystery remain. Certainly, Knight's "Stranger Station" and Lem's *Solaris* conclude with no feeling that the awesome alien nearby has truly been understood. Some lesser stories also end with an unresolved puzzle: in Gene L. Henderson's "Tiger by the Tail," a man constructing a space station is told to go rescue travelers in an errant spaceship; he flies to the designated area, picks up a spacecraft, and returns it to the station. Then he is told that the imperiled spaceship ended up returning safely to Earth, and there is no other vehicle unaccounted for. So where on Earth—or off Earth—did the spacecraft come from? The story ends without an answer. In Ted White's *Secret of the Marauder Satellite*, a space station is threatened by a mysterious alien ship, apparently programmed to destroy all space vehicles; the menace is removed for now, but the aliens who built the ship and what their motives were remain a mystery—and a potential threat. In Clarke's "The Other Side of the Sky," a space station resident, busy with other affairs, glimpses a mysterious vehicle; by the time he is free to investigate it further, it is gone, leaving him with only the suspicion that what he saw was an alien vehicle. In these stories, the strange and horrific possibilities of life in space are never made clear, and their open-ended conclusions imply there will be some future contact with the unknown. With such endings, the continuing dangers of space station life are validated, at least those involving alien beings.

Finally, those in a space station may investigate the horrible threat and discover that it was only an illusion. The author who most clearly contradicts the image of space station as haunted house, who rips the sheets off the fraudulent ghosts and reveals the machinery of the trap door, is Arthur C. Clarke in *Islands in the Sky*. There, the protagonist is a teenager named Roy Malcolm, who gets a chance to visit the Inner Station after winning a contest; he is naturally enthusiastic and imaginative, and he expects living at the station to be a thrilling adventure. However, he lets his imagination run wild and three times he reacts to dangers of the types listed above that turn out to be nonexistent. He sees a large meteor come crashing through the station wall—but it turns out to be an obvious training exercise staged for young spacemen. Walking through one space station, he looks at what he thinks is a huge alien creature—but it is only an ordinary Earth hydra, scientifically enlarged in weightless conditions. And he observes strangers engaged in suspicious activities near the Station and suspects that they are space pirates—but they are only actors and technicians filming an adventure movie in space.

I would argue that Clarke's achievement in this novel is significant, although *Islands in the Sky* is typically regarded as a minor work. Certainly, he is in some ways exploiting the conventions of juvenile space opera, and the supposed threats of meteors, aliens, and space pirates provide the few moments of drama in an otherwise uneventful narrative. Yet Clarke is also deconstructing the genre, as he demonstrates the absurdity of such threats: given our current knowledge of the solar system, there is extremely little chance of a large meteor ever hitting a space station; given the evident rarity of life forms in our vicinity, there is extremely little chance that an alien would ever visit a space station; and given our reasonable expectations concerning the logistics and economics of space travel, there is extremely little chance that space piracy would ever become a profession. In these ways, *Islands in the Sky* is both an example of, and a commentary on, juvenile space fiction.

"The Haunted Spacesuit," "Scratches in the Dark," and *Target: Terra* offer similarly prosaic resolutions: the noises in the spacesuit of Clarke's hero turn out to be kittens—the newly arrived space station cat had, unknown to the crew, just given birth and left her offspring in the suit. The scratching noises in McNeil's story are caused by geysers of surface rock triggered by the station's own force field: "The venting gases had become animated in his mind, forming a monstrosity. The gases became the dragons of his dreams" (117). And in Janifer and Treibich's novel, the atmosphere of mystery is finally dispelled when the protagonist discovers that one of his crewmates has gone insane and is trying to sabotage the station, producing all the mysterious effects. Again, after exploiting fears of supernatural assault, these authors completely dispel them and instead present more plausible explanations.

Stories of this sort also acknowledge that there are genuine dangers which may endanger in a space station: *Islands in the Sky* concludes with a real emergency involving an injured crewman, the spaceman in "The Haunted Spacesuit" is dealing with the threat of a horrible collision, the station in "Scratches in the Dark" is constantly on the watch for alien invaders, and the possibility of a madman controlling the atomic weapons on the station in *Target: Terra* can hardly be dismissed. Still, these works suggest that the feelings found elsewhere of omnipresent danger and constant, impending doom are simply not accurate; they are rather only illusions in the minds of overly anxious or imaginative residents. The reality of space station life, they indicate, will be more likely the monotony of repetitive routine suggested by the image of an office building, and those who crave excitement and adventure had best go elsewhere.

And going elsewhere is exactly what Roy Malcolm, the hero of *Islands in the Sky*, plans to do. While he initially dreams of someday returning to the Station as a regular crewman, he finally turns down an offer to do just that; instead, after meeting colonists from Mars visiting the Station, he becomes interested in the drama of conquering an unknown world and concludes the novel by saying that "The space stations were too near home to satisfy me now...When I went into space again, the Inner Station would only be the first milestone on my outward road from Earth" (157). Other stories follow a similar scenario: in Robert Silverberg's *World's Fair 1992*, for example, another young hero is first thrilled to be working in a gigantic space station, and constant speculation about sabotage provides a sense of impending menace; but later, as things remain calm during the World's Fair, he jumps at the chance to join a hastily organized expedition to Pluto and finally resolves to pursue his interest in exobiology on other worlds: "The real work was just beginning. And there was Neptune, and Jupiter, and Uranus, and Saturn, and all the many moons, and maybe someday the stars—" (239). The same transition occurs with amazing rapidity in Lester del Rey's *Mission to the Moon*: while he is initially a bit excited to be back at the station, the protagonist quickly "found he was bored with it...His mind needed more than bare walls and the feeling that he was out in space" (53). Clearly, the sense of excitement involved in space station life fades quickly in these stories, and those with an adventurous spirit soon develop the desire to travel further into the unknown.

All three possible endings to the story of the haunted space station indicate, in different ways, that such an environment will not be a satisfying place to live. The fainthearted will flee back to Earth to avoid the dangers they see; those who find genuine mystery will be forever tormented by it; and the heroes who discover that the menaces are not real will want to travel further into space, where true excitement and peril might be found.

In all these resolutions, then, we see one of the fundamental problems posed by the space station in science fiction. In striving to achieve excitement, science fiction authors can somewhat undermine the picture of space stations as bland, functional places of businesses; they do offer in some ways a true sense of danger and mystery. However, not enough of this atmosphere can be plausibly generated to make the space station a satisfying arena for sustained adventure, which ultimately drives away the heroes and would-be heroes that characterize so much of the genre.

Still, not all of science fiction is fast-paced melodrama, and not all writers need their space stations to provide constant thrills and excitement. There remains another option for space station writers: to portray the station as a placid domestic community, like a settlement on Earth, and develop stories of an entirely different nature; however, this approach brings difficulties of a different sort.

6. *City in the Sky*:
Space Stations as Communities

If space is going to be conceived of as something like land, then it instantly seems more reassuring and more safe, and space stations can reasonably be expected to serve as permanent communities for contented residents. This shift in perspective has practical as well as metaphorical ramifications: obviously, if this image is not applicable, and if people are not going to enjoy life in space stations, then there is no point in attempting to build them as residences. In examining various depictions of space stations as homes, one first finds some implausible attempts to portray space stations as universally pleasant, trouble-free communities for all; then, there are more realistic stories that suggest the difficulties as well as the possibilities; and finally, some scenarios indicate that space station life will be rewarding only for a few special kinds of people now existing, or for new and different kinds of people who might emerge in the future.

The first inhabited artificial satellite that appeared in fiction—Edward Everett Hale's "The Brick Moon"—is also the most utopian community ever found in a space station. A resident there exclaims, "Go to thunder with your old law-books. We have not had a primary meeting nor a justice court since we have been here, and, D. V., we never will have.... You can't quarrel here, where you are never sick, never tired, and need not be ever hungry" (116, 119). However, Hale's vision of human society now seems as quaintly fantastic as his notion of a brick space station catapulted into space by gyroscopes. Although based on more solid science, Tsiolkovsky's numerous rhapsodies about the pleasures of life in space are also less than realistic: "Here life is a virtual paradise" (*Beyond the Planet Earth* 251).

A later series of novels which seem as sociologically and scientifically naive as Hale's and Tsiolkovsky's visions are E. C. Eliott's Kemlo books, which argue that a community in space would be as blissfully domestic and ordinary as any on Earth: "Life was organized very similarly to that on Earth, apart from the restrictions forced upon them by living in space" (*Kemlo and the Sky Horse* 55). In Satellite Belt K, there are apparently no major disputes, no difficulties to interfere with harmonious family life, and everyone has happily adjusted to life in space: "as the rolling plains and swelling seas of Earth satisfy and somehow soothe and feed the minds of men who live their wildness, so did the blue [?] void of space satisfy those who, like Kemlo and his friends, were born and raised in its empty vastness" (*Kemlo and the Sky Horse* 135).

If Hale's, Tsiolkovsky's, and Eliott's visions of societies in space can be dismissed as blatantly unrealistic, however, there remain three other space station communities whose harmonious state seems a bit more credible: Curt Siodmak's *City in the Sky*, *Earth II* in the television movie of that name, and Sector Twelve General Hospital in the novels of James White. All three depictions suggest two necessary—if not sufficient—conditions for a successful space community.

The first is that the station be established specifically as a model of international or interplanetary cooperation. As one character in Siodmak's novel observed, "The ISC [International Space City] is neutral ground, a visual symbol of unity of the countries on the globe" (13), and he asks rhetorically, "Can the ISC prove that the people of the world need no boundaries to work harmoniously together? That nationalism and chauvinism belong to a barbaric past?" (14) In the opening sequence of *Earth II*, the station is launched by the President of the United States as a new nation, with residents recruited from all over the world, with the expressed aim of promoting a new spirit of international unity; in keeping with this goal, even toy guns are banned from the station to maintain an atmosphere of peace there. And a similar motive, on a grander scale, inspired Sector Twelve General Hospital: a story in White's *Sector General* describes how two war veterans, continually traveling to various planets in a fruitless effort to achieve better communication between different intelligent species, are involved in a traffic accident involving several types of beings; the experience convinces them that a space hospital, staffed by and serving members of all alien races, could be a means to and model for more cooperation. In addition, the policy described in White's *Star Healer*—that doctors never work on members of their own race—reflects the idea that a secondary purpose of the facility is to improve contact between species. In all three cases, the special goal which created the space community serves as an obvious incentive to maintain its harmony; a society so inspired which succumbs to dissension and dissatisfaction would defeat its own purpose.

The second factor which makes these three stations work as communities is that they acknowledge the possibility of conflict and establish mechanisms to deal with it. In Siodmak's novel, the system is judicial: one character is a judge, empowered to settle disputes which arise in the International Space City. In *Earth II*, major arguments are resolved politically: when residents of the avowedly pacifistic community confront the problem of a Chinese nuclear weapon in nearby space, they convene a meeting of all citizens of Earth II, discuss whether they should take action or not, and decide the question by popular vote. And in White's Sector Twelve stories, the model for conflict resolution is, appropriately enough, medical: Chief Psychologist O'Mara has the responsibility of constantly observing all personnel for signs of instability or dissension and immediately intervening to diagnose and treat any troubled personnel.

While White's Sector Twelve General Hospital is inhabited only by specialists, the other two works argue that people of all types, with a great deal of effort, can indeed achieve a permanent, harmonious community in space. This is, however, distinctly a minority viewpoint. Most stories carefully define a space station as a suitable home only for particular persons: the dedicated, the elderly, the handicapped, the insane, and the exiled.

In addition to the mentioned factors, White's Sector Twelve functions well because it is staffed by particularly dedicated people: namely, doctors. Indeed, unlike other heroes, who are often eager to go out in search of adventure, doctors are expected to sit and wait for problems to come—the more challenging, the better; hence, since Sector General handles the largest and most difficult cases in the Galaxy, medical personnel of all kinds—and species—are pictured as anxious and willing to spend their lives working there. Other types of committed professionals might also be attracted to a space station: the engineers and communication experts in Smith's *Venus Equilateral* seem happy to be where they are, in an ideal locale for working on solving problems and developing new equipment; Hal Clement's "Answer" depicts a scientific research station equipped with a supercomputer which has apparently contented—and permanent—residents; and with his tongue in cheek, Michael Moorcock in *The Fireclown* describes the Scientologists happy to live in a space monastery.

Another group of people who might prefer life in a space station are the elderly, for weightlessness or low gravity would be better for their frail bodies and could even lengthen their lives. This was anticipated as early as 1920 in Tsiolkovsky's *Beyond the Planet Earth*, where his complete assertion was, "Here life is a virtual paradise, especially for the weak and ailing" (251). Thus, the commander of the station in Clement's "Answer" is incredibly old, presumably kept alive by the absence of gravity; in Clarke's *2061: Odyssey Three*, a now-elderly Dr. Heywood Floyd is enjoying his retirement living in a space station; a space habitat in Dean Ing's "Down and Out in Ellfive Prime" is "a natural choice for a retirement community" (98); and in Frederik Pohl's *The Annals of the Heechee*, the Gateway asteroid is eventually renamed Wrinkle Rock and "converted into an old folks' home. It was perfect for the geriatric cases" (8-9). Even some young and healthy people might retire to a space station because of its environmental advantages; for example, a newscaster in Clarke's "The Other Side of the Sky" decides to become a permanent resident because of "two things he liked in particular. 'This air you make,' he said, 'it beats the stuff we have to breathe down in New York.'...He also relished the low gravity" (36).

For similar reasons, the physically handicapped could prefer—or even be forced—to live in a space station. Indeed, in a genre often derided for focusing on Aryan stereotypes, it is remarkable to see how many space stations feature individuals who are deformed in some way. These include four men without legs—the commander of the Inner Station in Clarke's *Islands in the Sky*, who lived there because "it was the only place where he wouldn't be a cripple" (32-33), Shikitei Bakin working in Frederik Pohl's transformed asteroid in *Gateway*, Frederick Malone in Ben Bova's "Isolation Area," and chief controller Tanaka in Paul Preuss's *Breaking Strain*. In addition, there are: the crewman missing only one leg in Correy's *Space Doctor*; the woman with an artificial leg in Appleton's *The City in the Stars*; John Ogelby, a hunchback in Joe Haldeman's *Worlds*, who chose life in a space habitat "because low gravity was the best, safest anodyne for the constant aching in his joints" (23); the blind commander of the S. S. Randolph, orbiting Earth in Heinlein's *Space Cadet*; "About half the [asteroid] station personnel" in Jerry Pournelle's "Bind Your Sons to Exile" who "were missing something: fingers, an arm, a leg, one eye; one chap was missing one of each" (144); the dwarfs serving on space stations in Leinster's *Space Tug* and Janifer and Treibich's *Target: Terra*; Heinlein's "Waldo," living in a space station because he suffers from myasthenia gravis; the gravely injured station resident in del Rey's *Siege Perilous* who remains there because of "The fantastic healing power of space" (19); the crippled cosmonaut permanently assigned to space station Kosmograd in Bruce Sterling and William Gibson's "Red Star, Winter Orbit"; and George Walt, the one-headed, two-bodied mutant running the 5000 Doors Moments of Bliss Satellite in Dick's *The Crack in Space*. In the last case, the motive for life in space may not be comfort, but the desire to avoid the stares and ridicules of everyday people—a feeling that might also affect other handicapped individuals, and one that was mentioned by Haldeman's Ogelby: "a small world was like a small town: people got used to you and stopped staring" (*Worlds* 23).

There is also the suggestion in some stories that people with psychological problems—the mentally handicapped, as it were—may be better suited to life in the unnatural environment of a space station more than to normal life on Earth. Certainly, Rory, the man suffering from Mongolism in the Steven Gould story of that name, seems perfectly content to live in his space station home. In some cases, the space station environment even seems to attract people already diagnosed as mentally ill: the hero of Ted White's *Secret of the Marauder Satellite*, described as paranoiac, has a burning desire to live and serve in a space station and finally succeeds in earning such a position despite his condition. In one of the most moving tributes to a space station in science fiction, he describes his new sense of belonging there:

> [Home] must really exist, I guess. Even in my darkest, most paranoid moments, I've never thought the whole world was a sham—that everyone lived lives as empty and distorted as mine...Now, I sensed my life was changing...*Home* was a tiny pinprick of light, hanging above and behind me, in cold and empty space, orbiting hundreds of miles above the Earth's surface, at thousands of miles an hour. (116, 120)

While he was never happy on Earth, he finally becomes well adjusted by living in space—a transformation similar to that undergone by a troubled young girl in Vonda N. McIntyre's *Barbary*. Oddly enough, a similar outburst of emotion occurs to the protagonist of Edward Gibson's *Reach*, the first novel by a former resident of a space station (Skylab 3): "this part of the space station seemed the same. Each shape, each color, each shading of the sun-drenched surfaces had a familiarity to it, an open friendliness and warmth, like the well-worn footpath to home's back door" (174).

In other cases, living in a space station seems to cause derangement—and contented acceptance of life there, as is the case with the crewmen aboard the Doughnut in James Gunn's *Station in Space*. A visiting psychologist examines them and offers this gloomy assessment: "They all sounded like depressives on the verge of becoming manic...[he] could classify the crewmembers with certainty: schizoids, cycloids, paranoids, homosexuals, sadists, incipient homicides...psychopaths all" (89). Yet the men are all fiercely devoted to their jobs on the station, and the psychologist acknowledges their competence and does nothing to have them replaced or treated: "As neurotic as the crew members certainly were, as psychopathic as many of them seemed to be, on the job they did only those things they were supposed to do and forgot nothing" (90).

While Gunn's Doughnut is a grim madhouse, one sees the space station as a comic madhouse in Janifer and Treibich's *Target: Terra*, where all the residents have seemingly been driven mad with amusing results: the hero who keeps putting in absurd requests for "flight pay" and "travel pay" (15), the by-the-book commander, the engineer obsessed with protocol, the drunken cook, and the sex-crazed biologist. Yet while they complain about being forced to live in the station, they appear to be reasonably well adjusted to it, and they manage to cooperate successfully to solve the mystery of the strange problems plaguing the station and identify and thwart the saboteur in their midst.

Another interesting picture of slightly addled people living happily in space is in Fritz Leiber's "The Beat Cluster," which sees a complex of individually constructed space homes as an ideal place for Earth's eccentrics, where they can happily indulge in activities like "sunbathing, algae tending...yeast culture...reading, studying, arguing, stargazing, meditation, space squash," "vacuum chemistry," "space pong," and "space pool" (199, 201, 202).

The clearest statement of the benefits of madness in space station life comes in Charles L. Harness's *The Paradox Men*, where, after observing in the solar stations near the Sun that "every one of these creatures was stark mad" (146), the hero explains:

> "Let us examine a society of some thirty souls, cast away from the mother culture and cooped up in a solarion. Vast dangers threaten on every side...it is the normal lot of people who live this life to be—by terrestrial standards—insane. Insanity under such conditions is a useful and logical defense mechanism, an invaluable and salutary retreat from reality.
>
> "Until the crew makes this adjustment— 'response challenge to environment' as we Toynbee-

ans call it—they have little chance of survival. The will to insanity in a sunman is as vital as the will to irrigate in a Sumerian...."

Shey smirked... "Would you say, then, that the *raison d'être* of a solarion psychologist is to drive the men toward madness?" (155-156)

Thus, insanity, undesirable on Earth, becomes beneficial, even necessary, when one is living and working in a space station.

Finally, prisoners in space stations are obviously destined to be permanent residents; they have no choice. But they will hardly be contented in their situation; indeed, virtually every story about a space prison I have read—Ellison's "The Discarded," Siodmak's *City in the Sky*, Bova's *Exiled from Earth*, Long's *This Strange Tomorrow*, Simak's *Empire*, the anonymous "Rough Justice," Maxwell's "Prisoner 794," Sheffield's "Dinsdale Dissents," and Forstchen's *Into the Sea of Stars*—depicts space convicts as either longing for or actively plotting an escape to Earth or another planet; there is no sense that these people are becoming reconciled to space station life. And in Patricia A. McKillip's *Fool's Run*, even the commander of a space prison longs to be transferred back to Earth.

Indeed, the survey above suggests that the prognosis for permanent human life in space is not good: obviously, handicapped persons, madmen, and criminals are not the stuff from which to build a space civilization, and there are indications that even residents of the few apparently harmonious space communities will eventually grow discontented with their lot. In the early pages of one Kemlo book, *Kemlo and the Zones of Silence*, a resident of Satellite Belt K refers to "something we have lost—the spirit of adventure" (16), and the rest of the novel, significantly, concerns a trip into a mysterious area of space. The Sector Twelve stories of James White take a curious turn: after a while, protagonist Dr. Conway is assigned to serve on the "ambulance ship" *Rhadbar*, which goes out to investigate and handle medical emergencies in space or on other planets, and he begins to spend most of his time on missions instead of in the hospital itself. Apparently, even the huge and multifaceted Sector Twelve General Hospital is starting to seem humdrum, and adventures in outer space are now required to hold Conway's—and the reader's—attention. The dénouement of Smith's *Venus Equilateral* is rather startling: even though the engineers and technicians on board the station appeared completely at home in their station, as soon as their new scientific developments make the relay station unnecessary, commander Don Channing abruptly declares that its residents should "all go home to Man's Natural Environment. A natural planet"—namely Earth (422). Even the hero of White's *Secret of the Marauder Satellite*, soon after proclaiming the station to be his home, laments its envisioned destruction by saying, "The station was our beachhead. It was our first important outpost in space" (151)—as if he regretted not the loss of his "home" but the chance to go further into space. And the hero of Gibson's *Reach* quickly loses interest in the space station and prepares for his deep space mission. In short, the feeling of dissatisfaction with space station life seen clearly in Clarke's Roy Malcolm seems likely to eventually develop in almost all station residents.

Is there an answer? A possibility raised in some stories is that current human beings might someday *evolve*, due to natural selection, the effects of weightlessness, or bioengineering, into people who would naturally prefer life in space. Bishop's *The Shuttle People* sees this happening in a matter of a few years:

> What had happened to [astronaut] Hamilton and to the dozens like him was really evolution speeded up, thousands of years covered in less than a decade. A gradual process accelerated until an entirely different species was being created before man's very eyes. As the shuttle program grew, the crewmen and women withdrew more and more from their earthly environment. (23)

However, these people are finally viewed as lunatics—"Emotionally and mentally unstable" (69)—and a danger to all people: one character observes, "For the first time in history, a human species has been formed that is powerful enough to enslave us and eventually kill us off" (84).

Other works see human evolution in space in a more positive light. In Katherine MacLean's "Incommunicado," residents of a space station begin to change in response to the noises given off by a library file system—noises which in fact constitute a new language they are subconsciously learning which is "raising the intelligence level" (30), creating in effect "a new human race" (32). In Jack Vance's "Abercrombie Station," long-term residents of Earth-orbiting space stations have grown immensely fat, too fat to move around in Earth's gravity. A more extravagant prediction of evolutionary change in space is briefly presented in Pelham Groom's *The Purple Twilight*: "without gravity muscles would eventually weaken and waste away...I saw huge shapeless jellyfish-like creatures which wobbled about in space" (80). Lois McMaster Bujold's *Falling Free* envisions the genetic engineering of people with two additional hands replacing their feet—since feet are generally useless in zero gravity—as ideal residents of a space habitat. In Dan Simmons's *The Fall of Hyperion*, there is a brief glimpse of space-dwelling humans who have grown wings (436). And Spider and Jeanne Robinson's *Stardance* envisions the residents of a dance studio in space being transformed, with the help of friendly aliens, into beings who can live in the vacuum of outer space and commune as a group intelligence.

One extensive look at the evolution of human life in space is provided by Fritz Leiber's *A Specter Is Haunting Texas*, where the inhabitants of the Sack, a space station orbiting the Moon, have the choice of becoming "Fats" or "Thins"; the protagonist, a Thin, is described as over eight feet tall and incredibly thin and frail—so much so that he requires an exoskeleton to walk on Earth and looks so strange that revolutionaries plotting against the oppressive government of Texas can present him as the Angel of Death to superstitious citizens and have him speak for their cause. Since his physique makes life in gravity a continual torment, it is hardly surprising that he returns to the Sack at the end of the novel, and that he appears both physically and psychologically adjusted to permanent life in free fall, which he calls "a most harsh environment, yet I believe life and man were meant for it" (243).

One particular physiological change frequently envisioned as a result of space life is immortality. A new process that seems to promise eternal life to space-dwellers is what finally motivates Bishop's "shuttle people" to take action against Earth. Fritz Leiber posits that people living in weightlessness will by nature become virtually immortal—"who ever dies in free fall?" (243)—a further incentive for permanent life in space. One of the space habitats in Forstchen's *Into the Sea of Stars* in inhabited by a group of contented, though sepulchral, immortals. A form of immortality also figures in Charles Sheffield's *Between the Strokes of Night*, where residents of a space station learn how to greatly slow down human activity, so that weeks, or even years, are perceived as minutes; these elevated states, called S-space and T-space, are seen as a way to indefinitely extend one's life span, and, it is finally argued, to truly understand the cosmos and the mysterious space beings called Kermel Objects that inhabit it:

> He began to see the Universe as they must see it, from that unique vantage point of the longest per-

spective of evolutionary time. With the T-state available, humans had a chance to experience that other world-view....

And now the T-state became essential. Planet-based humans, less than mayflies, flickered through their brief existence in a tiny fraction of a cosmic day. The whole of human history had run its course in a single T-week, while mankind moved out from the dervish whirl of the planets into the space surrounding Sol. Then S-space had given the nearer stars; but the whole Galaxy and the open vastness of inter-galactic space still beckoned. And in that space, in T-state, humans could be free to thrive forever. (325-326)

Grand visions of long-lived space civilizations have their place, but they hardly provide a solution to the problem of establishing a community in a space station: if a radical physical change in humanity and the prospect of immortal life are necessary requirements for a such a community, then it is clear that not many of these communities are going to get off the ground, so to speak. And in fact, the extreme developments in human evolution observed in Leiber's, Forstchen's, Sheffield's and Simmons's novels may never have taken place had there not first occurred widespread devastation of Earth in all cases. It is also worth noting that in *Between the Strokes of Night*, some of the Immortals finally opt for a normal life span— N-space—on the grounds that it provides a more vivid and stimulating experience, and they commit themselves to more contact with planetary dwellers, suggesting that even such transformed residents ultimately may not be satisfied with permanent life in space.

One overall conclusion to be drawn from this survey of the three basic functions of space stations in science fiction is that they illustrate the full dimensions of the critical dilemma Hugo Gernsback bequeathed to the genre: namely, the need to meet both scientific and literary standards. With scientific logic, writers can devise any number of useful businesses for space stations, but these do not in themselves seem suited for an engrossing narrative. They can create scenarios for action and adventure on a space station, but these often conflict with scientific logic. And stories about contented communities in space sometimes fail on both grounds: as interesting literature and as scientific predictions. Yet stories about space stations are not always failures, and there are particular types of narratives where, as is made clear below, the space station serves unusually well.

Before considering exactly what kinds of roles space stations have often settled into, however, I must first examine repeated attempts to transform the space station, as one strategy to make it a more satisfactory element in science fiction. The three major transformations which can be observed are clearly designed to intensify one of the station's three functions and downplay the other two, thus simplifying and, in theory, improving the station: to achieve new opportunities for adventure and danger, writers transform the space station into a spaceship, eliminating its roles as business and community; to create a more pleasant and satisfying community, they create the space habitat, a larger structure not as well suited for business and adventure; and to improve the business of space travel, they build the space elevator, although that provides little in the way of homelike comfort or exciting drama.

Despite their novelty and promise, however, these transformations ultimately prove dysfunctional: the traveling space station simply avoids the problems of space stations without confronting them; the space habitat creates a host of new scientific and literary problems; and the space elevator, even more so than the space station, tends to fade into the background without impact. Thus, a survey of current literature reveals that the small, traditional space station is still the most common type of space structure; and its endurance suggests that the space station has, without any need for transformation, indeed assumed an important position in the universe of science fiction.

PART THREE

TRANSFORMATIONS

7. *Exiled from Earth*:
The Traveling Space Station

Changing a space station into a spaceship is an attractive resolution of the problems generated by space stations for several reasons. If there is some doubt about the station's usefulness as a business, providing a mission and a destination eliminates all doubts; if the station starts to become unpleasant as a residence, moving into the unknown might generate a new sense of community and offer the prospect of an eventual home on another planet; and most importantly, if the station seems too placid and uneventful to offer adventures, going out into space promises such adventures.

While this transformation is appealing as a narrative device, it is also eminently reasonable as a scientific speculation. The images we have of rounded space stations and long, angular rockets are hardly justified by their situations; in the vacuum of space, no streamlining is necessary, so an unwieldy-looking object can travel just as well as a sleek rocket ship. Furthermore, many of the "space stations" of science fiction, like the S. S. Randolph in Heinlein's *Space Cadet* and Williamson's "Dead Star Station," are, as I have noted, nothing more than spaceships which have been permanently parked in one area of space—so why not move in the other direction and turn a space station into a spaceship? All that is required for the transformation is some sort of engine to move the station, and a reason for the station to begin traveling.

The first problem—providing an engine—is usually a simple matter; space stations typically are equipped with small rockets to maintain a stable spin which can be modified to move the station more purposefully, or a more powerful rocket can be attached to it. The second issue is more complex: although, as already observed, the space station usually proves unsatisfactory either as an opportunity for constant adventure or an acceptable home, unhappy individuals can usually leave the station without difficulty and go elsewhere; thus, the need to convert a space station into a spaceship arises in two special situations: when there is no chance for individual escape, and when the station has ceased to serve any useful purpose—when it is no longer a viable business.

This transformation is seen most clearly in Ben Bova's *Exiled from Earth*. In the novel, the world's genetic engineers, all exiled to a space station to maintain the stability of the world, are initially depressed by their tiny quarters, inadequate research facilities, and the lack of any meaningful goals in their lives. Then one of the scientists has an idea: by attaching a rocket engine to the station, it could be transformed into a starship to Alpha Centauri. He exclaims, "Heading for the stars gives everybody an aim, a purpose. Staying here is riding an orbital merry-go-round for the rest of your life" (198). As they start working on transforming the station, the scientists are suddenly optimistic and cheerful, even though nothing in their immediate environment has changed. The metaphor of a "merry-go-round" perfectly expresses the frustration noted in stories about heroes anxious to move beyond space stations; for example, in Sam Merwin, Jr.'s "Star Tracks," an astronomer says to a frustrated space pilot stuck in a space station, "It's been hard on you, hasn't it—being cooped up here for so long, going nowhere?" (148) In Bova's novel, since the station inhabitants are not allowed to leave, and since the station has no other function, the entire station and all of its inhabitants undertake a journey to the stars.

A space station becoming a spaceship occurs as the resolution of several other science fiction works. Three works are set in the near future and involve human beings: in David Duncan's *Dark Dominion*, because the preparations for the launch of an armed space station have generated so much tension and hostility, the commander of the station, once it is in space, decides it would be best to travel on to other worlds instead of remaining in orbit around Earth; the station's intended business seems counterproductive, so it is given a new mission.

In Long's *This Strange Tomorrow*, rebels seize control of space station Molidor, declaring that "space therapy has failed" (84); the station is not performing its proper function. For that reason, they send it moving out of orbit, whereupon it promptly vanishes into a space warp, to reappear years later as a settlement on Mars.

And Thomas N. Scortia's *Earthwreck!* depicts a nuclear war that destroys all life on Earth, which leads the residents of the American and Russian space stations to join forces to change one of their stations in a spaceship headed for Mars, where, it is believed, there will be sufficient resources for them to survive. In this case, there is no one else for the station to serve and nowhere to escape to, so the entire station travels to another world to preserve the human race.

Four other examples involve more advanced space stations created or manned by aliens or robots. John Brunner's *Sanctuary in the Sky* involves a mysterious visitor to a massive structure that was found abandoned and occupied as a space station; he finally reveals that he is a member of the alien race which built it and that the structure was actually a starship, designed to establish life on different worlds throughout the Galaxy. Therefore, he forces the residents to leave and the structure moves out into space—here, to return to its original purpose. In A. A. Jackson IV and Howard Waldrop's "Sun Up," a space station manned by robots near a distant star is threatened when the star is about to explode; so its robots build a huge platform and essentially ride away safely on the wake of the explosion, with the platform acting like a giant surfboard. In Ralph Williams's "Bertha," astronauts investigating an abandoned alien space station in Earth orbit are suddenly trapped in it as it flies off to the stars—it was, they deduce, a "mousetrap" set long ago by aliens anxious to study intelligent life should it develop. And in Frederik Pohl's *Heechee Rendezvous*, a structure named Heechee Heaven, previously regarded as a fixed structure in space, is revealed to be a huge spaceship and is used once again in that manner by Robinette Broadhead and his companions. In addition to works like these, there are several similar transformations from station to starship involving large space habitats, as discussed in Chapter 8.

In other cases, a traveling a space station is proposed as a solution to a problem, though it never actually happens: in White's *Secret of the Marauder Satellite*, residents propose moving their station to avoid the mysterious spaceship that is attacking them, but they fear that "the whole Station might just come apart at the seams" (150); and in Mike Resnick's *Eros Ascending*, the owner of the Velvet Comet wants her space brothel to travel as a necessary method to increase her profits—"I want the ship to have motive power. We can do much better traveling from one solar system to another" (224). Here, moving is viewed as a way to keep the space station in business, to eliminate a threat, but the problem is ultimately solved by other means.

Certainly, the peripatetic space station can provide a happy ending, or at least the chance for one; but there is another possibility. A space station free of its moorings, so to speak, may be capable of soaring to the stars, expressing what John Wyndham referred to as *The Outward Urge* that is basic to all humans; but such a station can also go back to Earth. And while there is something hopeful and exhilarating in the outward voyage, a way to solve problems and maintain progress, a space station's return to Earth is invariably associated with failure and a sense of loss. Thus, in Dean McLaughlin's *The Man Who Wanted Stars*, a novel whose first half is filled with pessimism about humanity's future in space, it is only appropriate to learn that the abandoned Orbitbase fell to Earth and "turned into a meteor" (149).

There is also the specific danger that a space station may fall out of orbit and strike the Earth, causing tremendous loss of life and property damage. The possibility is first suggested seriously in Robert Courtney's "One Thousand Miles Up" (1954)—"One of us could probably break away and cripple the station so it would fall back to the Earth" (99)—although an earlier work, Katherine MacLean's "Incommunicado" (1950), presents the threat as a plot in an absurd space movie being watched by space station residents: a character in the film "was supposed to have been subtly and insanely disarranging the Pluto Station orbit so that when it was finished it would leave Pluto and fall on Earth like a bomb" (8). Ironically, the first space station I know of in science fiction to fall out of orbit toward Earth was in an actual "absurd space movie"—*The Green Slime* (1968)—although the station there, abandoned and sent towards Earth to destroy the monstrous aliens on board, burns up along with the invaders before reaching the surface. Other absurd space movies involving a falling space station include the puppet film *Thunderbirds in Outer Space*, where a damaged space station drops out of orbit and threatens to strike a major oil refinery, and a *Doctor Who* adventure, "Revenge of the Cybermen," where the titular villains fill a space station with cobalt bombs and aim it at the surface of the planet Voga.

Some science fiction novels explore the scenario of MacLean's space movie more seriously; for a space station which remains intact as it falls to Earth might indeed pose a threat to humanity, especially if it is approaching a major population center. The first novel to depict this occurring is Harry Harrison's *Skyfall*, where a station launched in spite of safety concerns experiences a series of mechanical failures and accidents, achieves a dangerously low orbit, and seems doomed to crash into a large American city—indeed, a part of the station breaks off and destroy a small town in England, although the station itself is finally deflected and crashes in the ocean. Martin Caidin's *Killer Station* follows a similar scenario, except that the problem here is sabotage, a deliberate effort to send the station falling toward New York City; again, while the station is doomed, last-minute heroics involving the space shuttle nudge the station away from the populated area. And Joe Haldeman's *Worlds* describes how Jacob's Ladder, due to atmospheric drag and a faulty correction maneuver, was sent plunging into Earth's atmosphere to land, fortunately, in the Indian Ocean; but Haldeman's protagonist, anticipating Caidin, has a dream in which Jacob's Ladder crashes into New York. Finally, a less hazardous return to Earth is proposed in Dale Brown's *Silver Tower*, where the commander of a damaged military station intends to send it down to be destroyed in the atmosphere so its facilities cannot be captured and studied, although his plans are never carried out.

While events of this sort definitely make the space station an arena for temporary excitement and adventure—indeed, as one problem after another afflicts the doomed station in *Skyfall*, the place seems truly haunted—the crash destroys the station in every way— as a location for adventure, as a business, and as a home.

Even when a space station comes back to Earth and makes a safe landing, the results are depressing. In the film *Gorath*, the three major space stations orbiting Earth are ordered to return to Earth to avoid being damaged in a close encounter with the wandering star known as Gorath. However, a later scene shows one of the stations, now parked on Earth, falling underground as a major earthquake devastates its landing area. An action designed to preserve the station instead results in its destruction. (Left unexplained is the reappearance of the station and others in the final scenes of the movie.) Another grounded space station—although one teleported to the surface of Mars—is briefly seen in *War of the Planets*, although it is later destroyed.

More interestingly, Tyrone C. Barr's *The Last Fourteen* offers the same scenario as Scortia's *Earthwreck!*—a disaster destroys all life on Earth while a space station is in orbit—but here the decision is made to return to Earth after five years. Once landed, the fourteen survivors attempt to establish a utopia, but bitterness and feuding soon lead to murders and the dissolution of the group, with only the faint hope that two sympathetic survivors might manage to maintain human civilization. Thus, while the move to Mars in Scortia's novel is seen as a positive and optimistic development, the return to Earth in Barr's novel seems like a doomed gesture, with the future of humanity very much in doubt.

A peculiar variation on the theme of space stations returning to Earth occurs in James P. Hogan's *Endgame Enigma*. Here, the protagonists discover that the Soviet space station they thought they were imprisoned in is actually a huge mock-up in an underground chamber in Siberia, and that the investigations they thought they were clandestinely carrying out were actually officially sanctioned, as a way to delude the American government. And with the realization that the station is in fact on Earth comes the fear that the charade might work, and that the United States might be conquered by the actual military space station in orbit—though this eventuality is avoided in the novel when the prisoners manage to escape and communicate their information to the government. Here, the return to Earth is a matter of changed perception, not travel, but the sense of regression is identical, as a facility apparently devoted to forward-looking, peaceful research is instead revealed as a fortress with weapons aimed at Earth.

Overall, these transformations reveal the space station in its role as a transitional stage—a *Step to the Stars*, in del Rey's terms—a place which can assist in further travel to space, yet a place that also remains close to Earth. Since the most celebrated stations in science fiction are often designed to bring about such space exploration, there is a strange sort of satisfying logic in a space station which become a spaceship and ventures into the unknown; hence, there is a feeling of triumph in these transformations. In contrast, since the most criticized stations in science fiction are so strongly oriented toward earthly affairs—the military space stations—it is equally and understandably unpleasant when a station returns to Earth, acting out the unfortunate terrestrial orientation of some stations; it seems to be going backwards, not accomplishing what it should be doing, and hence is associated with a sense of failure and gloom.

Of course, a traveling space station, however satisfying it may be to its restless inhabitants, leaves the question of permanent life in a space station unanswered. To achieve a comfortable and constant life in space, to transform a station into a suitable home, the most common answer in recent times has been the space habitat—a space station which, in theory, offers all the comforts of planetary life with none of its problems.

8. "Home on Lagrange": The Space Habitat

The basic concept of a space habitat is ingenious: begin by building a large enclosed structure in the shape of a sphere, cylinder, or torus; place dirt and vegetation on its interior; and rotate the structure to simulate Earth gravity on the inside surface. Alternative types of space colonies that seem related to the space habitat, and are featured along with them in modern science fiction, are the hollowed-out asteroid, celebrated in George Zebrowski's *Macrolife*, and the vastly enlarged space station seen in the novels of C. J. Cherryh.

As already noted, the idea of a space habitat can be traced back to the "star cottages" and other space dwellings of Tsiolkovsky, and to the gigantic celestial spheres envisioned in J. D. Bernal's *The World, the Flesh, and the Devil* and described in Williamson's "The Prince of Space"; however, it is not difficult to see why Gerard O'Neill's revival of the idea in the 1960s met with such widespread interest. By that time, planetary science had more or less revealed that all planets in the Solar System were basically inhospitable to man; no world offered a breathable atmosphere, comfortable climate, or easy access to necessary resources. Indeed, there seemed to be no life at all on these worlds. So, if there were no paradises available on nearby planets, then the next best answer would be to build them in outer space.

Indeed, it can be argued that they are a better answer: while there is a disconcerting sense of the alien, the unknown, on the new world one travels to, the world one constructs should provide a feeling of familiarity, a homelike environment. And it is this spirit that also distinguishes this type of structure from the conventional space station. Typically, this unusual structure gleaming in the blackness of space was seen as a new type of environment, and their inhabitants regarded themselves as part of something new—like the commander building a space station in Bernard's *The Wheel in the Sky* who exclaims, "We're space men now, and we've got to make a different set of rules to live by. We're being forced into a different way of living—an unnatural way" (24). In contrast, space habitats are designed to look as much like Earth as possible to their inhabitants, and residents like to feel that they have returned to an old way of living; thus, they seem to provide the perfect setting for a comforting community in space.

While in theory, a space habitat could be built with almost any kind of environment as possible, their physical appearance, more often than not, resembles the landscape of a small town in the American Midwest. There are references to possible or actual habitats with unconventional or unusual environments: a character in Arthur C. Clarke's *Imperial Earth* suggests transforming some smaller moons of Saturn into "orbiting zoos" or "islands in space for experiments in super-technology life styles" (18-19); a genetic engineer in Isaac Asimov's "The Greatest Asset" proposes hollowed-out asteroids for trying out different types of closed systems in order to "develop a science of applied ecology" (49); and William John Watkins's *Going to See the End of the Sky* refers to one large habitat where "Some of the segments were environments that hadn't been found on Earth in a century, and others had never been found there at all and never would be" (78). However, except for the Mesozoic jungle of Robert Silverberg's "Our Lady of the Sauropods" and the water world of Charles Sheffield's *The Web between the Worlds*, these unusual space environments are simply proposed or mentioned; the typical space habitat is well described by Isaac Asimov's "For the Birds" as "a vista of suburbia" (85), and by the reaction of a young immigrant in Sam Nicholson's "He Who Fights and Runs Away": "Hey, this is super, Dad! It's like a TV sit-com house" (24)—odd responses, it seems, to one's strange new world. In fact, this approach to environment design in space is specifically ridiculed in Allan Steele's *Clarke County, Space*, where someone reminisces about "early artists' conceptions" of habitats "as wall-to-wall tract housing, complete with backyard barbecue grills. Looked like New Jersey in orbit. Space as a giant suburb" (91).

This spirit of familiarity, of returning to the past, takes many forms, the most explicit being the idea of a *homeland*: in a world of cultural uniformity and suppression of unique lifestyles, a space habitat can be a place where any national, religious or cultural group can establish its own society and maintain its special sense of identity, free from the interference of others. As a character remarks in Richard A. Lupoff's *Sun's End*, "After a long period of growing homogenization on earth, the development of the Islands has encouraged renewed cultural diversity" (73). Thus, we see a space habitat literally becoming the new Promised Land for six million Jews in W. D. Yates's *Diasporah*, where the new Hezora Ysroel is necessarily built and inhabited after extremists destroy Israel with nuclear weapons. Other examples are the Rastafarian space colony in William Gibson's *Neuromancer*, the Amish colony briefly seen in Suchariktul's *Mallworld*, and the traditional Japanese space colony in Lupoff's *Sun's End*. Two novels—Mack Reynolds's *Chaos in Lagrangia* and William Forstchen's *Into the Sea of Stars*—offer lists of various cultural havens in space: Reynolds mentions, among others, the all-black Promised Land, the all-Chinese Han, the Victoria—"Back to the old values of the Victorian age," the Pericles—"Devoted to the arts...More far-outs per square foot than Athens ever dreamed of," and the Marx—"determined to establish pure scientific socialism" (15, 16); while Forstchen's 700 space habitats include "the Botswanian Liberation Group," "the Pan-Zionist Russian Nationalists," and "the 'peace experiment' units" (54, 77).

Beyond specific returns to the real or imagined lifestyles of the past, space habitats generally hearken back to simpler, happier times. In a world of mechanized transport, space habitats bring a return to earlier vehicles—bicycles (in Ben Bova's *Colony*), rickshaws (in William John Watkins's *The Centrifugal Rickshaw Dancer*) or gliders (in Watkins's "Coming of Age in Henson's Tube" and Larry Niven and Jerry Pournelle's "Spirals"). And in a world of crowded cities and stifling bureaucracies, space habitats offer a return to a easy, hassle-free existence and the preservation of individual freedom, best symbolized, perhaps, by the common practice of gliding; a character in "Spirals" says, "I knew already why people who came here wanted to stay. I'd never experienced anything like it, soaring like a bird...Putting on wings does things to people" (38, 56). In "For the Birds," Isaac Asimov offers another metaphor for free movement through space—swimming: "When we fly through zero-gravity water, we call it swimming. In Space Station 5, where there's no gravity in this region, the air is for swimming, not flying. We must imitate the dolphin and not the eagle" (89-90).

This sense of simplicity and freedom comes through in the most frequent image of return in space habitat stories, the American West. This is seen in the persistence of the word "frontier": Kennedy's "New Frontier" becomes "the High Frontier" of the L-5 Society and *The Endless Frontier* in three Jerry Pournelle anthologies about life in space. While the theme of the New West is never as literal as having boys in cowboy suits riding mechanical horses through space—

the subject of E. C. Eliott's *Kemlo and the Sky Horse*—a few stories approach this ludicrous level: John F. Carr's "Shapes of Things to Come" concerns an Native American mounting a sneak attack on a space factory, and Katharine MacLean's "The Gambling Hell and the Sinful Girl" describes a simple-minded mother living in a "home barrel" in space who must struggle to keep her children free of the corrupting influence of the "Belt Foundry living barrel" nearby; it is the old story of the Ozark hillbillies confronting the city slickers. In keeping with this spirit, Bill Higgins and Barry Gehm rewrote the old cowboy song "Home on the Range" as "Home on Lagrange," with lyrics like these:

> Home, home on Lagrange
> Where the space debris always collects
> We have, so it seems
> Two of man's greatest dreams
> Solar power and zero-gee sex. (264)

Another novel about space habitats, Michael Swanwick's *Vacuum Flowers*, frequently invokes the mood of another past period—the English Renaissance: during one fight, the protagonist thinks, "In a giddy, crazily gleeful corner of her mind, she felt like a Renaissance dandy. This was how they had fought in Spain, in Greece, all those centuries ago" (74); and she later "felt like an Elizabethan lady riding to the hawks with her retinue" (85). More broadly, Swanwick takes an underlying theme in such metaphors—that space represents a return to freedom, while Earth represents increased repression—to a new level; in his future world, all people on Earth have merged into a hive mind called the Comprise, so that individual personalities continue to exist only in outer space. In a contrasting mood that also reflects a notion of return, Watkins's *Going to See the End of the Sky* presents the old tenets of Eastern mysticism—that all is illusion, that all is one, and so on—as a new religion developing in a space habitat; while the sheriff of Steele's *Clarke County, Space* is a Native American who follows the old Navajo religion and occasionally communes with the trickster spirit, Coyote.

Overall, the general mood of the space habitat is definitely pastoral, an image of beauty and simplicity in life that ultimately suggests a return to the Garden of Eden, to life without original sin; indeed, Asimov's "For the Birds" describes a habitat's weather as "Garden of Edenish" (85). Gardens and gardening are recurring themes in these stories: gardens are mentioned above as a feature in the habitat of "The Prince of Space"; a "Japanese landscaping team" (12) prepared the beautifully balanced landscapes of Ben Bova's *Colony*; Port Hesperus of Paul Preuss's *Breaking Strain* is famous for its immense gardens representing various regions of Earth, so much so that its main section is known as the "Garden Sphere"; and in the space habitat of Victor Appleton's *The City in the Stars*, "Each house had its own small garden, and the predominant theme was Japanese, with the precise, artistic and somewhat miniaturized attitude of the Oriental toward his environment" (32). Space habitat residents thus seem like Voltaire's Candide, retreating from the world to tend their gardens.

Visions of a new Eden are also raised by the casual nudity seen in the space habitats of Ben Bova's *Colony*, Charles Sheffield's "Transition Team," and Niven and Pournelle's "Spirals"; a character in the third story says, "Why wear clothes inside? There wasn't any weather" (40). Thus, space habitats seem to offer an environment of unchanging perfection—virtual utopias in space.

In addition to images of Eden, space habitats sometimes offer other forms of return to prehistory or mythology. In Robert Silverberg's "Our Lady of the Sauropods," a space habitat becomes the new home of dinosaurs, reborn through genetic engineering, who turn out to be intelligent and telepathic—and intent on reconquering the Earth; and in Kevin Christensen's "Bellerophon," a space colony is the scene where a bioengineered Pegasus is mounted to reenact its mythological battle with a recreated Chimera. Suchariktul's *Mallworld* offers all this and more in the Earthscape Safari Park: "distant dueling triceratops...a passably convincing tyrannosaur...winged pterosaurs...their unicorns...a chimerical half-Pegasus" (63, 64, 77, 164, 181). There is also a primordial atmosphere in the "complete water-world" (95) built out of an asteroid in Charles Sheffield's *The Web between the Worlds*, with a gigantic squid providing the feel of a prehistoric ocean.

Finally, to carry the theme of return to its most extreme form, the space habitat is sometimes depicted as a new type of living creature, or as an extravagant type of womb, with both images suggesting a gigantic, mothering presence. A character in Niven and Pournelle's "Spirals" says, "I was a tiny chick in a vast eggshell" (36); the gigantic Waystation in John Brunner's *Sanctuary in the Sky* is said to be "like a living organism" (40); a space habitat is described as a "protective egg" and a "cocoon" in Chad Oliver's "Meanwhile, Back on the Reservation" (91, 94); Dan Simmons's *The Fall of Hyperion* likens "zero-g globe cities" to "improbable amoebae filled with busy flora and fauna" (435); and Swanwick's

Vacuum Flowers offers this extended analogy:

> Think of it as an enormous cell. The tank towns
> at the center are the nucleus. The sheraton is...oh, the
> centrosome, I guess. The air plant would have to be
> the mitochondria...And behold! A new form of life
> floats upon the winds of space. What vast, unimag-
> inably complex creatures will evolve from this first
> simple cell, a million years hence! (68)

Similarly, George Zebrowski's *Macrolife* describes a space colony as "an organism which can move and grow, as long as it can
obtain resources and maintain a food supply within its ecology. It's
a living organism because it can respond to stimuli through its optical and sensory nervous system. It thinks...And it can reproduce"
(30). In Steele's *Clarke County, Space*, the computer controlling the
space habitat becomes self-aware; one character tells him, "You're
Clarke County" (220). The ultimate personification of the space
habitat comes in Peter Dillingham's "House," a poem in which such
a habitat speaks:

> I am house
> House made of sun
> House made of wind
> House made of rain
> I am house
> Daystar house
> House made of sunbeams
> Starwind house
> House made of breezes
> Cloudburst house
> House made of snow....
> Occupancy by human organisms is
> welcomed because, like plasmids, they
> confer a certain transient evolutionary
> advantage—resistance to antibodies
> and the ability to colonize other
> specific environments for instance—
> which enables me to adapt quickly to
> immediate, short-term ecological pres-
> sures. (257, 259)

In becoming personified and alive, the space habitat develops into the ultimate mother—rounded, warm, protective—and residents seem to act out a journey back into the womb.

Of course, this idea of returning, especially in its aspect of reestablished ethnic enclaves, can have a negative aspect, as pointed out in Isaac Asimov's *Nemesis*:

> "What all the Settlements [space colonies] fear and hate most is variety. They don't want differences in appearance, tastes, ways, and life. They select themselves for uniformity and despise everything else."
>
> Fisher said, "You're right. And it's too bad."
>
> Wyler said, "That's a mild, unfeeling way of putting it. 'Too bad'...We're talking humanity here. We're talking about Earth's long struggle to find a way of living together, all cultures, all appearances. It isn't perfect yet, but compare it to how it was even a century ago, and it's heaven. Then, when we get a chance to move into space, we shuck it all off and move right back into the Dark Ages. And you say, 'Too bad.' That's some reaction to something that's an enormous tragedy." (118-119)

Here, the space colonies are seen as "returning" "right back into the Dark Ages"—retreating from centuries of social progress on Earth; and the hero of Asimov's novel, no matter how much time he spends in space colonies, always ends up despising their narrowness and longing for the diversity of Earth.

We thus begin to see a special spirit of fundamental conflict appearing in space habitat stories, one of a sort that is surprising in science fiction. Traditional space stations, as part of man's exploration of space, seemed a natural extension of human progress into the future, a fit subject to celebrate in the visionary genre of science fiction. In contrast, space habitats apparently interrupt progress and return to past patterns of life; they do not naturally extend human progress but argue against it. In supporting these structures, then, science fiction writers find themselves in the unusual position of supporting the past over the future—which leads to a recurring theme that never arose in stories about space stations: namely, emotional and sometimes violent conflict between the planet-dwellers and the space-dwellers.

Typically, residents of Earth resent space habitats as a expensive drain on the world's scarce resources. People trapped in the overcrowded, polluted environment of Earth may feel that they are doing nothing more than subsidizing a paradise for a lucky few—which is literally true in the case of Ben Bova's *Colony*, where one of the habitat's two sections is maintained exclusively as a haven for the rich and powerful. Such angry sentiments are seen in the protest signs carried by demonstrators greeting a visitor from a space colony in Oliver's "Meanwhile, Back on the Reservation":

NO MORE PIE IN THE SKY—WE EAT PIE!
SPEND OUR TAXES ON EARTH—WE AIN'T DIRT!
DOWNERS BE COUNTED!
SEND 'EM FURTHER OUT!
PULL THE PLUGS! (89)

Thus, there are frequent stories involving proposals from Earth to cut off supplies to the habitats, as in Niven and Pournelle's "Spirals" and Juanita Coulson's *Tomorrow's Heritage*, or to maintain oppressive control over them, as in Watkins's *The Centrifugal Rickshaw Dancer* and Melisa Michaels's *First Battle*.

And, as Earth residents come to dislike those in space, the people in space habitats develop similar feelings about people on Earth. Space habitat stories offer an entire new lexicon of contemptuous expressions used by space-dwellers to describe people who live in Earth and other planets: "groundpounder" (Gregory Benford, "Dark Sanctuary" 94), "earthworms" (Mack Reynolds and Dean Ing, *Trojan Orbit* 62; Lee Correy, *Manna* 37; D. H. Yates, *Diasporah* 158), "groundhogs" (Joe Haldeman, "Tricentennial" 105 and *Worlds* 15), "Mudballers" (Haldeman, *Worlds* 40), "Mudeaters" (Alexei Panshin, *Rite of Passage* 16), "Earthie" (Sucharitkul, *Mallworld* 146), "Grounders," "Earthers" (both in Melisa Michaels, *First Battle* 15, 56), "downers" (Oliver, "Meanwhile, Back on the Reservation" 89), "Downsiders" (Sheffield, *Between the Strokes of Night* 26), "planet-siders" (Coulson, *Tomorrow's Heritage* 86), "Groundsiders" (Dian Girard, "No Home-Like Place" 125), "Flatlanders" (Ben Bova, *Peacekeepers* 229), and "Planet-lubbers" (Lupoff, *Sun's End* 193). The view develops that there is something wrong, something unclean, about living on a planet, a theme developed at length in Zebrowski's *Macrolife* and reflected in a comment in Michaels's *First Battle*: "Children are...our future...our proof that what we're doing can be done: that Humankind doesn't have to root around on Earth like a bunch of grubby animals forever" (73). Residents of space habitats feel that people on Earth do not understand their problems and are unreasonably hostile; thus, another common story line involves the effort of space colonists, usually requiring a war, to achieve their independence from a repressive, uncaring Earth. One novel, Alexis A. Gilliland's *Long Shot for Rosinante*, argues that such developments are virtually inevitable: "The habitats lend themselves to autarky very naturally" (151).

In all this literature of extreme conflict, there are surprisingly few voices for compromise and reconciliation. Asimov's *Nemesis* works to generate sympathy for both planetary and space dwellers; Nicholson's "He Who Fights and Runs Away" has a protagonist in a space habitat who longs to return to Earth, and remains in space solely as a way to continue working on solutions to terrestrial problems; and one work explicitly advocates cooperation and mutual respect: "Meanwhile, Back on the Reservation," written—significantly—by anthropologist Chad Oliver. In that story, one character concludes, "There could not forever be two human races, one bound to the Earth, and the other riding mechanical toys through the deeps of space. That was not the way to go...They needed each other" (101). Despite these noteworthy exceptions, science fiction writers generally embrace the idea of conflict between planets and space colonies as something natural and inevitable; and that is an attitude which is noticeably new in the genre, and one that requires explanation.

To be sure, there were stories of conflict featuring space stations, but these were typically man struggling with the unknown, or with aliens, or with enemy nations; confrontations involving space habitats are more like family disputes—as is literally the case in Coulson's *Tomorrow's Heritage*, where members of the Saunders family represent feuding interests on Earth and in space. The other image is that of civil war, as innumerable stories explicitly or implicitly mimic the progress of the American Revolutionary War. In this way, models of international or interplanetary combat are replaced by those of internal dispute.

One might attempt to explain this special spirit of hostility between Earth and space in more recent fiction as the result of outside events: most stories of space stations were written at a time when there was enthusiastic public support for the space program; today, when budgetary restraints and widespread indifference plague that program, supporters of space travel may well feel isolated and different in an environment that seems hostile to further progress in space and consequently might cast their stories in this light. However, the root cause of this theme of conflict, I would argue, is a paradox at the heart of the whole idea of space habitats.

In their examinations of space stations, science fiction writers often found them rather static and unsuitable settings for their fictions, although immensely useful in the future conquest of space. In contrast, I would argue, writers have found space habitats to be wonderful settings for their stories but inherently implausible and impractical; and these aspects of space habitats cannot be ignored. For these reasons, almost all of the stories which appear to enthusiastically support space habitats end up presenting powerful arguments against them; and if there is a constant atmosphere of conflict in these stories, this may be in part a reflection of the inner conflicts these writers confront.

The arguments against building and occupying space habitats can be summarized in the framework of the three basic functions of the space station: first, unlike space stations, space habitats do not seem practical as places of business; second, ever more so than conventional space stations, they are continually threatened by natural and man-made disasters; and third, like space stations, they ultimately do not emerge as attractive homes for their residents—despite their apparent beauty and appeal.

Traditional space stations are in general rather modest structures; they are designed rather like a large spaceship, they usually have small crews with modest needs, and while the initial investment may be large, as noted in Chapter 4 above, they generally seem able to justify the expense, and eventually support themselves, by providing some useful service: transportation, observation, research, recreation, and the like. Space habitats are a completely different proposition: they literally involve the complete creation of a small new world, they typically have thousands of residents requiring tremendous amounts of supplies, and while they can provide the same services as space stations, there does not seem to be a compelling need to build such huge structures to perform them, and questions arise as to whether they can generate sufficient income to pay back investors and make a profit. This provides another explanation for the hostility toward space habitats: people trapped in the overcrowded, polluted environment of Earth do not feel they are getting their money's worth from these costly structures. And space habitat residents longing to be free no doubt resent their continuing need to depend on Earth—a point that comes out in David Brin's "Tank Farm Dynamo":

> There were some old SF stories I read when I was a kid, about space colonies rebelling against Earth bureaucracies. I had a brief fantasy of leading my crew in a "tea party," and kicking these two jerks

off our sovereign territory...Of course, the rebellion idea was absurd...We might be ninety-five percent free of Earth logistical support, but that last few percent would be with us for a hundred years. (198)

An issue related to economic feasibility is scientific feasibility, sharply raised in Mack Reynolds and Dean Ing's *Trojan Orbit*: is such an immense structure even possible? Since the conventional space station is little more than an expanded spaceship, building one seems to present no special challenges, and indeed, the Russian and American space programs have moved or are moving from space vehicles to space stations with little difficulty. However, building a complete ecosystem that reproduces the environment of a planet is quite another matter: in *Trojan Orbit*, a space habitat that is apparently progressing smoothly, with ample financial support, is quickly revealed as beset by scores of unsolved technical problems. In explaining this situation, one character in the novel makes a telling analogy:

> I feel the Lagrange Five Project is something as though one were to go to the...Wright brothers in 1903, and offer them a hundred billion dollars to embark upon a project to build an aircraft that would carry three hundred passengers at a time across the Atlantic at a speed exceeding that of sound....
>
> My point is that no matter how much you were willing to contribute to the building of such an aircraft, the Wright brothers were in no position to do it. Nor would anyone be for half a century and more. My first impression...is that the Lagrange Five Project is in the same position. That it is premature. We do not as yet have the knowledge to build a valid space colony. (232; first ellipsis authors', others mine)

And the novel vividly illustrates just how unpleasant—and even dangerous—life might be in a space habitat that is built without sufficient knowledge.

This argument might explain a curious omission in the literature of space habitats: whereas scores of stories—including Lester del Rey's *Step to the Stars*, Murray Leinster's *Space Platform*, Robert A. Heinlein's "Delilah and the Space Rigger," and Gene L. Henderson's "Tiger by the Tail," to name only a few—describe the process of building a space station, only a few works depict the construction of a space habitat—Richard A. Lupoff's *Sun's End* and Bob Shaw's "Small World" are the only two that come to mind—and they do so briefly; and significantly, both Lupoff's and Shaw's anecdotes involve fatal accidents which occur during the process. Perhaps authors are understandably reluctant to explore just how difficult and problematic the building of a space habitat might turn out to be.

Whatever differences there may be in the economic and scientific feasibility of space stations and space habitats, they share one feature: the constant threat of danger. In sharper tones than those of space station stories, works concerning space habitats repeatedly raise the issue of a space habitat's basic *vulnerability*: Coulson's *Tomorrow's Heritage* speaks of "the terrible vulnerability of these structures" (328); a character in C. J. Cherryh's *Downbelow Station* asks, "Do you know the vulnerability of a station?" (126); someone in Mack Reynolds's *Chaos in Lagrangia* similarly asks, "Do you realize the vulnerability of space Islands?" (29); and Christensen's "Bellerophon" speaks of "the feeling of vulnerability in riding a tiny bubble of life in a great sea of darkness" (255).

Although I argued that this feeling is sometimes illusory in a space station, circumstances seem more genuinely frightening in a space habitat. For one thing, while space stations are typically divided into small compartments, which can be quickly sealed off if there is a problem in one section, space habitats usually consist of one large chamber; a leak is an immediate problem to every inhabitant. In addition, space station crewmen are ready to respond to any danger, with spacesuits hanging nearby and emergency procedures worked out beforehand; space habitat residents, enjoying their earthlike environments, have no spacesuits handy—they may not be wearing anything at all—and they often have no systems for dealing with emergencies. Finally, in a space habitat, the stakes are higher: a disaster in a space station might mean, at worst, the death of several dozen crewmen; a disaster in a space habitat could wipe out thousands, even millions, and could bring an end to an entire culture or civilization.

The particular dangers facing space habitats are the same as those facing space stations, although there are differences in degree: concern over alien invasion recedes, as stories of space habitats generally envision a future solar system where there are no other life forms in the vicinity of Earth, and madness is more an undercurrent, a long-range problem, than an immediate threat; on the other hand, the dangers of accidents or armed attack loom even larger than before.

Assuming that space habitats are feasible—and even the skeptics in *Trojan Orbit* acknowledge that they eventually will be—these structures will still be susceptible to a variety of accidents. Meteors remain a potential hazard: someone in Reynolds and Ing's *Trojan Orbit* asks, "Suppose one was struck by that king-sized meteor that nobody expects to come, given percentages" (164); and both Niven and Pournelle's "Spirals" (39) and Victor Appleton's *The City in the Stars* (133) describe the danger of solar flares. A collision between the space habitat and a spacecraft would be disastrous: *The City in the Stars* says, "There was always the danger of collision" (188) and a character in Haldeman's "Tricentennial" speculates, "If the shuttle hit the mating dimple too fast, [the space colony] would fold up like an accordion" (103). Handguns are strictly forbidden in the space habitats of Watkins's *The Centrifugal Rickshaw Dancer*: "The inhabitants of the Lagrange League had an abhorrence of guns found nowhere on Earth...They were obviously too dangerous when the habitats were being built...A stray bullet could puncture a wall, and more than one in the same area might cause an immediately fatal decompression" (103); and Shaw's "Small World" extends the prohibition to include "explosive devices" and even toy catapults (66). And in some ways, the complex interactions which occur in a space habitat could make the entire construct more vulnerable to accidents; for example, in Dean Ing's "Down and Out in Ellfive Prime," a malfunctioning sprinkler system oversaturates part of the soil, which triggers "the nightmare more feared than meteorites by every colony manager: spinquake. Small meteors could only damage a colony, but computer simulations had proved that if the spin axis shifted suddenly a spinquake could crack a colony like an egg" (108).

As mentioned, alien invaders rarely threaten a space habitat; still, there is the mysterious—though not greatly threatening—being that bothers Cheryl Harbottle in Dian Girard's "Invisible Encounter," and two stories point out the danger of disease: in Yates's *Diasporah*, a virulent plague kills many residents of Hezora Ysroel—"The virus was more frightening than the dangers of the space environment" (37)—and Heinlein's *Friday* observes that if a new outbreak of the Black Death reached Ell-Five, the habitat would be a "ghost town in a week" (236). And, recalling Arthur C. Clarke's concern over mice in a space station, the residents of Appleton's New America in *The City in the Stars* must endure the infestation of cockroaches.

Furthermore, there is no reason to believe that space habitats will be less susceptible than space stations to sabotage or attack.

Ben Bova's *Kinsman* deflates a proposal for a space habitat by observing, "Your colony would be wide open to a small nuclear bomb" (213); Steele's *Clarke County, Space* has to be evacuated when a religious fanatic aims a nuclear weapon at it; missiles launched by hostile Earth forces severely damage Goddard Space Colony in Coulson's *Tomorrow's Heritage*; Cherryh's *Downbelow Station* comments that "Mariner [Station]...had been blown. Sabotage. From the inside" (154); Ing's "Down and Out on Ellfive Prime" reports, "The first Ellfive...got snuffed by the Chinese in 2012...a nuke was intercepted just off the centerline of Ellfive Prime" (98); in Alexis A. Gilliland's *Long Shot for Rosinante*, a space habitat is threatened by a nuclear missile; a character in Yates's *Diasporah* explains, "What we are principally worried about is sabotage by other cities—principally, particles of stone accelerated to high velocity" (83), and describes "four attacks that have been made against Hezora [Ysroel] since the beginning of the month of Elal" (91); and in Joe Haldeman's *Worlds*, missiles launched from Earth destroy several habitats and severely damage all the others—except for New New York, which was built inside an asteroid.

In addition, despite their larger size, space habitats are also vulnerable to manned attack: a group of terrorists seize control of Island One in Bova's *Colony*, a similar band of revolutionaries take over a space telescope near a space habitat in John Alfred Taylor's "Grave-11," and Reynolds's *Chaos in Lagrangia* mentions that "Twenty-five years ago...a bunch of gunmen from Earthside came up in an attempt to sabotage the Island" (23).

Finally, although outright madness in space habitats is rare, there are ominous signs of its widespread imminence. The space habitat in Reynolds and Ing's *Trojan Orbit* is said to look like "a madhouse...a lunatic asylum" (141, 143), and Haldeman's "Tricentennial" speaks of "a deep-seated paranoia about Earth and Earthlings" (110). In Appleton's *The City in the Stars*, "The permanent director of the colony had had a heart attack—from the pressures, it was told" (20) and a character in Coulson's *Tomorrow's Heritage* observes "Isolation syndrome" (287) in residents of the space colony. A character in Haldeman's *Worlds* describes the residents of New New York as "slightly wonky people" (32), and the sequel, *Worlds Apart*, repeatedly refers to widespread "paranoia" (52, 108, 141) and a growing number of suicides (55).

Perhaps more disturbing are the observations of two writers who have repeatedly described large colonies in space, William John Watkins and C. J. Cherryh. In Watkins's *The Centrifugal Rickshaw Dancer*, the Grand Sphere is described as a "paranoid's paradise" (19); and in his *Going to See the End of the Sky*, a popular drug called Blink is said to cause "generalized paranoia and blind rages" (159). (Walter Jon Williams's *Voice of the Whirlwind* also says "Paranoia is becoming a way of life...in space" [76].) And the multiple crises which threaten the space residents in Cherryh's *Downbelow Station* lead to "bizarre hysteria" (154), "Madness" (157, 220), and "a rising number of suicides" (157). As for the over-all attitude of the residents, it is reported in *The Centrifugal Rick-shaw Dancer* that "Most Granders bet like a religious obligation" (31); in contrast to this tendency to wild, compulsive gambling, the people of *Downbelow Station* are described as passive in times of crisis: "things which went wrong onstation went wrong sitting still, by quadrants and by sections, and there was a certain fatalism bred of it; if one was in a safe zone, one stayed there; if one had a job which could help, one did it; and if it was one's own area in trouble, one still sat fixed—it was the only heroism possible" (20). The atti-tudes depicted in both novels, in fact, suggest an unhealthy sense of fatalism, the feeling that one is helpless in the face of danger, so crazy risk-taking or complete inaction are appropriate responses.

In addition, when I first presented a paper on my space station research, Gregory Benford made an interesting observation regard-ing a difference in the attitudes of space station and space habitat residents which has disturbing implications: while the life of a space station resident usually involves regular exposure to the new envi-ronment of space—excursions and repair missions outside the sta-tion and large viewports showing the stars and planets— the daily life in a space habitat involves little contact with space—no trips outside, no windows—as if residents did not like to be aware of their surroundings. Indeed, a character in Reynolds and Ing's *Trojan Orbit* says, "Inside the island, we don't consider ourselves actually to be in space. This is our Brave New World and we try to carry on as similarly to Earthside as possible" (103). Since space habitats are unquestionably "actually. . .in space," this attitude can only be de-scribed as a type of denial, a sign of psychological distress; and such feelings are specifically ascribed to the family that built Freeside space colony in William Gibson's *Neuromancer*: "Tessier and Ash-pool climbed the well of gravity to discover that they loathed space...We [are] growing inward, generating a seamless universe of self" (173).

A fundamental denial of reality of a different sort can be ob-served in Alexei Panshin's *Rite of Passage*, a novel about people living permanently in space who seemingly refuse to accept the fact that they are living permanently in space. That is, although Panshin speaks of their transport ship being converted into a city, residents still refer to it as "the Ship"; their efforts to rigorously limit population make perfect sense for a spaceship on a long voyage, but little sense for a true space colony, which should seek to expand and nurture offshoots; and their determination to maintain strict control over the colony planets reflects a twisted dedication to their original mission—to set up planetary colonies—instead of a more reasonable resolve to leave the planets alone and build a space civilization. Here, members of space society acknowledge that they are truly in space but insist upon wrongly characterizing themselves as travelers in space, not inhabitants of space; and their final decision to exterminate an entire planet for not-particularly-provocative behavior plainly suggests that residents are becoming completely irrational.

In addition, a desire to escape from, to refuse to accept, reality is manifest in the members of the younger generation in both Watkins's *The Centrifugal Rickshaw Dancer* and Reynolds's *Chaos in Lagrangia*, both depicted as bored and decadent, driven to hedonism, drug abuse, and flirtations with fascism; space residents in Swanwick's *Vacuum Flowers* are driven to escape by voluntarily reprogramming their minds to resemble popular marketed personalities; and Bob Shaw's "Small World" foresees the development of gangs in outer space, another sign of decadence. Overall, Watkins's *The Centrifugal Rickshaw Dancer* describes "the nearly insane pursuit of pleasure that was a way of life for...the third-generation elite of the Grand Sphere" (10); Reynolds's *Chaos in LaGrangia* reports that "alcoholism...is growing geometrically...So is the use of trank" (54-55) in the space habitat—developments also noted in New New York in Haldeman's *Worlds Apart* (55); and residents of the space habitat Aurelian in Arthur Byron Cover's *Stationfall* are all devoted to bizarre religious cults, drugs, and casual acts of violence.

With all these signs of psychological distress in evidence, the residents of space habitats are acutely aware of the possibility of mental breakdown and the danger it could pose: a character in Reynolds and Ing's *Trojan Orbit* says, "I suppose there's always the chance of some crackpot. Can you imagine how much damage a terrorist with his eggs scrambled could do out in space?" (45-46), and Arthur C. Clarke's *The Fountains of Paradise* comments, "today, it would not be difficult for a deranged engineer to assassinate a city. The narrow escape of O'Neill Space Colony 11 from such a disaster in 2047 has been well documented" (157).

If the residents of space habitats will forever be haunted by danger, there are also factors which make these structures less attractive as homes. For one thing, the supposedly earthlike environment of the space habitat may not truly satisfying: the Lagrange Five Project of Reynolds and Ing's *Trojan Orbit* is said to have "an artificial feeling far and beyond anything he had seen before...an unlived-in feeling" (83, 85); a woman living in Port Hesperus in Paul Preuss's *Breaking Strain* regularly visits Earth because she gets tired of "artificial luxury" (70); a resident of a space colony in Josephine Rector Stone's *Green Is for Galanx* exclaims, "We need real flowers, real sky, a real world, our own world...no more artificial, pointless existence" (47, 80); the hero of Nicholson's "He Who Fights and Runs Away" resists continued life in a space habitat because "I'd be potbound...I'd be cramped by artificial skies and fake horizons" (50); a character in the Grand Sphere of Watkins's *The Centrifugal Rickshaw Dancer* "had never been Earthside, but like many Granders, he shared a human longing for a sea he had never seen" (87); and Isaac Asimov's *Nemesis* suggests that humans may always possess "some dim atavistic memory of Earth...a feeling for a huge endless world in [one's] genes; a longing that a small, artificial turning city-in-space could not fulfill" (271). In a similar spirit, David Brin's "The Crystal Spheres" says that if humans do not need to actually live on a planet's surface, they will at least have to have one in the vicinity: "Simply put, men could live on asteroids, but they needed to *know* that there was a blue world nearby—to see it in their sky. It's a flaw in our character, no doubt, but we cannot go out and live in space all alone" (138); people who tried to live in faraway space colonies "simply lost interest in procreation" (138).

In addition, several stories suggest that space habitats will be plagued with disharmony and dissension. George Zebrowski's *Macrolife* laboriously argues that there will never be conflict in a space colony, simply because people can always build another one and leave; and a similar observation is voiced in Haldeman's *Worlds*: "You don't meet many real political dissidents in the Worlds; too easy to go someplace else if you don't like it at home" (63). However, this opinion is almost certainly naïve. After all, at a time in Earth's history when there were vast regions that were virtually uninhabited, people still fought war after war over possession of small areas of Europe. Similarly, one can expect dissidents in a space habitat to attempt a revolution instead of meekly withdrawing to some new habitat. Thus, all sorts of factional disputes break out in Reynolds's *Chaos in Lagrangia*; Aurelian in Cover's *Stationfall* verges on anarchy, with various sectors separately controlled by petty barons; traitorous political intrigue threatens the independence of Cherryh's *Downbelow Station*; residents of the Ship in Panshin's *Rite of Passage* split almost evenly over the question of whether or not to destroy a hostile planet; a group of young Marxists challenges the government of space habitat Rosinante in Gilliland's *Long Shot for Rosinante*; and the revolt against Earth in Watkins's *The Centrifugal Rickshaw Dancer* almost fails because of the inability of various groups of space dwellers to work together: "nobody had ever known the six habitats to agree on *any* subject...Certainly there was a generalized animosity toward cooperation" (17-18). And while there are no overt acts of rebellion in Preuss's *Breaking Strain*, his protagonist senses an overall "message" of "tension in reserve, of time bided, of a feeling close to indentured servitude. And there was something more, partly among the recent, reluctant immigrants but especially among the younger residents, those who had been born on the station—a sense of humdrum, a certain resentment, that half-conscious undercurrent of brewing discontent" (166).

In addition to such general atmospheres of dissension, the political structures of space habitats are repeatedly depicted as repressive. Despite the singular claim in Donald Kingsbury's "To Bring in the Steel" that "Small space colonies were made for village democracy" (201), Gregory Benford argues in "Redeemer" that in fact there is a natural tendency for them to become dictatorships: "The colony environments aren't a social advance. You need discipline to keep life-support systems from springing a leak or poisoning you. Communication and travel have to be regulated for simple safety. So you don't get democracies, you get strong men" (415). Indeed, in an environment where a single gun, or bomb, or even a push of the wrong button could destroy the entire community, a strong and even repressive government may become a virtual necessity. Thus, while there are often pluralistic pretensions in space habitats, they tend to be dominated by one leader or small faction, an echo of the military style of command common in space stations. In Bova's *Colony*, the habitat leader defensively argues, "a democracy works only as well as its citizens want to...See to it that they have jobs, that their garbage is collected regularly, and that the communications media are under your control. Then you can become a pretty effective dictator yourself, even in a democracy" (93). Elsewhere, the development of autocratic rule is described less positively: a character in Reynolds's *Chaos in Lagrangia* exclaims, "I never expected [dictatorship] to spread into space" (17)—although it did; in Appleton's *The City in the Stars*, the evil head of the space habitat argues, "Independent thinkers had no place here. Absolute loyalty was the only acceptable attitude" (41); VitaCon, a space habitat under construction in H. M. Hoover's *Away Is a Strange Place to Be*, is a cruel corporate empire which ruthlessly employs children virtually as slave laborers; Cherryh's *Downbelow Station* comments, "They had democracy in the council, but it was dynasty in the station offices" (40); and the habitats in Swanwick's *Vacuum Flowers* are generally repressive, with mysterious authority figures who periodically attack the populace and force them to have their personalities reprogrammed.

Even where the situation is less extreme, less dictatorial, there remains a necessary element of control in space habitat life that might be especially damaging to younger people, as discussed in Benford's *Jupiter Project*:

> That was the danger of compression, of packing people so close together they *had* to get along. In those circumstances, everybody had to back down, live life according to the concensus [sic] rules. That might be okay if you were already an adult...But to grow up you had to take *risks*. (166)

Another novel with a juvenile protagonist, Panshin's *Rite of Passage*, expresses similar disenchantment with life in space for youngsters; indeed, one hidden motive in the practice of sending young people to a planetary surface for their "rite of passage" is surely to provide the feeling of adventure and danger that their huge spaceship could not provide.

Given the gloomy picture of space habitat life that ultimately becomes apparent, it is not surprising that many residents would want to leave, just as many wished to leave space stations. Those who find the environment unpleasant may simply wish to return to Earth, like the disgruntled inhabitants of the space habitat in Reynolds and Ing's *Trojan Orbit* who says they have "the WITH-AW-DOH syndrome. The letters stand for What In The Hell Are We Doing Out Here?" (90-91) Similar disenchantment with space life is reflected in the graffiti decorating an elevator in the habitat of Haldeman's "Tricentennial":

> Stuck on this lift for hours,
> perforce:
> This lift that cost a million bucks.
> There's no such thing as
> centrifugal force:
> L-5 sucks. (104)

However, the more typical response to disenchantment with the space habitat is the familiar desire to travel to other worlds expressed so frequently at the end of space station stories; and a number of novels about space colonies conclude in exactly this way. In Joe Haldeman's "Tricentennial," space colony residents eagerly volunteer to serve on board a starship heading for the constellation Cygnus; the inhabitants of Goddard Space Colony in Coulson's *Tomorrow's Heritage* are frantically working to launch a mission to colonize Mars; the residents of the space habitat in Nicholson's "He Who Fights and Runs Away" want to go "Out"—"to establish a base [in the asteroids] and begin Waystations to Proxima Centauri" (25); a starship is constructed by inhabitants of New New York in Haldeman's *Worlds Apart*—a project undertaken, the narrator suggests, "for obvious morale purposes" (139); and a new project to build starships is created to ease the tensions in the habitat of Reynolds's *Chaos in Lagrangia*: "We don't build Island Five, but we'll build Starship One...It won't be a space Island floating without motion in Lagrange Five but will go to the nearest star system...It was the original dream!...We got bogged down, so far as the solar system is concerned, but the stars are still beckoning" (217-218). One citizen of the Ship in Panshin's *Rite of Passage* condemns his society's "meddlesome, paternalistic, repressive course" and proposes a project to "explore the stars...travel to the end of the Galaxy. That is within our power and it would certainly add to the knowledge we claim to be interested in" (249). Finally, although there are no specific plans developed, both Bova's *Colony* and Appleton's *The City in the Stars* end with similar speeches calling for further space exploration: Tom Swift exclaims, "that was the very best argument for the establishment of cities in space, of moving out to explore the other worlds around them, and then—in time, with luck and diligence, the stars" (183); and Bova's hero declares, "Island One is the beginning, the take-off point...the first real step outward from planet Earth. We can see to it that the human race spreads through the whole Solar System" (438).

Given the continuing appeal of exploring unknown worlds, the attitude seems to be, why settle for life in artificial constructed environments? In two novels, however, humanity is forced to settle for such development. Somtow Sucharitkul's *Mallworld* posits that an alien race, the Selespridar, will decide to isolate the human race in the Solar System within a huge force field until it becomes sufficiently mature; while David Brin's "The Crystal Spheres" imagines that all solar systems are for some reason surrounded by gigantic, invisible spheres that can only be broken from the inside—permanently keeping humanity away from the worlds orbiting other stars. In these situations, people naturally build large numbers of space stations, habitats, and colonies; there is no alternative.

If humans, given the chance, will never be permanently satisfied with life in a space habitat, there remains the suggested solution to space station life seen in Jack Vance's "Abercrombie Station" and Fritz Leiber's *A Specter Is Haunting Texas*: the evolution of new people who will be better adjusted to this new environment. This possibility is briefly raised in Reynolds's *Chaos in Lagrangia*, where a colony resident says, "I think we're beginning to breed true. *Homo superior*, you might say" (35), and in Oliver's "Meanwhile, Back on the Reservation," which speaks of people who have "adapted culturally and psychologically [and] biologically" to life in space (95). A more dramatic change in a single generation is described in Charles Sheffield's "Transition Team," where a psychologist is sent to study the "space-borns," the troubled children of space habitat residents. She concludes that the children are depressed because they are confined by the conventional expectations of their elders; since they are a new breed, the adults must leave them alone to develop in their own way: "I'll say it flat out: we don't *belong* here...This is their home. Earth is an alien place...we've served our purpose. We were just the transition team, essential to getting the place started. Now, we do more harm than good" (347, 350). Here, the problem is that people born on Earth will forever be limited in their attitudes, and hence unsuited for space life; only those born in space can live there happily. Moving farther into the future, Lois McMaster Bujold's *Falling Free*, as noted, envisions a new race of four-armed humans to live in space, and Bruce Sterling's *Schismatrix* sees space as the natural place for the development of many new forms of humanity, memorably including "Lobsters" who can live in the vacuum of space.

While all these works are optimistic in envisioning these new space beings, a less sanguine picture of evolution in space can be found in Richard A. Lupoff's *The Forever City*, where his time-traveling heroine visits a space habitat where there are first battles between ordinary humans and genetic mutations that seem cruel and repulsive; and appearing in a later time period, she discovers a form of collective intelligence has developed, represented by strange whispering voices and depicted as vaguely sinister. Here, new forms of life have emerged that do not appear to be particularly desirable, and these beings do not appear to be particularly happy. More ambiguous is Chad Oliver's "Ghost Town," where only a few people reduced to savagery live in the largely abandoned space habitats, although some remaining chimpanzees offer the possibility of a new civilization evolving.

In contrast, Zebrowski's *Macrolife* offers a grand and celebratory picture of the development of new beings in space, which occurs after all members of the human race have come to live exclusively in hollow-out asteroids. Gradually, these space colonies evolve into the "cells" of one gigantic group being called Macrolife, and people's sense of individual identity melts into this collective mind. Thus, while in Vance's and Leiber's works, space residents come to *look* like aliens, and in Sheffield's story, they start to *act* like aliens, people in Zebrowski's novel truly *become* an alien being.

Since evolution into a new form of life is never a viable option in the near future, one also sees with space habitats the same transformation that affected some space stations: namely, the entire habitat becomes a spaceship and travels into the unknown. In Niven and Pournelle's "Spirals," when it can no longer get needed supplies from Earth, a space habitat called the Shack renames itself the Skylark and decides to move out to the asteroid belt to obtain what it needs; in Yates's *Diasporah*, Hezora Ysroel becomes a starship and travels to another solar system so that the Jewish people can finally escape from persecution; in Asimov's *Nemesis*, a space habitat seeking to build a new society free from the influence of Earth travels to a newly discovered nearby star; in Lupoff's *Sun's End*, at least one or two of the space habitats have elected to travel to other stars to steer clear of the coming destruction of Earth; in Lois McMaster Bujold's *Falling Free*, the unhappy genetic freaks with four arms revolt, take over their habitat, and move it into unknown space; in Forstchen's *Into the Sea of Stars*, all 700 of the space habitats near the Earth decide to move into deep space when a deadly war breaks out on Earth—"the colonies broke their bonds and headed off into the unknown—looking for freedom and an escape" (2); and in Swanwick's *Vacuum Flowers*, habitat residents negotiate with Earth to learn the secret of interstellar flight, and the novel ends with the heroine returning to her home "dyson world" to travel with it into deep space: "It's going to the stars...and I want to go with it" (235).

While these developments are similar to the transformations of space stations into spaceships, there is an interesting difference: although space stations typically move out into space in order to search for something new, space habitats travel in order to escape from something old—the planet Earth. Thus, even in a gesture traditionally associated with adventure and novelty, the space habitats reflect their preoccupation with "escape" and retreat from life. And even though residents of peripatetic space habitats rarely land or settle on other worlds, there remains in their decision to leave the Solar

System a sense that permanent life in space is not satisfactory, that travel of some sort, to some other place, is more desirable.

For perfect parallelism, one might argue that the huge artificial worlds of science fiction—like Larry Niven's *Ringworld*, Bob Shaw's *Orbitsville*, and John Varley's *Titan*—represent another transformation of the space habitat, an attempt to make the space station even larger and even more earthlike in an effort to resolve its fundamental problems. However, I have no sense that this is in fact a useful framework for discussions of artificial worlds.

First, as in the three stories mentioned above, these huge structures are typically discovered in outer space—products of ancient alien civilizations—and the problem facing heroes in stories like Niven's *Ringworld* and Varley's *Titan* is not to build and inhabit these worlds but to explore them. Thus, artificial worlds function like transformations of alien worlds, a new type of unfamiliar environment to provide adventure and excitement, not as forms of the space station.

There is another reason for not considering these constructs space stations: since these artificial worlds are so similar to natural worlds, reasonable distinctions between space stations and planets begin to blur. One must consider, for example, the suggestion in Robert Sheckley's *Dimension of Miracles* and Jonathan Brand's "Encounter with a Hick" that the Earth itself was constructed by alien beings; if this scenario is accepted, then Earth emerges as a kind of space station, and I would need to add the Book of Genesis to my bibliography!

Finally, space habitats cannot lead naturally to artificial worlds because these huge structures contradict the basic logic supporting the establishment of space colonies. Proponents of space habitats, after all, argue that worlds are not suitable homes for humanity, and a multitude of small space colonies is seen as the ideal situation. Expanding a space habitat into a Dyson sphere or Ringworld would violate the whole idea of the structure, which was to serve as an alternative to large inhabited worlds.

Therefore, space habitats seem to represent the true end of space station expansion—a dead end, perhaps—although there is one other grandiose transformation of the space station of an entirely different character which still must be examined: the space elevator.

9. *The Web Between the Worlds*: The Space Elevator—and Beyond

The space elevator is the most striking variation on the space station to be proposed in recent decades: first suggested in two articles published in the 1960s, it burst into the literature of science fiction in the late 1970s with the simultaneous publication of two novels on the subject: Arthur C. Clarke's *The Fountains of Paradise* and Charles Sheffield's *The Web between the Worlds*. The plan is remarkable: since a space station in geosynchronous orbit 22,300 miles above the Earth is essentially motionless in relation to the planet below, one could theoretically establish a physical link between the station and Earth—like a long, super-strong cable. Then, with some sort of gondola or vehicle attached to the cable, people and materials could ride up and down between the surface of Earth and outer space.

The reasons why such a structure would be appealing to both the adventurous and timid space traveler are seen in the three names commonly given to it: the "space elevator, "the "beanstalk," and the "skyhook." As the first name implies, a space elevator offers a reassuring, even boring method of getting into space—there is no need to strap oneself into a rocket, blast off beneath tons of explosive fuel, and navigate to a precise location in space while avoiding hazards; now, one simply enters a small chamber, presses the "Up" button, and slowly and steadily rises towards one destination. As William Forstchen puts it in *Into the Sea of Stars*, "The trip into space was reduced to a simple elevator ride; a very long elevator ride, to be sure, but lacking the thundering grandeur of so long ago" (22). Indeed, since the space station one travels to is physically attached to Earth, one could argue that it not a separate building at all; rather, it is like the "top floor" of some immense skyscraper. Presumably, this aspect of the space elevator would make living in a space station more attractive to the faint-hearted, because if some problem or accident afflicted the station, one could escape to safety simply by going down the elevator.

On the other hand, no one is proposing to build a space elevator simply as an easy way to get to a space station; instead, it is designed to solve what has emerged as the major problem in space travel: the tremendous expense of getting out of Earth's "gravity well" into space. That is, it is relatively cheap and easy to move from point to point in space but incredibly expensive and difficult to fight the immense gravity of Earth to get off its surface. So the appeal of the space elevator is that it would facilitate the exploration and exploitation of space by simplifying the hardest part of the process; as Clarke posited in *The Songs of Distant Earth*, the space elevator "marked the very beginning of planetary colonization, by giving mankind virtually free access to the Solar System" (162). Hence, there are the images of a "beanstalk," a magical way to climb above the clouds into the exciting world of outer space, and the "skyhook," evoking a mountain climber who throws a rope with a hook into the sky and, when it is attached, climbs up the rope. Indeed, space elevators typically appear as only one element in an imagined future of intense activity in space of all kinds: space stations, space habitats, planetary settlements, and interstellar travel.

Despite the undeniable appeal of this proposal, two problems emerge in the stories about space elevators. First is the immense logistical difficulty of constructing a structure, however minimal, that is 22,300 miles long. However, though the issue of building space habitats has largely been ignored in science fiction, the two major novels about space elevators directly address this tremendous engineering challenge. In *The Web between the Worlds*, Sheffield offers a quick method—essentially attaching a weight to the end of a long cable and "dropping" it from the station onto the Earth—but Clarke argues in his preface to Sheffield's novel that such a procedure "is hair-raising, and I don't believe it would work. I'm damn sure it wouldn't be permitted!" (v) However, Clarke's process in *The Fountains of Paradise*—painstaking, step-by-step construction through a series of intermediate stations—may also have hazards, and the final part of the novel describes the dangerous rescue of some scientists stranded halfway up the incomplete structure.

Once in place, the space elevator faces no special new problems; but there is one old problem in the literature of space stations which repeatedly emerges—sabotage. In *The Web between the Worlds*, one character asks, "What about sabotage? Suppose some lunatic got at it with a fusion bomb?" (101) And Sheffield's story "Skystalk," after mentioning that "sabotage was one thing that could never be fully ruled out" (53), describes exactly such an event: terrorists plant an atomic bomb on the compartment traveling on the upward cable of a space elevator, and a desperate rescue attempt requires riders in the compartment on the downward cable to leap across empty space to the rising compartment and defuse the bomb. The point is that the easy access to a space station provided by the space elevator might also provide another way to attack the elevator or the station. Another space elevator—the Quito Skyhook in Robert A. Heinlein's *Friday*—was actually destroyed by saboteurs prior to the novel. This is, no doubt, a danger inherent in any large structure: Sheffield's "Skystalk" describes a preventive system of "the best screening in the world, with hefty rewards for information even of *rumors* of sabotage" (53) but it does not prevent the near-disaster depicted in the story.

Despite the problems of constructing and protecting a space elevator, the concept remains attractive as a method to travel into space, and at least one work envisions a transformation of the space elevator into a gigantic home; at the end of Clarke's *The Fountains of Paradise*, someone proposes "To join [the geosynchronous stations] together, thus forming a ring completely around the world...No—not a ring—a wheel. This tower was only the first spoke. There would be others (four? six? a score?) spaced around the equator" (289). A postscript set further in the future describes the completed "Ring City that encircled the globe....the thin, shining band that split the sky into two hemispheres was a whole world in itself, where half a billion humans had opted for permanent zero-gravity life" (296). Here, several space stations attached to space elevators combined to form one huge structure in space—the biggest "wheel in the sky" of them all, and one that had not been seen in science fiction since the inhabited rings around asteroids proposed by Konstantin Tsiolkovsky. And although there is no explicit reference to space elevators, a similar structure, also called a "ring-city," is glimpsed in the far future world of David Brin's "The Crystal Spheres," where the hero contemplates "the gleaming, flexisolid belt of habitindustry" above him (138).

However, this bold development is relatively uncommon; more frequently, the space elevator simply recedes into the background, as in Heinlein's *Friday*, where the heroine's trip down the Kenya Beanstalk is a minor event, barely described at the beginning of the story; other novels which include space elevators only in brief episodes include Sheffield's *Between the Strokes of Night*, Joe Haldeman and Jack C. Haldeman II's *There Is No Darkness*, Richard A. Lupoff's *Sun's End*, and M. S. Murdock's *Rebellion 2456*.

More surprisingly, space elevators sometimes figure in stories of the far future as elements of the distant past, fondly remembered. Thus, in Clarke's *The Songs of Distant Earth*, the space elevators are just another memory of the destroyed planet Earth; in Sheffield's *The Nimrod Hunt*, "the Old Beanstalk" (31) is a relic, made obsolete by the development of teleportation; and in Forstchen's *Into the Sea of Stars*, the historian protagonist reminisces about the space elevators built in the twenty-first century. It is remarkable that what once was an exciting new idea should become, in a few years, a structure associated with a sense of nostalgia.

This abrupt change in attitude may simply reflect the fact that there is something inherently unsuitable about the space elevator as a subject for extended narrative, making it instantly obsolete as an element in a story; indeed, one may consider the basic analogy in the name and ask how many successful stories have been written about elevators. More broadly, the concept of the space elevator may transform the aura of outer space into something too routine, too ordinary, so that writers are naturally impelled to devise more exciting possibilities for space travel—such as teleportation in Sheffield's *The Nimrod Hunt*—to remove it from the scene. In short, while transformations into space habitats were not really successful in making those structures happy homes, the transformations into space elevators may be too successful in making those structures effective businesses; they no longer offer any sense of adventure, one of the usual businesses of the science fiction writer.

As the space elevator receded into the background of science fiction, some writers continued developing other extravagant new ideas for structures in space. One prominent example, featured in Rachel Pollack's "Tree House," is a Dyson Tree: a huge, genetically modified tree growing on a comet with tunnels and domes where large numbers of people attempt to live in harmony with the cosmos. The proposal certainly offers a powerful image, combining the novelty and adventure of space life with a primal appeal to humanity's ancient arboreal life. Another intriguing possibility is a space station which combines the nonliving and the living, a possibility first glimpsed in C. E. Fritch's "Many Dreams of Earth," and one arguably presented in Gregory Benford's novel, *Tides of Light*, where one finds gigantic cyborgs which are partly organic and mechanical, capable of inhabiting either the vacuum of space or the surface of a planet. Bruce Sterling's *Schismatrix* presents an extravagant vision of a genetically altered human, expanded to immense size in space, who effectively becomes an organic, living space station. In one passage in *The Fall of Hyperion*, Dan Simmons offers a glimpse of an immense variety of space structures and space organisms developed by the space-faring Ousters:

> massive comet farms, their dusty surfaces broken by
> the geometries of hard vacuum crops; zero-g globe
> cities, great irregular spheres of transparent mem-
> brane looking like improbable amoebae filled with
> busy flora and fauna; ten-klick-long thrust clusters,
> accreted over centuries, their innermost modules and
> lifecans and 'cologies looking like something stolen
> from O'Neill's Boondoggle and the dawn of the
> space age; wandering forests covering hundreds of
> kilometers like immense, floating kelp beds...hol-
> lowed-out asteroids long since abandoned by their
> residents, now given over to automated manufactur-
> ing and heavy-metal reprocessing...immense spheri-
> cal docking globes, given scale only by the torchship-
> and cruiser-size warcraft flitting around their surfaces
> like spermatazoa attacking an egg; and, most indeli-
> ble, organisms which the river came near or which
> flew near the river...organisms which might have
> been manufactured or born but probably were both,
> great butterfly shapes, opening wings of energy to the
> sun...(436-437)

And undoubtedly, writers will continue to envision many other types of extravagant space structures and habitations.

However, even as new and old types of immense constructs are still occasionally seen in the skies of science fiction, the small, conventional space station has stubbornly remained a part of the science fiction universe. Although the grave doubts about the feasibility and attractiveness of large space structures raised in Reynolds and Ing's *Trojan Orbit* and elsewhere have probably had an impact, one other reason for a continuing emphasis on traditional stations may be the inherently practical orientation in many approaches to science fiction—and the radically different atmosphere of the 1980s and 1990s.

In the 1960s and 1970s, when space travel seemed to be progressing with one triumph after another, unbounded optimism was the prevailing spirit, and dramatic predictions of future possibilities in space were complete appropriate. However, in more recent times, as space programs have repeatedly experienced cutbacks, delays, problems, and disasters, the very future of human activity in space appears to be threatened, and plans for grandiose space structures—like space habitats, artificial worlds, and space elevators—are, one might argue, at best distracting and at worst counterproductive; rather, there is a need to focus on short-term solutions, proposals and ideas for the near future that might maintain activity in space during an era of apparent hostility or indifference to the exploration of space. Thus, as interest in ambitious schemes started to fade, the small space station, which never entirely disappeared from the scene, reemerged as a major factor in science fiction, typically featured in one of four major roles.

First, space stations continue to serve the two main purposes outlined in earlier works: as orbiting fortresses, and as bases for further adventures in space. Despite the deep skepticism regarding military space stations in the 1950s, several later writers in the emerging genre of adventure stories which combine elements of the war novel, spy thriller, and science fiction have included space stations as part of the action, no doubt in response to the prominence of President Reagan's Strategic Defense Initiative. Thus, in novels like Hogan's *Endgame Enigma* (1987), Tom Cooper's *War Moon* (1987), David Drake's *Fortress* (1987), Brown's *Silver Tower* (1988), and Ben Bova's *Peacekeepers* (1988), space stations are again attempting to preserve world peace while at the same time increasing the possibility of a world war.

A practical suggestion for a space station as a "step to the stars"—its other standard goal—is featured in David Brin's "Tank Farm Dynamo" (1982). The protagonist, desperately trying to maintain a crude space station built out of discarded fuel tanks, has no time for extravagant proposals—"lunar mines and space colonies and other fairy tales" (201). He instead develops a new method for generating electricity that could make this type of station economically viable; and the story's main purpose, as Brin admits, is to serve as a "propaganda piece" (206) for this idea, which he claims could be accomplished with existing technology. But the hero's ultimate purpose in saving his station—and no doubt Brin's ultimate purpose in presenting the concept—is a familiar visionary dream: as the story ends, he imagines the unwieldy fuel tanks as "eggs" that will "someday transform themselves into great birds of space. And our grandchildren would ride their offspring to the stars" (204). Despite its updated scientific information, then, Brin's story is related in spirit to the many stories about building space stations written in the 1950s, when further space travel was always the underlying goal.

Elsewhere, space stations remain visible, albeit briefly, as launching pads for space flights: the first three *Star Trek* films (1979, 1982, 1985) all begin with the Enterprise parked at a space station of some sort in Earth orbit, being prepared for its missions to deep space, and the other three films all have brief glimpses of or visits to such stations. And in Isaac Asimov's *Nemesis* (1989), the first flight into interstellar space takes off from the traditional Space Station Four. In stories about space habitats, these new structures accompany, but do not replace, conventional space stations; thus, in Ben Bova's *Colony*, visitors to the space habitat Island One first stop at Space Station Alpha, already depicted in Bova's *Kinsman* and *Millennium*. There are also attractive space resorts, as in Resnick's Velvet Comet novels (1984, 1985, 1986) and Ron Goulart's *Everybody Comes to Cosmo's* (1988), space stations as places for visitors to stop for an extended vacation.

Third, space stations continue to be employed as settings for tales of madness, commonly involving a solitary resident under unusual pressure. Such protagonists may escape from their plight by either going back to Earth, as in Jayne Tannehill's "Last Words" (1982), or by venturing into unknown space, as in Graham Diamond's "Outcasts" (1984). Conversely, like the heroes of George R. R. Martin's "The Second Kind of Loneliness" (1972) and Mark McNeil's "Scratches in the Dark" (1982), they may remain at the station and remain mad.

Finally, in addition to continued interest in space habitats as homes and retreats, there are still efforts to portray the conventional space station as such a satisfying place. In Arthur C. Clarke's *2061: Odyssey Three* (1987), Heywood Floyd is thoroughly content in his space station residence and reluctant to leave. And novels like Lee Correy's *Space Doctor* (1983) and Allan Steele's *Orbital Decay* (1989) both depict the growth of true space station communities in Earth orbit, although they retain the rough-hewn atmosphere of a frontier town.

As one observes these recurring depictions of space stations as battle stations, places for beginnings and stopovers, outposts that inspire madness, and homes and refuges in space, there seems to be emerging a significant new element in the iconography of science fiction, one which plays certain small but important roles and fulfills certain natural narrative purposes. Examining science fiction in the context of space stations, then, one can obtain a glimpse of the genre's broad consistency and effectiveness—and intimations of the genre's fundamental problems as well.

PART FOUR

ICONOGRAPHY

10. "Stranger Station": Space Stations in the Universe of Science Fiction

When a critic begins to explore the iconography of science fiction, there are two pitfalls: first, assuming too readily that its iconography is straightforward and easily comprehended; and second, concluding that there is no iconography in science fiction at all.

The first danger is illustrated by the one major work on this subject, Gary K. Wolfe's *The Known and the Unknown: The Iconography of Science Fiction*. Wolfe refers to an impressive number of texts and seems to know the field well; yet his argument ultimately rests on detailed analyses of a small number of carefully selected works. And while his comments are no doubt accurate in a limited way, Wolfe blinds himself to large problems and numerous counterexamples that undermine his case.

Consider his discussion of the icon of the spaceship and its "nurturing, womblike aspect" (80). As one illustration of this characterization, Wolfe observes, "Stanley Kubrick has reported that his original intention in the film *2001* was to give the spaceship-computer HAL a woman's voice" (80)—as if that supported his argument. Yet the fact remains that the actual film provided the spaceship *Discovery* with a male personality, one which goes insane and attempts to kill all of its crewman—making it the farthest thing possible from a comforting, motherly figure. And there are no doubt many other works that do not fit Wolfe's thesis; from my own research, I can offer the examples of James Blish's "Solar Plexus," where an obviously masculine alien seizes control of a man's spaceship; James Gunn's *Station in Space*, where a spaceship to Mars is designed to project the image of a brotherly companion in order to prevent the crew from going mad during the long flight; and James Blish's four Cities in Flight novels—which Wolfe even discusses at length—where the computers that control the traveling space cities are called "the City Fathers." Clearly, the iconography of the spaceship is more complicated that Wolfe suggests, as the spaceship can at times assume both a feminine and a masculine personality.

Wolfe can hardly be blamed for failing to offer a comprehensive examination of the icon of the spaceship; after all, if there are indeed 150,000 works of science fiction, then there are surely at least 50,000 works which in some way involve a spaceship—obviously too many texts to be examined by one critic, or even several of them. However, there is no excuse for his similarly limited discussion involving the one aspect of his study which overlaps with mine—namely, "the space city."

Many of the space stations and space habitats I have read about are clearly described as, and clearly function as, cities in space—as evidenced by such titles as Mack Reynolds's *Satellite City* and Curt Siodmak's *City in the Sky*, as evidenced by names for space stations like Supra-New York in Robert A. Heinlein's "Space Jockey" and New New York in Joe Haldeman's *Worlds*, and as evidenced by comments that Venus Equilateral was "so much like a town on Terra" (Smith, *Venus Equilateral* 407) and "Small space colonies were made for village democracy" (Donald Kingsbury, "To Bring in the Steel" 201). However, Wolfe chooses to completely ignore such relevant texts and instead focuses narrowly on those few stories where a city on the surface of Earth is literally lifted up into space; and the only works he discusses at length are Blish's Cities in Flight novels—which, as I can demonstrate, are idiosyncratic, illogical, and unrepresentative depictions of life in space—in order to prove that the space city is simply another example of the future city which is automated, mechanical, and highly structured. Had Wolfe looked at any of the more illustrative works I have studied, he would have seen that in case after case, the city in space is deliberately designed to turn back the clock: to reject the futuristic mechanical city and instead establish a community like a small, pre-industrial village—as shown by the discussion in Chapter 8 of the space habitat as a means of returning to the past. Again, Wolfe's argument seems accurate but limited, in that it fails to leave room for the city of the future which aims to duplicate the city of the past.

In the face of apparently contradictory uses of one icon—the spaceship as female and as male, the future city as technological and as anti-technological—a critic may well be tempted to throw up her hands and declare that there must be no consistent iconography in science fiction at all. This is the argument of Vivian Sobchack in *Screening Space: The American Science Fiction Film*. In that study she begins, despite her announced topic, by discussing both written and filmed science fiction and denies there is a clear distinction between the two; evidently, she intends her conclusions to have some applicability to the genre as a whole. And, she claims, science fiction as a film genre is distinguished by the fact that, unlike westerns or gangster films, science fiction films have no coherent iconography:

> The fluctuating meanings of what superficially seem to be iconic objects in SF films can be demonstrated many times over...Inevitably, then, we must be led away from a preoccupation with a search for consistent visual emblems into more ambiguous territory. It is the very plasticity of objects and settings in SF films which help define them as science fiction, and not their consistency. (86-87)

I would instead argue that, in regards both to written and filmed science fiction, Sobchack is completely wrong.

Part of the problem in her analysis is the typical myopia of film critics, who often study motion pictures in isolation, without any consideration of other related genres; thus, in his *The Encyclopedia of Science Fiction Movies*, Phil Hardy absurdly regards the use of numbers as names in *THX 1138* as a borrowing from the obscure musical *Just Imagine*, when in truth George Lucas surely derived the device from the scores of other stories and novels that have employed it. More broadly, Sobchack illustrates the problem faced by all science fiction critics who base their arguments on a detailed examination of a few selected masterpieces; not understanding the context of those works, and not understanding their connections to a broader range of texts, they cannot observe true relationships and are instead obliged to offered overly simplified models, like Wolfe, or to assert that there are no relationships, as does Sobchack.

To illustrate the fallacy in her pronouncements, consider Sobchack's example of a fixed icon—the railroad in western films—and imagine a critic with little knowledge of the genre who watches a few films involving railroads. She would see the railroad associated with a feeling of progress and achievement in films like *Union Pacific*; she would view it as an image of impersonal, implacable doom in melodramas where the heroine is tied to the railroad tracks while the engine inexorably approaches; and she would observe the cozy domesticity of the railroad headquarters of agents James West and Artemus Gordon in the television series *The Wild Wild West*. With no other evidence available, she would conclude that there is no coherence, no connectedness in the genre's use of the railroad; the filmmakers are simply employing the image for their own individual purposes. In fact, it would only be after achieving familiarity with hundreds of western films and stories that the critic would see the inner consistency in the image of the railroad—a icon which, in Sobchack's words, "threatens the openness and freedom of the West and individual enterprise, but...also promises the advantages of civilized life and brings the gentling influence of the Eastern heroine who plays the piano" (67). However, one cannot get this full, satisfying picture from a handful of works.

Similarly, one can readily imagine Sobchack considering the topic of the space station in science fiction films. Watching several films which feature space stations, she would see the station as a threatening image of technological destruction in the film *Moonraker*; as a place to stop on the way to adventure in films like *Project Moonbase* and *2001: A Space Odyssey*; as a research base threatened by aliens in *Mutiny in Outer Space* and *The Green Slime*; and as a happy community in the film *Earth II*. Her ready conclusion would be that there is no cohesion, no connectedness, in the cluster of meanings linked to a space station; the image is simply serving the various individual preferences of different filmmakers.

With knowledge of hundreds of science fiction novels, stories, films, and television programs, I am now prepared to challenge this posited conclusion, and to argue that the space station has in fact evolved to become a reasonably fixed and consistent icon in the universe of science fiction—although it is a bit more complicated and multifaceted than the icons Wolfe creates in *The Known and the Unknown*. By extension, I will suggest that other familiar objects in the genre, like the spaceship and robot mentioned by Sobchack, will similarly emerge as reasonably fixed, though rather complex, icons, with little "plasticity," once large numbers of relevant texts are examined. In short, while I am hardly attempting to completely delineate the iconography of science fiction like Wolfe, I am offering a methodology for doing so, and one example of the pictures that might emerge.

As previously noted, there is a difference in the origin of the icons of science fiction and those in other genres: images in the western, for example, are clearly derived from the actual history of the American West. In the case of science fiction, the unifying impulse is the need for writers to adhere to scientific facts and reasonable extrapolations about future developments; within such a framework, writers are inevitably forced to consider space stations in certain ways. A further unifying factor is the science fiction community itself, in which writers read each others' works, discuss stories in progress, and regularly borrow from and build upon the achievements of their peers. And this is in fact what makes the iconography of science fiction so fascinating, and so rewarding to thoroughgoing study: it is not an iconography borrowed from outside sources, but one that has developed and grown within the genre itself. Thus, a complete examination of a given object in all works of all sorts in science fiction is as necessary and as interesting as a complete examination of the evolution of life on Earth, where the failed experiments and cut-off branches are as valuable to the biologist as are the glorious successes.

To regard an object as a true literary icon, one must demonstrate that that object is regularly associated with certain actions and themes, and that it resists association with contrary or unrelated actions and themes. In the case of the space station, I will argue that it is consistently linked to the actions and themes of *cycles in human history, transition, frustration and madness,* and *inward movement,* and that the space station resists linkage to other genre themes like *linearity, progress, achievement, discovery,* and *outward movement.* And, to demonstrate how a broad knowledge of science fiction is important in any analysis of a science fiction text, I will focus my explication of these iconic resonances on the four works in my bibliography which are universally regarded as masterpieces and are frequently examined in critical studies—*A Canticle for Leibowitz* by Walter M. Miller, Jr.; the film *2001: A Space Odyssey,* written by Arthur C. Clarke and Stanley Kubrick, and Clarke's novel of the same name; *Solaris* by Stanislaw Lem; and *Neuromancer* by William Gibson—employing each as a primary example of the four symbolic functions of the space station. However, I will hardly neglect other relevant works, and will also discuss several of them at length.

Of course, these novels and one film have never been regarded as "space station stories" and their use of space stations is certainly not their most important feature. Still, I would justify placing them in this context by making two points: first, all four creators are known to be familiar with a broad range of science fiction texts: Miller regularly published in the major science fiction magazines of the 1950s and presumably read their contents; Clarke's familiarity with science fiction is obvious; in his "Afterword" to *Solaris,* Darko Suvin describes Lem's awareness of American science fiction of the 1940s and 1950s; and Gibson's first published story, "The Gernsback Continuum," with its references to Hugo Gernsback and Frank R. Paul, reveals his broad knowledge of the genre. As a corollary, one must assume that all four authors had read at least some of the space station works I have discussed before writing their novels.

Second, the use of space stations in each work is in no way dictated by the story's contents: Miller could have easily established an atmosphere of increased world tension in Part Three of his novel without mentioning military space stations; Heywood Floyd might have taken a direct flight to the Moon instead of stopping at a space station; the scientific study of the mysterious being in *Solaris* could have taken place in an outpost on the planet's surface; and the Tessier-Ashpool family complex attacked in *Neuromancer* might have been situated on a privately owned island on Earth. Thus, each creator consciously chose to include space stations in his novel, and one may assume that he did so for some reason.

In approaching *A Canticle for Leibowitz*, one notes first that the space station, for a number of reasons, is an ideal vehicle for the theme of *cycles* in human existence. For one thing, the traditional space station—a spinning torus—is in itself an image of cyclical movement, and the normal movement of a space station, perpetually orbiting the Earth, is also an endless cycle. Many stories about space stations present their activities as benign continuations of positive cycles in the history of civilization; business as usual is being carried out in outer space. Thus, there is something reassuring in the familiarity of Basil E. Wells's "Factory in the Sky" which is so much like a factory on Earth, right down to the whistle that announces the end of the working day, or the space airport of Lee Grant's "Signal Thirty-Three," which seems to be managed exactly like an airport on Earth. Here, the honest, worthwhile work of typical people is simply transplanted to outer space. Depictions of space observatories, space hospitals, and space schools similarly suggest an extension of valuable, rewarding activity long honored on Earth.

However, there is a negative aspect to the idea of cycles, to business as usual in space: in the 1950s, repeated proposals for space stations armed with missiles evoked specific concerns about an old cycle in human history—escalation and counter-escalation inexorably leading to devastating war—being acted out again in the militarization of space; and novels of that era like Edmund Cooper's *Seed of Light* and C. M. Kornbluth's *Not This August* explicitly address this issue. Again such a backdrop, the minor references to military space stations in *A Canticle for Leibowitz* seem a bit more significant: in constructing a model of human development involving repeated patterns of war, the end of civilization, and slow progress back to civilization leading to another war, Miller would logically see the conquest of space as just another element in humanity's steady cycle back to self-destruction. And with this theme raised in many previous works, he would not need to emphasize the point; a single mention would trigger readers' memories of the lesser works which dwelt more on the dangers of military space stations.

The way to escape from a cycle is linear movement, and the typical image of such movement in science fiction is the spaceship venturing straight out into the unknown. Such travel is the method frequently used to escape from the space station; in novels where a visit to a space station is the first step in a cosmic voyage, like Arthur C. Clarke's *Sands of Mars* or Richard Marsten's *Rocket to Luna*, the departure from the space station represents the true beginning of the adventure, leaving an environment that the hero usually finds boring to seek the excitement available on another world. And outward travel into space, either by or from a space station, can serve as a signal that the cycle of rising military tension is ending: in David Duncan's *Dark Dominion*, the building of a military space station generates extreme tension on Earth, so when it is launched, its commander independently decides to travel into space as a starship instead of entering Earth orbit; the threat inherent in its cyclical movement around Earth is eliminated by linear movement away from it. In Clarke's "Venture to the Moon," American, British, and Russian spacecraft simultaneously depart from a space station in a cooperative effort to explore the Moon, symbolizing an end to national conflicts. And in Lester del Rey's *Mission to the Moon*, the first trip to the Moon comes at a time when nations on Earth have agreed to internationalize and demilitarize outer space, so that the lunar expedition proceeds in a new atmosphere of world harmony.

Thus, in ending *A Canticle for Leibowitz* with the launching of a starship to another solar system as a way to preserve human civilization as Earth approaches another disastrous war, Miller is drawing upon a common theme in science fiction—outward space travel as a method for escaping from old patterns of human behavior. As in many other novels, the linearity of the space journey contrasts with the cyclical movement of man's existence on Earth.

One 1959 novel, Edmund Cooper's *Seed of Light*, seems particularly similar to Miller's work in its structure and themes. In the prologue, a military space station is launched in an effort to maintain world peace; but the actions of its first two occupants, a paranoid and a traitor, directly provoke a devastating nuclear war. In the next part of the novel, humanity, huddling together in domed cities, is on the verge of extinction because of repeated wars; but one city manages to launch a starship in a desperate effort to preserve human life and civilization. After long years of fruitless search for an Earthlike planet, the space travelers finally create a device that will automatically transport them to a suitable world; to their surprise, they land on Earth—50,000 years in the past—and recognize that they now have an opportunity to begin human civilization anew, hopefully with different—and better—results. The parallels with Part Three of *A Canticle for Leibowitz* are apparent: the militarization of space is an aspect of an old, destructive cycle inevitably leading to war; and the launch of a starship brings the possibility of escape from that cycle.

However, there is a difference between the two novels: in *Seed of Light*, the starship represents secular, scientific progress, seen in the fact that its residents name themselves after great scientists and philosophers of the past—a device also used in Konstantin Tsiolkovsky's *Beyond the Planet Earth*, another paean to scientific progress through space travel. And science does in fact offer one possible avenue of slow linear movement from ignorance to wisdom, breaking traditional cycles of human activity, and presenting the tantalizing goal of ultimate knowledge of the universe. But there is another available model of linear movement in human culture—Christianity, which postulates that people, both as individuals and groups, are progressing toward a final purging of original sin and reunion with their God. Like science but on different grounds, Christian thought rejects cyclical patterns, seeing a final destination in human history—God.

In this respect, there is another science fiction novel of the 1950s—Kornbluth's *Not This August*—which provides illuminating commentary on Miller's novel. While Kornbluth's hero works frantically to achieve the launching of a military space station that will force the occupying Russian army to leave America, another character in the novel, a preacher, wanders through the country calling for prayer and repentance. He seems a bit deranged by the shock of Russian conquest and not at all a sympathetic figure in a novel describing active, scientific efforts to rid America of the Russians; one rather expects him to receive his comeuppance at the end of the book. But Kornbluth surprises the reader: after the satellite is successfully launched and the Russians withdraw, the hero announces that the space station is simply another step in a deadly cycle of military escalation, and he joins the itinerant preacher in a final prayer for peace. Implicitly, he rejects the model of linear movement through scientific progress and seeks instead the Christian pattern of linear movement towards God.

The genius of *A Canticle for Leibowitz* is that its climactic starship represents both models of linear progress: the scientific quest for knowledge and the Christian quest for redemption. Miller argues that the two forces are natural allies, not enemies; their common foe is traditional, destructive cycles of human behavior, and both secular culture and Christian belief are needed to break those cycles. Thus, just as the medieval church preserved both classical civilization and Christianity between the fall of Rome and the Renaissance, and the same church preserved both modern civilization and Christianity after Earth's first nuclear war, the church will continue to preserve, by traveling into space, both secular and divine knowledge after the second nuclear war. In the wider context of science fiction, then, Miller's starship both represents and deepens a traditional symbol of human progress beyond historical cycles, making it serve to represent both scientific and Christian progress.

In seeing the space station as a representation of cyclical movement, and space travel as a symbol of escape from cycles, one observes the second characteristic of the space station: a place of *transition* from Earth to space, from familiarity to the unknown. Without doubt, this is the single most common role that space stations play; and we also come to understand the peculiar importance of space stations in juvenile science fiction, a genre built on the theme of transition from childhood to adulthood. In thumbing through anthologies in search of relevant stories, I could always be sure to find one space station story in a collection aimed at boys or teenagers; and in that milieu, as in Richard Elam, Jr.'s "The Iron Moon," Robert A. Heinlein's *Space Cadet*, Ted White's *Secret of the Marauder Satellite*, or Blake Savage's *Rip Foster in Ride the Wild Planet*, the space station serves as a school, a training ground, a place to prepare for further adventures.

2001: A Space Odyssey is thus simply the best known illustration of the space station as transitional device. As in so many other stories, it is first a place to transfer from a vehicle designed for planetary landing to one used only in deep space; Kubrick's use of Strauss's *The Blue Danube Waltz* provides a contrast between traditional music and a bizarre new setting; the station's decor is a blend of the familiar—the Howard Johnson's sign—and the fantastic—the corridor curving up into the ceiling; and Floyd's conversation with his Russian friends is both guarded—reflecting age-old hostilities on Earth—and friendly—reflecting the new international camaraderie of space. Structurally, the space station episode comes between the cavemen's discovery of the monolith on Earth and the inspection of the monolith on the Moon, and Floyd's activities while there refer both back to Earth—his picturephone conversation with his daughter—and toward the Moon—his wary words concerning his mission to Clavius.

The role of the space station as a transitional stage is further emphasized by the elements in Clarke's original story outline which were omitted in the film but preserved in the narrative passages of his book *The Lost Worlds of 2001*. Although the film presents a structure of steady outward movement—the space station, the Moon, Jupiter, and the cosmos—Clarke at first envisioned additional scenes depicting the crewmen of the *Discovery*, working in various locations on Earth and in space, at the moment they are contacted to join the mission, and a scene of the *Discovery* being launched from Space Station One. Therefore, Clarke first depicted the film as the story of two voyages—from the Earth to the space station to the Moon, and from the Earth to the space station to Jupiter—with the space station as the transitional point in both journeys.

A space station also functions as a place of transition in three of Clarke's space station stories—*Sands of Mars*, *Islands in the Sky*, and "The Other Side of the Sky"—although the alien world at the end of the journey is Mars, not the Moon or Jupiter. In *Sands of Mars*, the hero—a science fiction writer and neophyte space traveler—briefly stops at a space station on his way to Mars. In *Islands in the Sky*, the young hero ultimately sees his return to the space station as simply a stopping point on a hoped-for trip to Mars, where he can join the other pioneers there. And in the final section of "The Other Side of the Sky," the protagonist reflects upon how he came to the space station despite the wishes of his father, who was committed to staying on Earth; now, he observes his son preparing to travel to Mars while he is committed to staying on the space station. In these last two examples, the exploration of space proceeds more slowly, and the space station stage represents several years, or even an entire generation; but its role remains the same.

By the way, while numerous commentaries on *2001* have detailed its debts to earlier Clarke stories like "The Sentinel" and "Expedition to Earth," I would argue these space station stories were also important influences on the film. Both *Sands of Mars* and *Islands in the Sky*, like *2001*, employ as a viewpoint character someone with no prior familiarity with life in space who is introduced to that environment due to special circumstances. The glimpse of the alien spacecraft in "The Other Side of the Sky" is another demonstration that the occupation of space may bring contact with ancient alien intelligences. And what is arguably the most exciting scene in the film, when Bowman must briefly expose himself to the vacuum of space in order to return to the *Discovery*, is directly taken from a similar episode in "The Other Side of the Sky"—a vignette which is sometimes published separately as "Take a Deep Breath."

In some cases, the space station symbolizes an intermediate

stage in human evolution without an embracing, ongoing narrative of exploration; in Juanita Coulson's *Tomorrow's Heritage*, for instance, the oldest son of a powerful family is trying to become president of Earth; the youngest daughter is married to the head of a rebellious space colony; and the middle son, with his headquarters on a communications satellite orbiting Earth, functions as the family peacemaker. Again, the space station symbolizes a halfway point between Earth and space.

Occasionally, a story like "The Other Side of the Sky" will linger at a transitional space station, describing the training and maturation of a young spaceman in some detail; thus, as already indicated, what might be described as the science fiction *bildungsroman* frequently takes place in this setting. More often, however, stations fulfilling this function are reduced to episodes in larger adventures, as happens in *2001* and countless other stories.

Then, as most science fiction works leave the space station, those that remain focused on this setting must discover a new theme: the predicament of those who are for some reason confined to space stations, unable to travel beyond them. That is the situation, for example, of the teenagers in Richard Elam, Jr.'s "The Ghost Ship of Space," working at the "space service station" only because they flunked out of the academy that would have qualified them for actual space travel. When ambitious people are obliged to remain at a space station, it loses its stature as a place of transition and becomes instead an icon of *frustration*. Sometimes, the situation is readily resolved, as in "Ghost Ship," where the boys get an opportunity to demonstrate their true merit and are rewarded with a chance to serve in the space forces; but when the situation is prolonged, the frustration grows.

Now, the appropriate resonance becomes not so much a cycle as complete, utter stasis; the space station resident is forced to sit and wait in a place that can be incredibly monotonous for long periods of time and then, when an accident or invasion occurs, can instantly become incredibly dangerous. In this essentially passive position, the dominant mood can move beyond fear to become sheer *madness*; as noted, Charles L. Harness's *The Paradox Men* points out the possible benefits of insanity in space, and I have already listed numerous cases of individual madness in space stations and described the communities of madmen in Harness's novel, James Gunn's *Station in Space*, and Laurence M. Janifer and T. L. Treibich's *Target: Terra*. Hence, it is completely appropriate that Stanislaw Lem should choose a space station as the setting for *Solaris*; as the crewmen confront figures from the past who keep appearing and reappearing without explanation, their sense of horror and growing madness recalls the reactions of many others forced to remain in space stations.

What makes some of these experiences so frustrating and maddening in many cases is, I would suggest, a feeling of *incomplete knowledge*: just beyond the station are vast, unexplored regions of space, offering new experiences and information, but access is denied to these possibilities by the limiting perspective of the station; one must be content with whatever knowledge happens to appear. The idea of tantalizing knowledge just beyond one's grasp occurs in other space station stories about unsolved mysteries: if the hero of Clarke's "The Other Side of the Sky" had not been distracted by other matters, he could have investigated the unknown spacecraft; but he missed his chance and will be forever haunted by what he missed. If the alien spaceship in White's *Secret of the Marauder Satellite* had not threatened to destroy the space station, it could have been studied; instead, it had to be destroyed. If the story had been longer, the hero of Gene L. Henderson's "Tiger by the Tail" would have been able to investigate the mysterious alien spaceship that he found and retrieved; but the story ends without giving him a chance to obtain any knowledge of it.

In Lem's *Solaris*, of course, the mystery of the huge oceanic being is similarly never solved. For this reason, in his afterword to the novel, Suvin stresses Lem's originality in asserting "the price of certain kinds of progress and the impossibility of a 'final solution'"; his "pet horror...is eschatology—a claim to final static perfection" (208). Placed in the context of great literary figures, who are typically grand system-builders, this is no doubt an innovation. Yet it is important to note that Lem, in writing a space station story that begins and ends with an alien mystery, is also making use of a traditional pattern in popular science fiction, where questions are often left unanswered.

To be sure, Lem is also broadening and deepening this familiar theme: in the stories I referred to, the alien mystery remains unsolved—but not unsolvable. In the spirit of optimism that often dominates science fiction, these works imply that, with more effort and investigation, the aliens can eventually be understood: perhaps the strange spacecraft will return, another alien marauder may appear, or the strange spaceship will eventually be studied. In contrast, Lem argues that the mystery of the alien is both unsolved and unsolvable; all the examinations of the being have brought no solid results, and further study will be equally fruitless.

In this way, I would argue, *Solaris* functions as a critique of both types of forward movement celebrated in *A Canticle for Lei-bowitz*—science and religion. The people who have studied the strange alien are scientists, who have succeeded only in recording masses of data, applying names to various manifestations of the creature, and creating numerous unsatisfactory theories to explain it. Arguably, this is all science does and can do—examination that does not bring understanding. However, in describing the various schools of thought that develop concerning the alien and the factional squabbles that divide the field, Lem makes the investigation of the being a commentary on religious inquiry as well, for the scientists disputing the nature of the alien resemble nothing so much as a group of medieval theologians arguing about the nature of angels. Thus, the alien in *Solaris* symbolizes both the never-ending mystery of the physical universe and the unapproachable mystery of God, and there is no way for humans to fully understand either mystery.

In its evocation of the alien as unsolvable puzzle, *Solaris* resembles one science fiction story of the 1950s, Damon Knight's "Stranger Station," published in 1959; indeed, since Suvin specifically mentions Knight as one of the American authors Lem was familiar with (207), it is certainly possible, even probable, that he had read the story before writing *Solaris*. The parallels between the two works are striking: both stories involve men on a space station encountering a huge, mysterious alien being; both quote from and mention accounts of previous contacts with the creature; both protagonists seem on the verge of madness during their experience and are haunted by memories of their pasts; and both stories end with the mystery of the alien's nature and motives unresolved.

However, there are also illuminating differences between the stories. For one thing, while Lem makes the study of the alien a matter of pure curiosity, Knight muddles the issue somewhat by giving humanity a utilitarian reason for studying the alien: Knight's creature secretes a fluid that prolongs human life, so people wish to understand the alien simply to ensure that their supply of the fluid will not be cut off.

Indeed, the heroes' motives for approaching the alien described in the stories are different in a broader sense: Lem's scientists relish the intellectual challenge of studying and learning more about the alien, and while Lem is satirizing their efforts, he also displays a sense of respect and sympathy for them—there is something ennobling about the quest for knowledge even when it is finally futile. In contrast, Knight's hero is not an intelligent or well-educated man, and his reason for wanting to learn more about the alien is described as a desire for love. In a way, one can argue that Knight is reducing the intellectual pursuits of scientific data and knowledge of God to one basic underlying motive: the scientist will feel more secure, more loved, in a universe he fully understands, and the theologian desires the love of God. Thus, Knight seems to trivialize human quests for knowledge to celebrate a motive that is prehuman, animalistic, demeaning humanity in the process. It is fitting, then, that Lem's protagonist manages to retain his sanity to some extent and continues to relate to other men, while Knight's hero is reduced to incoherent ramblings about childhood grief over a dead puppy and an emotional request for the company of a cat. To Lem, man remains a unique and admirable creature, though his desires for ultimate knowledge will never be realized; to Knight, man becomes more like an animal.

In a corresponding fashion, two other stories reduce the quest for the alien to an animal instinct—James Tiptree, Jr.'s "And I Awoke and Found Me Here on the Cold Hill's Side," and Richard A. Lupoff's "Stomping Down Stroka Prospekt." Here, humans desire to know the aliens in the biblical sense of the word; Tiptree [Alice Sheldon] posits that this interest is simply a reflection of the ancient, exogamous tendency to mate with strangers. But there is no satisfaction, only pain and futility, in this sexual attraction, and the man encountered by the narrator of Tiptree's story, who is trapped at the station by his desire for the alien, desperately urges the narrator to go back to Earth and escape the temptation. If there is little mystery in the aliens in this story, there is still a sense of frustration: true union between human and alien cannot be achieved, and the urge for such a union is only debasing and humiliating to the people who seek it. A powerful aura of the sordid and unclean also emerges from the sexual encounter between man and alien in Lupoff's story, with the intimation that the alien encounter is a metaphor for homosexuality. In these stories, an impulse that Lem keeps on an intellectual and somewhat ennobling plane is again brought down to a emotional and animalistic desire. Another story which describes unfulfilling contact between human and alien in a space station is William Gibson's "Hinterlands": here, after each trip from the station through the strange singularity, the travelers return dead—or insane.

If the possibility of outward progress toward knowledge of the unknown—or knowledge of God—is denied, there is still the option of *inward movement*, ignoring the haunting puzzles and uncertainties of the outside world to concentrate on tending one's garden. And this shift in direction toward inwardness characterizes the literature of space habitats. People typically stopped at space stations as outposts on the way to new worlds, with the station's wide windows showing the vastness of space; in contrast, people regard space habitats as their final destinations, places to hide from the reality of space, to huddle in the comforting illusion of a terrestrial landscape with no glimpse provided of the universe outside. While space stations symbolized progress toward a new future, space habitats embody a return to a simpler past, a longing for simplicity, for home, ultimately for the womb. The later stories about traditional space stations begin to reflect this mood, as works like *Solaris*, "Stranger Station," and Lester del Rey's *Siege Perilous* depict heroes increasingly obsessed with their pasts, with a desire to return, instead of being focused on the future. It is the construct of the space habitat, however, that fully embodies and celebrates this new concern.

In this context, it is appropriate that the latter half of William Gibson's *Neuromancer* should take place in a space habitat; for the novel represents, among other things, an allegory of inward movement. The central motif of *Neuromancer*, the journey into the shared illusion that is the world of Cyberspace, obviously manifests a quest for inwardness; the name of the hero, Case, suggests confinement; he lives in a tiny chamber called a "coffin" and is perpetually traveling down narrow alleys and into dimly lit rooms; his regular use of alcohol and drugs represents another kind of inward movement, an avoidance of reality; and the climactic penetration of the Tessier-Ashpool family complex is a convoluted maneuver through a Chinese box of rooms within rooms.

And in moving his story into a space habitat, Gibson reflects an awareness that life in such an environment represents another type of inward journey; the family that built it "loathed space" and chose instead to build "a seamless universe of Self." Even before the final assault, one sees a similar attitude in the young people Case meets in the habitat and buys drugs from. They are exactly the same as the younger generation depicted in Mack Reynolds's *Chaos in Lagrangia* and William John Watkins's *The Centrifugal Rickshaw Dancer*: bored with life, addicted to sex and drugs, decadent, even suicidal. Of course, these are the people Case establishes a rapport with; he can see in them his own obsession with inwardness.

If Case desires a life of inward movement, will he be happy if he achieves it? The paradoxical answer is—no. For all his love of Cyberspace, the thrill he feels when traveling through its colorful structures, it is not a place he would wish to spend his entire life. Though he expresses contempt for bodily pleasures—"meat things" (153)—he still seems to enjoy them; after a session in Cyberspace, he wants to return to his cigarettes, his drugs, his women, his friends. To emphasize that continuing existence in Cyberspace would not satisfy Case, there is the character of McCoy Pauley, the "Dixie Flatline," a legendary computer "cowboy" who three times survived a period of brain death induced by Cyberspace travel—having a "flat line" on an electroencephalograph. "Dix" is now dead, but he has been resurrected as an artificial computer construct. In essence, he is a human who has achieved complete inwardness—he lives entirely in Cyberspace. Yet he is not happy—in fact he is miserable—and he repeatedly asks Case to have him "erased," or killed. This character can be said to represent what Case would be if he lived only in Cyberspace; and he obviously would not be satisfied there. At the end of the novel, in fact, such a construct of Case may exist, in the man on the shore Case briefly glimpses in Cyberspace; but Case recoils from the sight, again rejecting permanent existence there. Similarly, many of the people who first seem to enjoy life in a space habitat—like the heroes of Ben Bova's *Colony* and Victor Appleton's *The City in the Stars*—ultimately long to leave the symbolic womb and seek out new realities.

People, it appears, are essentially creatures of outward movement; whether that movement is seen as a positive achievement—as in *A Canticle for Leibowitz*—or as a futile expenditure of energy—as in *Solaris*—it is an activity that humans must pursue. But if people cannot be ultimately satisfied by an inward quest, there is still the chance that other beings might emerge to happily inhabit inner space. In the literature of space stations, this possibility is glimpsed in Jack Vance's "Abercrombie Station," where people in a space station are evolving into immensely fat beings that can live only in a space station, and in Fritz Leiber's *A Specter Is Haunting Texas*, where a more extended evolution of this type has produced humans that are incredibly thin and frail. The physical transformation of people seen here implies a mental transformation as well, a sense of satisfaction in the confined existence of a space station that seems unavailable to normal human beings. A space habitat story on the same theme is Charles Sheffield's "Transition Team": a psychologist, sent to investigate why the children living in a space habitat are so unhappy, realizes that the adults are in fact the problem—their traditional earthbound attitudes are inapplicable and constricting to the new generation of the space-born. She tells the adults that they have been a "transition team," beings from Earth who came to a space habitat to develop a new race to live there, and that it is now time for them to depart; the space children must be left alone to live and develop in an environment only they are truly suited for. Finally, there is the complete evolution from terrestrial human to space human seen in George Zebrowski's *Macrolife*: living generation after generation in a mobile space colony, inhabitants merge their minds and make their home one "cell" in an immense galactic being called Macrolife. Here, the pursuit of inwardness, the retreat into the womb of the space habitat, is ultimately transformed into an outward gesture, as residents embrace and become one with the universe.

While different in theme and mood, Sheffield's story and Zebrowski's novel are in many ways comparable to Gibson's *Neuromancer*. In that novel, Case and his cohorts are essentially functioning as a "transition team" in Cyberspace: able to visit Cyberspace, but not to permanently live there, they enter that realm to assist in the creation of a new being—an "Artificial Intelligence"—that is perfectly adapted to permanent life in a computer-created world. When that new being achieves independent existence, their mission in Cyberspace is over, and Case and the others return to the world of "meat things." They continue their outward existence, but they have engendered a new type of intelligence oriented to inwardness. It is finally revealed, though, that something more has occurred: Wintermute/Neuromancer, the new being, is not only alive in Cyberspace—he has *become* Cyberspace. "I'm the matrix," he tells Case (271); the inner world is not only inhabited, but personified, like the space habitat which speaks in Peter Dillingham's poem, "House." And this conclusion recalls the shift in *Macrolife* from inward to outward movement, as Wintermute/Neuromancer uses his new powers to make contact with similar creations from places like Alpha Centauri. In both works, the commitment to complete inwardness finally emerges as a new kind of outward quest involving the loss of individual identity—if Wintermute/Neuromancer has become the matrix, he has absorbed and merged its attributes—and a sense of uniting with the entire universe—although this culminating achievement is available only to humanity's successors, not to humans themselves. In this way, the final story of the space station seems to come to an end by beginning a new and different story.

This second story may be continued, of course, beyond the initial burst of excitement and new possibilities seen at the end of Gibson's *Neuromancer*, and the successors to humanity may eventually find that they too are frustrated in their efforts to live successfully in space. As in Olaf Stapledon's *Star Maker*, the conclusion of Zebrowski's *Macrolife* suggests both ultimate triumph and ultimate failure, as the immense construct of Macrolife finally begins breaking up back into its constituent elements as the end of the universe approaches.

However, the greatest feeling of pessimism regarding the development of life in space emerges in Richard A. Lupoff's *The Forever City*, which remarkably and uniquely presents the entire story of the birth and death of a space habitat. In the beginning, his heroine Mariel is living in the space city Yukawa, which seems like a functional and satisfactory home for its residents. When she comes into contact with a strange meteor that sends her traveling through time, however, she arrives at another space city, Hawking, where residents are in the grip of "terror and paranoia" (199) as they conduct forbidden genetic experiments; this represents the growing sense of withdrawal and madness that can develop in a space habitat. When she shifts into the future, she finds the habitat ravaged, as battles rage between normal humans and strange genetic mutations which are ugly and menacing; the evolution of new beings in space is occurring, although the results hardly seem desirable. After another leap through time, she finds the habitat apparently barren, inhabited only by soft whispering voices which represent a form of group intelligence; again, individual humans in space have merged into a single being, the development celebrated in *Macrolife*, but here this group mind seems weak and pathetic, albeit sinister in its efforts to absorb Mariel. A final time shift brings the heroine to a completely deserted Hawking; all life forms have died, bringing the development of space beings to an end. Thus, while ordinary humans are unable to achieve a satisfying life in outer space, their successors may ultimately face the same fate, frustrated and doomed by an implacable universe which remains inhospitable and inaccessible even to those beings which developed as a specific response to its challenges.

If one looks at the genre in its entirety, therefore, the space station clearly emerges as a powerful, consistent icon in science fiction, although its consistency paradoxically emerges from conflicting images and assigned functions.

It is first seen as akin either to a ship at sea or to a settlement on land; the metaphor of the ocean then suggests two narrative functions—as a place of business, and as a setting for thrilling adventure—while the metaphor of the land suggests its proper function is as a contented community. Finally, the function of business gives rise to two characteristic themes, cycles in human history and transitions; the function of adventure evokes the theme of frustration and madness; and the function of community leads to the theme of escape and inward movement. These different motifs are reconciled, I suggest, by assigning them to different stages in the imagined future history of the human race, just as the railroad takes on different roles in the history of the American West.

In the beginning, the space station is conceived of as an old business in a new environment, an extension of the cycles of human existence. This first theme of continuity and cyclical movement may be seen in a positive light, as in "Factory in the Sky," or, especially in the case of military stations, may emerge as a negative, destructive pattern, as in *A Canticle for Leibowitz*.

Escape from such cycles mandates linear movement, and the second characteristic theme associated with the space station is transition between Earth and space, a place to stop while moving from the known to the unknown; thus, the station can be the setting for an extended *bildungsroman,* like *Islands in the Sky*, or can simply serve as a brief episode in a larger epic of space adventure, as in *2001: A Space Odyssey*.

Those who are forced to remain in the space station, for whatever reason, are prone to become frustrated and insane, and such madness is the third characteristic theme in space station stories. In particular, they may be bedeviled by an alien mystery that they cannot solve, or that cannot be solved, as in "Stranger Station" and *Solaris*.

Another response to outward mysteries is to ignore them and seek fulfillment in an inward journey, a journey back into one's past—the true motive for building earthlike space habitats, and the fourth characteristic theme of the space station. However, since such inward quests apparently cannot satisfy something basic in human nature, station residents may ultimately assist in the creation or evolution of a new being more suited to the inner world, one which can achieve complete inwardness and loss of identity, while at the same time finding that the inward quest has now become a new outward journey toward union with the universe itself, as in *Macrolife* and *Neuromancer*.

In studying what might be described as the saga of space stations in science fiction, one tentatively glimpses a possible reason why they have been relatively neglected objects in the genre. For its typical iconic resonances, as characterized here, seem largely uncharacteristic of the genre. Science fiction, far more often, celebrates linear human progress—while the space station tends to represent a cyclical repetition of old patterns; demands outward movement—while the space station can only serve as the starting point for that movement; depicts the exploration of the unknown and discovery of the alien—while the space station can only illustrate the frustration of being unable to explore and discover, and the madness brought by that confinement; and applauds outward investigation and involvement with the entire universe—while the space station may only provoke inward movement and concern with oneself. With such thematic tendencies, apparently at odds with much of the genre's characteristic spirit, the space station, it could then be argued, is virtually doomed to function as a minor element in most science fiction works and as a major element in only a few works.

This conclusion, if accepted, has disturbing implications: for science fiction has so often been praised as the ultimate expression of human hopes and aspirations; and if space stations in some ways run counter to those hopes and aspirations, then there is something fundamental inhuman about them. Perhaps, this conclusion offers one explanation for the ongoing uncertainly over, and opposition to, plans for the international space station; a nation that could be become very enthusiastic about a trip to the Moon simply cannot muster a similar enthusiasm about constructing a home in space. The whole idea, it seems, may be in some ways unappealing, even repellent, in contrast to the other possibilities in space travel.

But if this analysis is correct, then a paradox appears to emerge: for another fundamental role often assigned to science fiction is to probe into and examine matters which people find unsettling or disturbing—to provide, in Harlan Ellison's phrase, "dangerous visions." If space stations do not harmonize with conventional attitudes and with conventional themes in the genre, that should in theory be all the more reason for writers of science fiction to confront and explore them.

Thus, having summed up what science fiction has done with space stations, I must finally examine what science fiction has not done with space stations.

And as work continues on the international space station, as engineers, science fiction writers and space enthusiasts continue to develop plans for further habitations in space, and as space stations continue to play their assigned roles in the genre of science fiction, this examination will have significant implications regarding the future of humanity in space, in life and in literature.

11. *This Strange Tomorrow*:
The Future of Space Stations
in Life and Literature

All science fiction writers and futurists agree that there will be space stations in humanity's future; there is a difference of opinion, however, concerning how important they will be.

The more traditional thinkers are what might be called the Planetary Chauvinists—to borrow Isaac Asimov's term. In the foreseeable future, they argue, Earth and other planetary settlements will be humanity's primary residences; space stations will exist, but they will be small, functional facilities with few inhabitants and little influence.

A second, more innovative group can be called the Space Chauvinists. As a natural step in humanity's evolution, they claim, people will gradually give up their homes on the surface of Earth and other worlds and choose the superior lifestyle of outer space; and only a few planetary settlements will endure, as places for research, alien contact, or residence for those unfortunate people helplessly attached to life on a planet.

A third group, which attempts to reconcile these two attitudes, can be called the Biculturalists. According to these people, a large proportion of humanity will continue to live on Earth and the planets, while at the same time a significant number will opt for space stations and space colonies. Thus, two human civilizations will emerge, typically seen in a state of continuing conflict.

As a point of departure in examining the implications of these scenarios, one might ask why it is that stories of Earth and its space colonies inevitably involve war, hostility, and tension. To be sure, there have been many cases of antagonism between colonial powers and their former possessions on Earth, but there have also been times when the parting was friendly and relations remained good; and to be sure, there may be natural economic or cultural reasons behind some of this hostility, as described in Chapter 8, but such disputes, like the continuing friction involving trade between Japan and the United States, have not always led to the kind of open conflict so often seen in the literature of space colonies. Why should it *always* be true that space dwellers despise Earth residents and Earth residents despise space dwellers?

The answer is that people living in space stations or space habitats are going to think differently than people living on the surface of a planet.

The reasons why this will be so are numerous and, perhaps, beyond our ability to completely predict, but several are immediately evident. The simple state of isolation from a larger group will in itself produce cultural and attitudinal change, and space station residents will be more isolated from previous environments than any group in history. The close proximity of the vacuum of outer space will change one's viewpoint, bringing among other things both a heightened sense of community—in the face of common danger—and, no doubt, a heightened need for privacy. A state of weightlessness or variable gravity will affect a whole set of assumptions and metaphors virtually built into terrestrial culture and language. The overarching sense of nature or the natural world—personified as either benevolent or threatening—will vanish in the manmade, artificial and controlled world of the space habitation. Fundamental perspectives will change: on Earth, despite scientific advances, one can still see the world as essentially a flat plane—as in Euclidean geometry—and regard the sun, moon, planets and stars as revolving around the Earth—as in Ptolemaic cosmology. Living in a confined habitat with curved surfaces and visible landscapes in the sky, residents will be forced to conceptualize in terms of non-Euclidean geometry, and deep in the vastness of space, will be forced to think of the universe in Copernican terms. And living in space may effect subtle and overt physiological changes which will also affect psychological states. In short, more so than any residence on a planetary surface, a space station will inevitably bring about truly alien thoughts and attitudes.

With this idea in mind, a number of things about space stations are quickly explained. We see, for example, the complete absurdity of employing a space station to cure the insane, as in Frank Belknap Long's *This Strange Tomorrow*. Insane people, by definition, are not well adjusted to their environment, and any successful therapy will involve helping them to better adjust to that environment. Placing such people in the utterly strange setting of a space station can hardly achieve this goal; instead, as Long himself acknowledges, it will only in most cases make the insanity even worse. We understand also why madness and insanity are so often associated with space stations, in the cases of both isolated individuals and entire crews which go mad; as Charles L. Harness pointed out in *The Paradox Men,* what an Earth dweller might regard as madness in fact represents mental adjustment to the bizarre new environment: "Insanity under such conditions is a useful and logical defense mechanism, an invaluable and salutary retreat from reality" (155).

More broadly, we can see why many science fiction writers have avoided space stations, and why those who deal with them tend to describe them in familiar terms, assign them to familiar functions, and characterize them with familiar themes; simply put, they are seeking to ignore or avoid the implications of the station's fundamental alienness.

Both of the basic metaphors for space associated with the space station—the ocean and the frontier—are clearly inaccurate and inadequate: the strangeness and hazards of outer space far exceed those of the open sea, and the cold vacuum of space can in no way provide the security and comfort of a planetary surface.

The three characteristic functions of the space station reflect a similar desire to treat the unknown as something known and knowable: a new place to carry out the old business of Earth, a setting for the sorts of thrilling adventure already available on the surface, a new community that duplicates the spirit of a terrestrial settlement.

The four themes associated with the space station, finally, continue this tendency to avoid confronting the true novelty of life in space. First, making the space station an emblem of cycles, of continuations in human activities and tendencies, simply denies the existence of the problem, and while a common strategy, remains unconvincing.

Second, emphasizing the space station's role as a place for transition from Earth to space reduces the space station to a minor matter, a place for brief visits that do not allow for full considerations of the fact that a space station may in fact be much more alien than any planet one might travel to.

Those stories which present the space station as a setting for frustration and madness come closest, no doubt, to expressing the essential and significant nature of such environments. One must note, however, that the madnesses depicted, despite all the novel terminology I have noted, are typically versions of familiar mental problems on Earth. Thus, we repeatedly see the sorts of paranoia, violent behavior, withdrawal and claustrophobia that occur when people live in isolated places on Earth instead of some genuinely novel form of insanity generated by life in space. It is also an evasion of sorts that in Stanislaw Lem's *Solaris* the residents' madness manifests itself in the form of reappearances by people from their pasts, instead of some genuinely alien visions; that Damon Knight's "Stranger Station" resolves into another evasion, as the protagonist's confrontation with the unknown leads to a simple reversion to childhood behavior instead of a real conceptual breakthrough; and that James Tiptree, Jr.'s "And I Awoke and Found Me Here on the Cold Hill's Side" depicts the desire for the alien as nothing more than an expression of the ancient urge for exogamy. Even in acknowledging that the strange world of the space station may lead to strange thoughts and thus madness, writers cast those strange thoughts and those madnesses in familiar terms.

Finally, transforming the space station into a place for returning and withdrawal is the grandest evasion of them all. Considering the limitless possibilities for creating absolutely any environment at all in a space station, one finds it truly depressing to see, again and again, the neat lawns and gently sloping landscapes of a suburb in the American Midwest. And considering the innumerable ways in which a space habitat will irrevocably change human nature, one finds it truly incredible to hear claims that such habitats will in fact function as the perfect environment for the rebirth of old cultures, particularly those of good old fashioned rugged individualism and the American frontier. Treating a miniature artificial world with infinite capacity for strangeness, writers stubbornly think in the most conventional ways imaginable.

There are other stories which in some ways attempt to explore the fundamental alienness of space stations; and while these are not always the best stories that I read—indeed, at least one is among the worst—they stand out as interesting, though largely unsuccessful, efforts to evoke a truly unique environment.

There is first of all a long tradition of science fiction works driven more by the surrealistic illogic of nightmares than by the extrapolative logic of science; and Charles L. Harness's *The Paradox Men*, Gordon R. Dickson's *The Pritcher Mass*, and Michael Swanwick's *Vacuum Flowers* are three novels involving space stations which all evoke an atmosphere of furious action and ever-changing realities, a definite sense of the alien. However, their space stations seem little more than incidental backgrounds for works impelled by other concerns, and the peculiar strangeness that might emerge from life in a space station is never really examined.

In the conclusion of *Down to Earth*, when residents decide to turn off the comforting illusions of Earth and confront the harsh re-

ality of their environment, Louis Charbonneau remarkably anticipates the problem in most depictions of space habitats and insists
that the residents of unusual places must observe those unusual
places clearly; but he offers no other insights about how that clear
vision might affect them.

In his story about a space habitat, "Small World," Bob Shaw
comments that his young hero's "imagination was not fully able to
cope with the old Earthbound concepts of 'above' and 'below'"
(63)—although there are no further signs of this new attitude in his
later adventures. Indeed, the feelings of the young woman in her
house seem a typical case of agoraphobia, and the terrified reaction
of the young man who attempts to run across the "sky"—the huge
windows which display the universe outside—is completely predictable: any resident of Earth would be frightened, reduced to shivering
in a fetal position, in these surroundings; one might expect instead
that someone who grew up in such an environment would respond
more calmly. Here, Shaw claims to be describing a completely different attitude emerging in a space habitat, but he ultimately depicts
thoroughly predictable attitudes.

Another work which purports to depict a new type of person
emerging in the environment of space is Spider and Jeanne Robinson's *Stardance*. Repeatedly, we are told that the dancers in zero
gravity are obliged to develop an entirely new attitude—to "think
spherically"; yet the characters in the novel do not seem to think any
differently than residents of Earth. Indeed, the fact that the Robinsons are ultimately unable to describe the space dances, except in
metaphorical terms—at one point the narrator says, "What can I tell
you of *Mass*, if you have not seen it? It cannot be described, even
badly, in mechanistic terms" (55)—indicates their similar inability
to describe the new personality of space residents. And at the conclusion of the novel, instead of pursuing the notion of new attitudes
in space, the Robinsons fall back on one of the oldest clichés in the
genre: the development of group intelligence, which also functions
as the unsatisfactory resolution of George Zebrowski's *Macrolife*
and as an element in the evolution of space life seen in Richard A.
Lupoff's *The Forever City*. By trotting out this ancient idea as something new and exciting, then, all these works raise—and ultimately
evade—the question of a new perspective arising from life in space.

Stories about the transformation of humans in space into new
and different beings suggest that the environment of the vacuum is
truly alien, but their evocation of that transformation is usually halt-
ing and incomplete. In the immensely fat residents of Jack Vance's
"Abercrombie Station," one sees only the beginning of the process

of change, as is the case in works like Charles Sheffield's "Transition Team" and William Gibson's *Neuromancer*. Bruce Sterling's *Schismatrix* argues that life in space will lead to the birth of many new and strange forms of humanity, but actually devotes little time to depicting them. And, despite its occasional power, Richard A. Lupoff's *The Forever City* fails to fully describe or characterize the strange creatures that he sees evolving in a space habitat, as they are only glimpsed briefly by his heroine.

By focusing on a space station inhabitant as its protagonist, Fritz Leiber's *A Specter Is Haunting Texas* occasionally manages to convincingly evoke the alien perspective brought on by such an environment; and, in a digression on the conventions of weightless theater, the novel gives one small hint as to just how completely our entire civilization will change when it is transplanted to outer space. But the novel paradoxically devotes most of its time to that station resident's visit to Earth, thereby avoiding a complete look at the new civilization flourishing in the space station. Leiber's "The Beat Cluster" goes further in describing how an entire new way of life might evolve in the weightless conditions of space; but since it is only a short story, it cannot begin to offer a full picture of that new life. Dan Simmons's *Hyperion* powerfully asserts that while life on planetary surfaces will produce only stagnation, life in space can radically transform humanity:

> I will not try to describe the beauty of life in a Swarm—their zero-gravity globe cities and comet farms and thrust cultures, their micro-orbital forests and migrating rivers and the ten thousand colors and textures of life at Rendezvous Week. Suffice it to say that I believe the Ousters have done what Web humanity has not in the past millennia: *evolved*. While we live in our derivative cultures, pale reflections of Old Earth life, the Ousters have explored new dimensions of aesthetics and ethics and biosciences and art and all the things that must change and grow to reflect the human soul. (468)

However, Simmons focuses his novel on planetary residents and, except for the brief and tantalizing glimpse of the Ousters in *The Fall of Hyperion* already cited, says little about these "new dimensions of aesthetics and ethics and biosciences and art."

Katherine MacLean's "Incommunicado" is unique in suggesting that space station residents may be transformed by a new language—in this case, the strange noises made by a library file system which they subconsciously learn and employ to help solve various problems. It is an intriguing idea, although MacLean does not fully develop it, and indeed does not really convey exactly what this language is like and how it is helping to raise people's intelligences. Still, in an interesting application of the Sapir-Whorf Hypothesis, MacLean does at least raise the possibility that the development of a new language may make space station residents become unusual, or even seem insane to outsiders.

Finally, there is Long's remarkable *This Strange Tomorrow*, which represents not a case of conscious artistic intent to explore, but an inadvertent stumbling toward, the strangeness of space life. As his sane protagonist is inexplicably committed to the space asylum Molidor, and as readers observe the peculiarities of "space therapy"—evil guards who stand ready to beat any patient who steps out of line, ballet dancers and clowns who randomly prance across the stage in order to somehow reawaken the spirit of childhood, and patients continually urged to simply sit and stare at the vastness of space, as if that could in any way be therapeutic—they can only feel that they are in some sort of surrealistic dream. Considered as a plan of action that might actually be carried out, Molidor truly seems like an asylum where the lunatics are in charge. And apparently horrified or baffled by his own vision, Long himself, in an extraordinary gesture of artistic despair, completely abandons his own story halfway through the manuscript, and, in a few pages, abruptly shifts into an entirely different story with entirely different characters. The novel thus records a spiritual journey toward the edge of the abyss—and an author backing away from the strangeness he has accidentally created.

What is unusual about *This Strange Tomorrow* is that such an abortive experience is recorded in the published version of the story—no doubt due to some pressing deadline or financial need; perhaps the wastebaskets of other science fiction writers are filled with space station stories which similarly led to impossible complications or unsolvable problems and which were abandoned by their authors in a more conventional fashion.

All of these stories, and a few others I might have mentioned, represent, in the end, a few anomalies amidst scores of works which do not even begin to wrestle with the implications of life in space. It seems, I submit, that science fiction writers are basically afraid of space stations and everything they might represent.

It is an attitude, to be sure, found not only the genre; one sees it in the planning of NASA administrators, who have tended to conceive of the international space station as just another space mission, with the same sort of daily schedule completely controlled by Earth, instead of seeing it as the start of a true space community; in the reports of a never-ending series of commissions and committees on America's future in space, which invariably conclude by suggesting a moon base or trip to Mars instead of habitations in space; in the indifference to space stations among the general public, who get excited, it seems, only about manned and unmanned missions to other planets and moons; and in the blind optimism of Gerard O'Neill and the L-5 enthusiasts, who simply refuse to see the intractable problems in their dreams of space utopias. No one is willing to admit that space station life will be utterly different from any previous form of civilization and to explore the full dimensions of those differences.

It is not surprising that many people prefer not to ponder the unknown, the alien; but one does not expect to find this attitude in the field of science fiction. After all, the encounter with the alien has long been celebrated as a central motif in the genre; I myself have said in print that anticipating and describing the successors to humanity are one frequent resolution to its stories. And throughout the upper and lower reaches of science fiction, there are thousands of alien worlds and alien beings.

But how alien are they, really? On examination, alien worlds, with a few exotic colors and effects, seem to resemble the remote regions of Earth, and alien beings, with some anatomical oddities, seem to look and act much like human beings. The genre's fixation with the alien, then, emerges as a fascination with external features and trivial differences in behavior and speech. Both writers and readers of science fiction, it might be maintained, do not really want to confront the alien; rather, they seek "aliens" who are simple transformations of parents, children, Christ figures, barbarians, and other archetypal figures of life and literature. Offhand, I can think of five major exceptions in modern science fiction, five works which actually struggle with the genuinely alien, and significantly, four of them—Knight's "Stranger Station," Lem's *Solaris*, Clarke's *2001: A Space Odyssey*, and James Tiptree, Jr.'s "And I Awoke and Found Me Here on the Cold Hill Side"—involve space stations (the other is Terry Carr's "The Dance of the Changer and the Three"); for the problems are inextricably linked: the truly alien being and the truly alien environment. And by and large, science fiction does not want to have anything to do with them.

I realize that in a way I am asking for a lot—for stories of exploration that do not involve physical exploration; stories which might take place over a span of several centuries, not several days;

stories that are dedicated to explaining the inexplicable or, to use Gregory Benford's memorable phrase, "effing the ineffable." Still, many standard arguments for science fiction rest on the assertion that works in the genre can accomplish goals that cannot be accomplished by ordinary fiction; and surely, if any form of literature can be challenged to, and be expected to, achieve the impossible, that genre is science fiction.

Thus, I return to the question with which I began this study—why are space stations relatively unimportant in science fiction?—and see in the answer a powerful indictment of the entire field: overtly committed to an exploration of the unknown, the alien, the unexpected, the genre instead is covertly committed to an exploration of the phony unknown, the comfortingly familiar alien, the expectable unexpected. In short, we find in science fiction a genre theoretically committed to the alien and practically wedded to the familiar.

And, at the risk of echoing the insufficiently forceful lament of the hero in Isaac Asimov's *Nemesis*, this is too bad.

For when people are living in space stations, there really will be a strange tomorrow; and nothing in our conventional expectations, analogies to previous situations, or lifeless computer projections can adequately prepare us for that strange tomorrow. For that reason, one of the cardinal purposes of science fiction has always been to consider, to anticipate, to grapple with the implications of coming change before we are overwhelmed by events.

And in the case of space stations, science fiction is just not doing the job.

PART FIVE

APPENDICES

12. *Step to the Stars*: The International Space Station in the Context of Science Fiction

To be completely effective, a consultant should be a member of the management team, aware of all ongoing developments and participating in the decision-making process. As I endeavor to apply the ideas in science fiction to the practical problems of building and maintaining a facility like the international space station, I obviously do not enjoy such a position. In 1985 and 1986, when I was working with Dr. Lindsay Moore, I briefly had access to some privileged—though hardly top-secret—materials regarding the negotiations between the United States, the European Space Agency, Japan, and Canada about the management structure of the station; but since that time, Dr. Moore has lost contact with NASA and the Jet Propulsion Laboratory, I have lost contact with Dr. Moore, and today, I must honestly say that all I know about the progress of the international space station is what I read in the newspapers.

Since I am handicapped by my position as an outsider, and since I lack any particular expertise in these areas, my suggestions regarding both politics and engineering may well be inherently impractical, precluded by decisions that have already been made, or already incorporated into the official plans. Nevertheless, I offer them for three reasons. First, as I have discussed, my research began with this utilitarian purpose, and I still feel a lingering obligation to fulfill that original purpose, especially since the association between Dr. Moore and NASA did not last long enough for the following ideas to be conveyed through proper channels—with one notable exception, as shall be described below. Thus, I present them here in the hopes that they will in this indirect way eventually find their original intended audience and be duly considered. Second, beyond assisting in the success of the international space station, I have other purposes. When this station is completed (assuming that it will be completed), there will be other space stations and large-scale space projects, and if my ideas are inapplicable to this particular undertaking they still may be useful in other contexts. In addition, if one or two of these insights prove helpful, or if they have been reached independently by current experts, then I have some support for the original conclusions of Hugo Gernsback and John W. Campbell, Jr.: that the materials in science fiction can indeed have some practical value.

I can first offer one general conclusion about space stations found in the stories I have read: again and again, space stations, unlike space habitats, emerge as eminently sensible ideas. True, there are genuine dangers, though these are perhaps exaggerated, and there is something unsatisfactory in the space station as a permanent home. But in terms of the functions they can perform and the logical limitations commonly placed on their size and goals, the concept of the traditional space station has been thoroughly tested in the crucible of science fiction and found to be a worthwhile, viable idea. In particular, there is, as noted in Chapter 4, nearly unanimous agreement that a space station will indeed serve many useful purposes in the context of an energetic program of space exploration. The overall prognosis for the international space station and similar facilities, based on an examination of science fiction, is therefore good, and NASA can proceed with the reasonable expectation that their space station will be technologically feasible, economically successful, and a valuable if minor addition to human civilization.

In my view, the tasks confronting NASA in its space station project fall into four categories: obtaining and building support—both political and financial—for the program, constructing and furnishing the station, maintaining its security, and managing and governing the station on an ongoing basis; and I have located suggestions in science fiction relevant to all four concerns.

Support for the international space station may be NASA's most pressing problem: it is a relatively expensive program in a time of continuing budget deficits; many have questioned the need for such a facility at this time; and there is no great public interest in the project, possibly for the reasons I have earlier advanced, which may be the key reason its survival seems continually threatened. One difficulty as I see it is that the international space station does not appear sufficiently *new*; after all, there have been at least three previous structures—the American Skylab and the Russian Salyut and Mir—which could be described as space stations, and the fact that this station will be the first that was not cobbled together from old spaceship designs does not appear to constitute a significant breakthrough.

A possible answer to this problem lies in three of the ways that science fiction has found to make space stations dramatic. One of these, the military station, is here ruled out by explicit agreement among the nations building the international space station and in any event, as already discussed, is not a particularly good plan. However, there are two other possibilities: the space station as a launching point for further space exploration, and the space station as a new kind of international community in space.

To exploit either of these potentially powerful images, I suggest renaming the structure to better establish its novelty and clear up doubts about its purpose. There are two synonyms for "space station" found in science fiction that could be employed in this way: "space platform," first used by Otto Gail in *The Stone from the Moon* and later popularized by Murray Leinster's *Space Platform*, and "space city," notably employed in Curt Siodmak's *City in the Sky* (an alternative here could be "satellite city," found in Mack Reynolds's novel of that name). That is, if the international space station cannot really claim to be the first "space station," it might with more justice be called the first "space platform" or first "space city."

The first name would emphasize that this facility could be readily used as a base for launching manned and unmanned expeditions to other planets and into deep space; after all, that is the traditional function of the first space stations in science fiction, and one that Skylab, Salyut, and Mir were or are not designed for. Using the more suggestive term "space platform" might be a way to win over to the space station project those who feel the money might be better spent on other types of space exploration; the point would be that such missions would be much cheaper—and thus more frequent—if they could be assembled in, or launched from, the international space station, instead of being constructed on and launched from Earth. Although the space shuttle has sometimes been used to send unmanned space probes on their way, a permanent space station could perform this service with greater reliability and less difficulty.

The second term, "space city," seems a grandiose description of a facility that will initially have only a handful of residents in six-month shifts; yet it could be argued that the international space station is being planned so that it can repeatedly be expanded and upgraded, making it at least the beginning of or basis for a space city. This descriptive term would emphasize the spirit of international cooperation behind the project and suggest that the international space station might grow into a means to and a model for increased cooperation on Earth, exactly as suggested in Siodmak's *City in the Sky*. And this conceptual framework for the venture might appeal to those who say that the money for the space station might be better spent on problems at home; from this perspective, the international space station would be one way to encourage international cooperation and peace on Earth and thus may serve in an indirect way to solve some of those earthly problems.

As for financial support, Mack Reynolds and Dean Ing's *Trojan Orbit* offers an intriguing idea: the space habitat in that novel is supported by a broad-based private corporation whose capital comes from millions of individual shareholders who have both an idealistic commitment in humanity's future in space and a practical desire to eventually earn dividends from their stock. Without entirely privatizing the international space station, it would not be difficult to establish some sort of government-sponsored corporation as a "silent partner" in the project and have it sell stocks, backed up a vague promise of future profit-sharing when and if there are profits to share. I suspect that, just as in *Trojan Orbit*, there would be millions of customers anxious to make such an investment for both idealistic and practical reasons.

In addition, the film *2001: A Space Odyssey* provides NASA with a lesson: the Howard Johnson's restaurant seen in the space station there is not simply a visual gag, but a reminder that when space travel becomes a part of everyday life, there will be a need for such things as restaurants and hotels in space; and the best people to provide such services will be those who now do so on Earth. To be sure, such facilities as a part of the international space station are far in the future; but there is nothing to prevent NASA and its partners from selling the rights to them now. For example, I suspect that McDonalds might be willing to pay a substantial amount of money now for the eventual privilege of opening the first fast-food restaurant in outer space; if nothing else, the publicity alone might justify such an investment.

In short, if the international space station is conceived of as the first space city, one need only consider the many activities and businesses that characterize urban civilization, and any number of commercial possibilities in the present or future will emerge. To be sure, no one wants to see a large Pepsi sign on the outside of the station, but there would be, I suspect, methods for establishing business relationships which brought money into the project without compromising its basic integrity.

Plans for assembling the space station in Earth orbit have been a source of continuing controversy, at one point involving an embarrassing public dispute between NASA and its own astronauts, who objected strenuously to the amount and duration of work tentatively assigned to them. And the plan once put forth to have robots do much of the construction has little merit; with robots still a relatively new feature in terrestrial factories, it seems premature to employ them for a difficult job in an unfamiliar environment. The underlying problem is that the current group of astronauts—highly qualified pilots and scientists—are not suited by training or temperament for the long hours of monotonous welding and bolting that building a space station will surely require; as is said of the space factory in Jerry Pournelle's "High Justice," "There is a lot of construction work, and...repetitive labor...bores the big brains" (126). Here, novels like Lester del Rey's *Step to the Stars* and Lee Correy's *Space Doctor* provide an elegant solution: hire construction workers who are better prepared for such activity and send them into space. Surely a well-publicized national search would turn up a sufficient number of attractive candidates, and journalists tired of talking to ex-pilots and Ph.D.'s might pay more attention to these strange new creatures: the blue-collar astronauts. In addition, beyond the abortive publicity stunts of "teacher in space" and "journalist in space," this plan would allow NASA to offer a meaningful role in space to some "ordinary citizens."

From NASA's viewpoint, of course, there could be one eventual problem for NASA in this approach, first raised in Siodmak's *City in the Sky*: "The men belonged to the SWU, the Space Worker's Union, an affiliate of the AFL-CIO" [65]); and grumblings about the interference of labor unions figure in two novels, Spider and Jeanne Robinson's *Stardance* and Allan Steele's *Orbital Decay*. Still, space unions could also have the beneficial effect of vigilantly protecting the safety of persons working in space, a point emphasized in Elizabeth Moon's "ABCs in Zero G" and Michael Flynn's "The Washer at the Ford."

Regarding the overall design of the station, I will offer only one wistful comment: while I bow to the logic and practicality of having six or so modules attached to an enormous grid work in no particular configuration, I suspect that interest in and enthusiasm for the space station project would more than double if NASA unveiled revised plans showing an enormous metallic doughnut. To millions of Americans indoctrinated by the visual iconography of science fiction, only a structure of this kind will be a *real* space station.

Science fiction offers any number of practical suggestions that might be helpful to the specialists now working to perfect their plans for the international space station or future space stations. Some of these involve engineering—both mechanical and biological—while others are more a matter of environmental design.

One intriguing idea to consider in designing the station can be found in Hal Clement's "Answer," where the inhabitants of a space station communicate by means of "an efficient but amazingly archaic system of mechanical bells and speaking tubes" (160). While the purpose of this mechanism in the story is to avoid radio transmissions that might disrupt the station's sensitive computer, it occurs to me that such a system might have other values. If, for example, there is a catastrophic power failure in the station, the survival of the crew, when they are in different modules, might depend on their ability to communicate quickly with each other; but such a power failure would also disable all radios. In this case, a mechanical means to communicate could be crucially important; and even under ordinary conditions, a communications system that saves a little energy would certainly do no harm.

Other ideas for features that might be incorporated into the station may be less valuable but should still be presented. Victor Appleton II's *Tom Swift, Jr., and His Outpost in Space* suggests that the space station employ "an oxygen-helium mixture to breathe—it'll cut down the danger of your crew suffering from the bends in case of an air leak...It would also cut down on the weight of the breathing mixture" (159). Albert Saari's "Sitting Duck" offers what sounds like an interesting suggestion for generating a feeling of gravity in a space station: "a continuous fan-drawn suction created a substitute for gravity" (126). Arthur C. Clarke's *Islands in the Sky* envisions a simple and useful vehicle for traveling in space around the station called a "broomstick"—a spring in a hollow tube (32). Elizabeth Moon's "ABCs in Zero G" offers some reasonable proposals for improved medical care of space station residents, including spacesuits with limbs that unscrew for easy access and a "can-opener" device to quickly remove the cumbersome suits from injured space workers. And del Rey's *Step to the Stars* points out that a space station will need some kind of sprinkler system to deal with fires (143).

A more general reminder of value regarding a project that combines the efforts of four separate governments can be found in Harry Harrison's *Skyfall*; in that novel, a problem involving the joint American-Soviet space station is investigated, with these findings:

> "Exploding bolt.... Unexploded. An American bolt, I am unhappy to report."
> "And those supports and pistons are Soviet...The

interface between the two techniques, the weak spot where one meets the other." (141)

Perhaps NASA requires no additional reminder that there are possible dangers in combining the technologies of different countries; still, the points of "interface" in the international space station should be a matter of concern throughout the process of planning and building the facility.

Finally, while I do not feel competent to intelligently evaluate—or even fully understand—the proposed design for an energy-producing space station in David Brin's "propaganda piece," "Tank Farm Dynamo," I strongly suspect, given Brin's past work for the space program, that his ideas have merit.

While some of these suggestions involve redesigning a structure in space so as to better cope with the human body's requirements, some science fiction also suggests redesigning the human body so as to better cope with a structure in space. Michael Swanwick's *Vacuum Flowers* presents a possible solution to the problem of "calcium depletion" in weightlessness: "You could tailor a strain of coraliferous algae to live in the bloodstream. In the first phase they're free-swimming, and in the second they colonize the bone tissue. When they die, they leave behind a tiny bit of calcium" (49). And Michael Flynn's "The Washer at the Ford" involves the development of a special "nanny," a tailored microorganism that could protect astronauts against the effects of harmful radiation in outer space.

When it comes time to add decor to, and plan everyday life on board, the space station, science fiction offers a few suggestions. Several works—including Alan Ash's *Conditioned for Space*, Robert A. Heinlein's "Delilah and the Space Rigger," J. Lloyd Castle's *Satellite E-One*, Ted White's *Secret of the Marauder Satellite*, Siodmak's *City in the Sky*, and Correy's *Space Doctor*—stress the importance of using bright colors on spacesuits and the station for ready identification and, according to Correy's book, to improve general "crew morale, effectiveness and efficiency" (84). And Harrison's *Skyfall* proposes a system of Muzak in orbit: "In one of the cabinets, a microminiaturized tape player ran continuously, providing six channels of music that could be tapped at will" (229); I must point out, though, that the crewmen in Allan Steele's *Orbital Decay* object strenuously to the background music they are constantly obliged to hear.

In addition, while NASA is unlikely to allow smoking on board the station, at least in its first years of operation, two works—Robert A. Heinlein's "Waldo" (37) and Leinster's *Space Platform* (78)—go to the trouble of designing zero-gravity ashtrays, both featuring a suction tube to draw in the ashes. To be sure, the slightest mention of space smoking in the vicinity of the Secretary for Health and Human Services would no doubt provoke a burst of righteous indignation and the announced governmental goal of a "smoke-free cosmos"; still, although—as a former smoker—I am hardly an unbiased observer, I see no reason why smoking should be permanently banned in outer space. In Rafe Bernard's *The Wheel in the Sky*, the lighting of the first cigarettes in the space station is a solemn ceremony, a sign that the facility has truly become habitable; and in Caidin's *Four Came Back*, the station commander enjoys his occasional cigar as a well-earned reward for his hard work. A space station, I maintain, must be prepared to provide space for humanity's vices as well as its virtues. A different kind of smoking—marijuana—takes place in Steele's *Orbital Decay*, although the instigator of the practice later concludes, wisely, that it is not a particularly good idea.

Arthur C. Clarke twice raises the issue of having animals on board a space station. In "The Other Side of the Sky," a space station crewman's pet canary is driving everyone crazy with its singing until it suddenly becomes quiet; quickly, they realize that there must be some problem with the oxygen supply: "Half a million dollars of chemical and electronic engineering had let us down completely. Without Claribel [the canary], we should soon have been slightly dead" (32). Of course, Clarke is borrowing the idea from coal miners, who regularly brought canaries down with them to monitor the air; but the idea has merit when applied to a space station as well. No doubt there will be sensors and alarms to indicate any drop in air pressure, but life might be a little more secure if there was an "organic" backup system. And in "The Haunted Spacesuit," the narrator speaks of "Tommy, our recently acquired cat. Pets mean a great deal to men thousands of miles from Earth" (62) If, as other stories suggest, pests like mice and cockroaches will inevitably accompany man into space, we should at least bring along some more pleasant animal companions as well; certainly, there is more than enough evidence available that pets can be valuable companions for lonely people on Earth, suggesting they would be equally valuable for lonely people in space.

Once the station is functioning, avoiding natural disasters will be a recurring concern. Meteors are unlikely to be a threat, but as the space around Earth becomes more and more cluttered with old satellites and manmade debris, a collision becomes a real possibility; it may be necessary, as in Clarke's "The Haunted Spacesuit," to keep a constant outlook for nearby objects and eliminate them if they seem too nearby. Another genuine danger, stressed in Martin Caidin's *Killer Station* and elsewhere, is radiation from solar flares; since even now scientists cannot predict the sun's activity with complete accuracy, at least one of the modules should be heavily armored to protect astronauts from a solar flare of unprecedented strength. Fortunately, I recall reading that NASA has anticipated this problem and is providing exactly this sort of shielding. However, such intense radiation could also affect the station's orbit and lead to the other danger depicted in *Killer Station*—a station which falls into the atmosphere and threatens Earth; this has recently been aired as a possible problem, since the international space station is rather large and is going to be placed in a rather low orbit. It might be prudent to either downscale the station or place it in a slightly higher orbit; for, as the real-life example of Skylab demonstrates, one need not believe in Caidin's bomb-planting traitor to see a true threat in a big space station orbiting close to the surface of Earth.

On the subject of protection from intentional attacks of the kind Caidin describes, to be sure, I am no doubt a little paranoid, having read of so many attempts to destroy or sabotage space stations. Still, while one can safely dismiss fears of Martian invaders (as in del Rey's *Siege Perilous*) or impostors replacing legitimate station visitors (as in the film *Project Moonbase*), it remains the case that any space station will be extremely vulnerable to someone with the ability and the desire to destroy it. And although recently improved relations with the former Soviet Union seem to make a Russian attack on the station unlikely, a number of stories, including John Alfred Taylor's "Grave-11" and Ben Bova's *Colony*, describe the threat of Third World terrorist activity. After all, amidst fears that the likes of Saddam Hussein and Moammar Kaddafi might obtain the technology to build nuclear weapons, we must also remember that the technology to build orbiting anti-satellite weapons will soon be equally accessible.

The prospect of a deliberate assault on the international space station raises a troublesome issue, though: all partners in the project have agreed that the facility will be devoted exclusively to peaceful purposes; how then can the station be given a means for defending itself? One answer might be passive defense methods; for example, in Murray Leinster's *Space Tug* a space station neutralizes enemy missiles by throwing out bits and pieces of junk which the missiles hit instead of the station—a device that would work against the crudest kind of anti-satellite weapon, one set to explode on contact. And Ted White's *Secret of the Marauder Satellite* suggests a station that can move out of the way when danger approaches, although the station in that novel is not sturdy enough to do so; I have heard that NASA actually considered plans to give the international space station limited motive power, though to avoid space debris, not attacks. And to deal with the problem of interlopers or hijackers who actually board the station, Paul Preuss's *Breaking Strain* suggests the use of "stun-guns—air rifles using rubber bullets that were capable of severely injuring a human, even one in a spacesuit, although not likely to puncture crucial space station systems" (155).

Finally, there has to be some concern about members of the crew becoming mentally unbalanced. If the testimony of science fiction seems a bit hysterical here, one should recall that Russian cosmonauts, I am told, are no longer allowed to play chess in space—because while living at an isolated Antarctic base, one Russian killed another in a dispute over chess! It is also worth remembering that the nearest thing to a mutiny in the United States space program occurred during the three-month Skylab 3 mission, when the harried crewmen announced one day that they were going to stop following instructions for a while. Although a look at their workload suggests that they had legitimate grievances, their actions still represented a significant departure from normal behavior and may have partially resulted from the unbalancing effects of a long stay in space.

Unfortunately, science fiction seems to offer no convincing solution to the problem of potential madness in space. Preuss's *Breaking Strain* simply suggests that "hardened cops" will eventually get "used to dealing with...forms of insanity that commonly afflict the human residents of space stations" (230). Caidin's *Killer Station* suggests having a psychologist on board at all times, to look out for and deal with signs of incipient mental illness, but also acknowledges that the very presence of such an observer might increase tensions—and when the station faces a real crisis, the commander pointedly tells the psychologist to stay away from his crew. In addition, there is one old question: who will watch the watcher? That is, what happens if the psychologist starts to go crazy?

Regarding the governance of the space station—the original focus of my research—Dr. Moore's interests and my own gradually diverged: to him, the crucial issue was an equitable distribution of authority among the four international partners, while I was increasingly concerned with equitably distributing authority between those on Earth and those in space.

To Dr. Moore and his associates—and myself as well—the space station project at first represented a golden opportunity, a chance to foster a new spirit of international harmony and brotherhood on Earth with a cooperative effort in space. This was, of course, exactly the feeling expressed in such works as Siodmak's *City in the Sky* and the film *Earth II*. In discussions with NASA officials, Dr. Moore argued that the United States should offer its partners a genuine share of authority over the station, proportionate to each partner's investment in it. Since America was paying for about two-thirds of the station, such a proposal seemed to ensure a significant degree of American control over the station, while at the same time giving at least a limited veto power to the other three contributors.

Understandably, NASA seemed to have a different view. To them, it appeared, international participation in the space station was a necessary evil, brought on by the limited resources the government was willing to commit to the project; they were used to running space programs all by themselves and thought it would be best to operate this one in the same way. In fact, Dr. Moore's relationship with NASA may have ended prematurely because at one point in his meetings with their officials he exploded with anger at one of their proposals which he regarded as particularly unfair to the other partners.

Ironically, the one specific proposal of mine which reached the ears of NASA was offered in the spirit of international cooperation and received in a spirit of national self-interest. I noted that science fiction novels like Bernard's *The Wheel in the Sky* and Siodmak's *City in the Sky* envisioned a single international authority which, implicitly, would oversee all activities in space, not just a single space station. Though I knew that such an idea would not be warmly received in Washington, I thought of a suggested provision in the agreement to build the station that might nudge affairs in that direction. I proposed that all four partners agree that, should any of them decide to build another space station in the future, that nation or entity would commit itself to offering the other three partners the chance to participate in the second project as well; specifically, all entities building the international space station would have the right to provide at least 10% of the funding for the next station and in turn receive at least 10% of the control over that station. I saw this proposal as a device to ensure that a number of future space activities would be, like the international space station, multinational in design and committed solely to peaceful projects; and with two or more such stations in service, the idea of a single agency governing them all would seem only logical.

However, when Dr. Moore conveyed this suggestion to his contacts at NASA, he reports that they "loved" the idea—but for a quite different reason: they had developed the theory that the European Space Agency was playing along with the American project solely for the purpose of obtaining information about space stations so that they could turn around and build a better one; and they saw my idea as America's chance to grab a piece of it!

I shared some of Dr. Moore's frustration regarding NASA's attitude at the time, but now, having read many stories about space stations I have learned one simple lesson: people who have power are always reluctant to give it up, not so much because they are natural tyrants but because they are used to the old ways of doing things and fearful of something new. In retrospect, it seems naïve to have thought that NASA would willingly yield any of its traditional authority over its space activities; and although I no longer have any special knowledge of the subject, my impression is that, according to current plans, NASA has more or less gotten what it wanted: that is, while there will be some participation in decision-making by Russia, the European Space Agency, Japan, and Canada, the United States will basically be in charge. In this respect, Caidin's *Four Came Back* emerges as the most accurate prediction of the international space station: the station in that novel is rather small (eight people), involves a combined crew of Americans and Europeans, and is essentially controlled by NASA: "The United States had absorbed the bulk of the cost, and though there was an outward semblance of international cooperation, the United States really ran the show" (15).

The issue of yielding power seemed more important to me in reference to the role of the crew of the international space station. Here, there was a significant difference between the governance plans sketched in science fiction and those developed by NASA. Both structures involved three levels of authority: the "top," which finances and provides overall direction to the station, roughly corresponding to a company's stockholders; the "middle," which decides the functions and operations of the station, corresponding to a company's Board of Directors; and the "bottom," which actually oversees the station's daily operation, corresponding to a company's president and other executives. The difference was that in science fiction, the third and lowest level is the space station itself, which gives the commander a crew a considerable amount of autonomy; but in the initial NASA proposals, all three levels were on the ground, making the station personnel virtually powerless. Again, this suggested distribution of authority was completely understandable: NASA had always maintained complete control over its missions, and it sounded to me as if NASA planned to control the international space station like any other space mission.

Although I understand that NASA has now modified its plans to give its space station crew more autonomy, one can argue that the relatively absolute freedom enjoyed by space station crewmen in science fiction simply reflects those writers' failure to predict developments in telemetry; during space activities, thanks to the information provided in this way, monitors on the ground have just as much information—if not more—regarding what was happening in the station, justifying their firm authority over its operations. In contrast, science fiction writers thought that in times of crisis, only the crewmen on board would actually know what was going on and how to respond.

Still, I came to regard and still regard NASA's basic attitude as counterproductive. As space travel becomes more common, and stays in space become longer, at some point NASA will have to give up its micromanagement of space activities; there will simply be too many decisions for monitors on Earth to make. In addition, as more people, and more different kinds of people, go into space, the military model of command typically employed by NASA will become outmoded and obnoxious and will increasingly seem incompatible with the values of democracy and self-government which are shared by all the nations supporting the international space station. Indeed, I cannot help but think: how can a station originally named "Freedom" keep its residents in permanent bondage to distant administrators on Earth?

Furthermore, in the future, people surely will increasingly come to regard themselves as inhabitants of space, not of Earth, and inevitably they will want virtually total control over their own lives; there is again the example of Skylab 3, and the space station residents of science fiction continually complain about interference from Earth bureaucrats: in del Rey's *Step to the Stars*, one man grumbles about "Those bastards down there" and "the pigheadedness of the Earth-side brass" (7), and a character in Siodmak's *City in the Sky* asks, "Why did you call on Ground for these negotiations? They'll mess up everything, as usual" (155). This natural and inevitable hostility between Earth and space is not likely to emerge in the first few years of the international space station, when dutiful astronauts will be the only inhabitants; but it certainly will eventually become an issue.

A proposal to grant more power to space station residents, significantly, is strongly endorsed in the novel by a former member of the rebellious Skylab 3 mission, Edward Gibson: living in the middle of the twenty-first century, his hero comments, "We've had spacecraft and space stations operating autonomously since the turn of the century. Confidence in automatic scheduling and the judgment of the crew has long since replaced detailed specification of every decision and operation from the ground" (*Reach* 52-53).

For these reasons, I argue that NASA would be well advised to start working now on plans for some system of autonomy and self-government in space. It is no doubt hard to believe that the United States government would, as in *Earth II*, blithely allow a space station to declare its independence, but there are plenty of warnings in science fiction that if Earth fails to gradually let go of its citizens in space, resentment and, finally, revolt are the only possible outcomes.

Perhaps NASA officials would acknowledge the truth in what I am saying but maintain that such concerns are decades away; why worry about them now? To an extent, they would be right; but there is another issue to be raised here. In the course of doing this research, almost everyone I spoke to seemed fascinated by the problem of government in space; I am sure they would have been disappointed to hear about the arguments about division of station resources that actually occupied most of Dr. Moore's time, but they immediately grasped the broader issues raised by the project. If NASA were to announce that the international space station was now being conceived of as the foundation for a future space city, and that they were beginning to solicit ideas on how that city should be governed, I think there would be a surge of interest in and enthusiasm for the project.

My comments seem to keep returning to the subject of public relations and this is not, I suspect, accidental. Science fiction writers may have a great deal of scientific knowledge, but are usually not working scientists or scholars; and when I present their suggestions for station design or management, I no doubt sound a bit tentative. However, science fiction writers are people who have, in a sense, made their living by selling the future; if their stories were dull or unattractive, they surely would have found out about it and taken corrective action. In looking at their stories, then, one may not, despite the dreams of Gernsback and Campbell, find a wealth of good technical ideas or insights into the broader effects of scientific discoveries; however, these stories may reflect considerable wisdom in the technique of getting people interested in and excited about the future. Hence, when I pass along their ideas for making a space station seem glamorous or worthwhile, I feel I am on surer ground.

Thus, there may be some merit in another suggestion I shall pass along from Correy's *Space Doctor* about achieving a successful space station: "Looking back on it, maybe we should have hired a PR man" (235). However, in a sense I have done something better: I have examined the writings of hundreds of "PR" men and women who have spent their careers as specialists in promoting the virtues of space travel in general and space stations in particular. Perhaps NASA is already realizing the potential value of such expertise; as reported in his *Endless Frontier* anthologies, science fiction author Jerry Pournelle was approached by government officials early in the Reagan administration for his advice on future directions for the space program. But I would ask NASA this: why consult with one science fiction writer when you can "consult" with dozens of them? And essentially, that is what I have done.

* * * * * * *

Looking over all of these ideas, several months after they were originally written, I now realize that applying the practical wisdom of science fiction and improving the space program's public relations represent at best limited and short-range solutions to the problems that NASA now faces. That is, such steps as renaming the space station, adding some blue-collar workers as its construction crew, and emphasizing the spirit of international cooperation behind the station may win the project a few more supporters and may in fact mean the difference between its life and death in the congressional budget wars; but the difficulties involved in maintaining the commitment to the international space station are related to larger issues. Specifically, given the tremendous enthusiasm for space exploration once manifest in this country, given the public's continuing interest in science fiction books and films, given NASA's remarkable string of successes—which cannot be totally obscured by its few recent and conspicuous failures—given all these factors, why is NASA now forced to struggle to win support? Why is the construction of the space station—entirely defensible as "the next logical step"—still a matter of heated debate?

In pondering this question, I keep thinking of the striking thesis of Charles Sheffield's *Between the Strokes of Night*: that because the universe is so vast and slow-moving, it cannot be comprehended or appreciated within the normal lifespan of human beings. Therefore, Sheffield's protagonists argue, it is necessary to slow down or extend human life so that a civilization truly oriented to space can emerge.

The implications of this idea are, I submit, disturbing.

Someday, with data compiled from several intelligent species, sociologists may conclude that sentient beings normally commit themselves only to those projects which can be successfully realized within about one-sixth of the species' expected lifespan. For humans, the relevant figure would be about twelve years; and a remarkable number of human endeavors seem to occur within these limits. In education, one observes the typical twelve-year program of public education, and a person who wishes to become a doctor must, at the age of eighteen, commit herself to about twelve years of college, medical school, and internship before achieving her goal. Virtually all of the great building projects of human history seem to have been completed within this period of time. (Possible exceptions—the Great Pyramids, medieval cathedrals—appear to require a homogeneous, tightly controlled society motivated by religious fervor—conditions rarely present, and certainly not present today.) And the American space program itself, with almost eerie regularity, at first proceeded within such time frames: it was about twelve years from the earliest beginnings of space research in the late 1940s to its first successful satellite launch in 1958; about twelve years from that development to the triumphs of Apollo (1969-1972); about twelve years elapsed from that era to the establishment of the space shuttle as a regular, viable space transportation system (the early 1980s). More recently, progress in space travel has slowed a bit, but there remain dreams that the United States might perfect the international space station in the next few years, return to the Moon within the next two decades, and then advance to launching a manned expedition to Mars after a similar length of time.

However, as already suggested, this piecemeal, sequential approach to the exploration and exploitation of space does not really make much sense; to achieve truly worthwhile results, a broader, more ambitious program of several simultaneous activities seems necessary. The reason why such a program has not been put in place may be this: that in contemplating the logical steps in the conquest of space, the human race is finally confronting projects which cannot be accommodated to its normal attention span.

Consider the proposals typically put forth by space enthusiasts like G. Harry Stine [Lee Correy]: a string of solar power satellites circling the Earth, beaming microwave radiation down to Earth to be converted and sent to consumers by power stations built in deserts and other remote areas; a true factory in space, with needed materials catapulted to it from the Moon by a mass driver on the lunar surface; a huge, Earthlike space habitat; and, to mention some ideas not directly related to life in space, the construction of large colonies on planetary surfaces and the terraforming of Venus and Mars. No one can doubt that such projects would eventually generate massive profits; but the key word is "eventually." Actually constructing and putting into operation such plans would surely require truly astronomical sums of money and would take at least twenty, thirty, or forty years to be finished. Is it reasonable to expect a government or corporation to commit itself to such expensive and long-range projects? Mack Reynolds and Dean Ing's *Trojan Orbit* mildly suggests that grandiose proposals for space activities may simply be a bit premature; but perhaps they are by nature beyond the common parameters of human activities.

I can envision at this point only two developments that might actually bring about these ambitious proposals: first, new technological breakthroughs that would make them infinitely cheaper and infinitely easier to accomplish—although the harsh realities of gravity and outer space may rule out such achievements; and a noteworthy increase in human life expectancy. To be sure, the latter possibility would be tremendously disruptive to an already overpopulated world, and research efforts aimed at such increases may now be inadequately funded for precisely that reason. However, it is also possible to argue that a longer human lifespan may facilitate solutions to humanity's fundamental problems. That is, to people expecting to live two hundred years, the prospect of running out of fossil fuels and key minerals in the next century will seem real and imminent, and a forty-year plan to address those problems will seem logical and practical.

In a way, I am at this time going beyond my earlier conclusion: for having already argued that a permanent presence in space will inevitably cause a profound transformation in the human race, I now suggest that such a transformation may in fact be a necessary prelude to a space civilization. Again, life in space emerges as a matter of far greater consequence than either science fiction writers or other visionaries seem to realize.

These thoughts appear to be far removed in spirit from the practical frame of mind that I began with in this chapter; yet I offer them as an explanation, and perhaps as some consolation, for NASA administrators and others who are keenly interested in the space program and no doubt greatly disappointed by recent trends. All too often, the recent failures of NASA have been attributed to the fact that the agency is aging or losing its touch; and all too often, the failure to initiate vast space projects has been attributed to conservatism, short-sightedness, and sheer stupidity. I argue that these characterizations are inaccurate. Rather, problems in the space shuttle and space station programs may reflect the reality that NASA is now moving beyond such readily accomplishable goals as simple lunar landings and unmanned planetary missions and confronting challenges that cannot be overcome within the time and budgetary constraints which typically limit human efforts; and the absence of major new initiatives in space may reflect the reality that these plans, from the reasonable perspective of present-day human beings, simply cannot be justified. In sum, there are no villains to blame for the apparent lack of progress in the conquest of space; it is a matter of human nature.

In literature and in life, the human race simply may not be prepared for the strange tomorrow of life in outer space.

13. *A Handful of Stars*:
Space Stations in the Literature of the 1990s

The original version of this chapter was completed in 1994, to add to the text of the first edition some discussion of more recent works and developments involving space stations; for the second edition, this chapter is being expanded to discuss several more recent texts. Fortunately, there remains no need to update the essential points of my analysis, since none of these additional texts substantively alter the overall picture I developed from earlier data.

That is, while political developments have now muted concerns about armed space stations in Earth orbit, the pattern of the military station serving to perpetuate old patterns of human behavior can be observed in editors David Drake and Bill Fawcett's two volumes of *Battlestation* stories (1992, 1993), all involving a large mobile base for interstellar warfare, as well as in the "space fortress" that figures in Ken Kato's *Yamato—A Rage in Heaven, Part Two: The Way of the Warrior* (1992). Space stations continue to serve as transitional points, as way stations between Earth and outer space: thus, four novels about manned expeditions to Mars—Terry Bisson's *Voyage to the Red Planet* (1990), C. J. Sykes's *Red Genesis* (1991), Ben Bova's *Mars* (1992), and Jack Williamson's *Beachhead* (1992)—all feature early stopovers at Earth-orbiting space stations. Kim Stanley Robinson's *Red Mars* (1993) and its sequels develop the theme of the transition point from the opposite direction, depicting the construction of a space elevator from the surface of Mars to orbital space; although at one point destroyed by rebels, it is later rebuilt to function as a key element in the colonization and economic development of the planet. The tradition of space stations focused on medicine is maintained by Tess Gerritsen's *Gravity* (1999), a near-future medical thriller taking place in Earth orbit, and space stations as places for alien encounters and outbreaks of madness were recurring themes in the series *Star Trek: Deep Space Nine* (as discussed in more detail below). The space habitat as a place for retreat and inward movement is exemplified by Dana Stabenow's *Second Star* (1991), and the specific image of the nurturing, womblike station is featured in Anne McCaffrey and S. M. Stirling's *The City Who Fought* (1993), another example of the "living space station."

Stabenow's novel, and its sequel *A Handful of Stars* (1991), clearly illustrate the ongoing lack of imagination in many space station stories. One can pick any adjective typically used to describe terrible science fiction—trite, clichéd, juvenile, mechanical, formulaic—and it will apply to these books. Oblivious to a decade of research and thought indicating that space habitats are a highly questionable idea (summarized as noted in Mack Reynolds and Dean Ing's *Trojan Orbit*, Norman Spinrad's *Science Fiction in the Real World*, and elsewhere), Stabenow blithely presents a garden-variety space suburb in the L-5 position, and her feisty, tough-as-nails heroine Star Svensdotter fends off all the usual bad guys—anti-science "Luddites" determined to stop space travel, conniving Earth politicians ready to stab space pioneers in the back to win votes, and narrow-minded soldiers who see space only as a military base. In the sequel, Star takes her act to the asteroid belt, ostensibly to send mineral-rich asteroids back to her habitat.

For those reasonably familiar with the contemporary literature of space stations and habitats, it is depressing that Stabenow offers no new ideas about life in space; what is worse, the author pretends not to notice this lack of originality. In *A Handful of Stars*, when Star reveals her exciting new proposal—refurbishing asteroids and selling them as homes for Earth's oppressed minorities—her cohorts, who are described as devotees of old science fiction, should yawn and point out that the concept had already been described in scores of novels; instead, they gape in astonishment at her brilliant imagination. One passage in *Second Star* sums up the novel's staleness:

> "You don't believe in E.T., Tori?" Crip said. "Shame on you. Next you'll be saying there are no Vulcans."
> "Personally, I chose spacing because I hoped I'd meet a Wookie someday," Ariadne added, grinning....
> "I think it is reasonable to believe that intelligent life might, I say *might* exist on other planets," Tori said obstinately, "but simply believing don't necessarily make it so."
> "I'd settle for intelligent life on Terra," I said, and everyone laughed politely at the very old joke.

Old and still my favorite. (93-94)

As a storyteller describing humanity's possible futures in space, Stabenow is telling a very old joke indeed.

Also covering familiar ground, though with considerably more skill and intelligence, is Howard V. Hendrix's *Lightpaths* (1997), describing a utopian community in Earth orbit threatened by unexplained events. In the novel, familiar concerns about the fragility of life in space and the dangers of projectile weapons are briefly raised; there is a familiar emphasis on gardens as the perfect expression and epitomization of life in space; there are familiar scenes of low-gravity flight, idyllic interludes in bucolic settings, and democratic gatherings to resolve controversies; and residents have the familiar sense that their little society in space represents an important opportunity to begin human civilization anew, though that utopian impulse is stressed here more than elsewhere.

Only one plot development in *Lightpaths* is strikingly innovative: earlier space station literature is permeated with tales of disgruntled space residents, chafing under the control of a repressive, decadent Earth, who endeavor (usually with success) to rebel against Earth and make their habitat an independent nation. In Hendrix's Orbital Complex, a revolution would have absolutely no appeal to its placid and peaceful residents; yet when mysterious developments ensue in and around the station, people on Earth incorrectly assume that this must be the prelude to a revolution and respond accordingly with an unnecessary show of force. Thus, this is the first science fiction novel featuring a future Earth made senselessly paranoid by previous science fiction novels.

In regards to critical commentaries about space stations, one significant addition was Peter Nicholls's entry on "Space Habitats" in *The Encyclopedia of Science Fiction* (1993). The entry is first of all irritating because Nicholls, alone in the science fiction community, insists that all space stations should be called "space habitats"—even though that term has been universally reserved for immense hollow structures with Earth-like landscapes on the interior; and this idiosyncratic pattern of usage leads to several misleading and anachronistic references, including descriptions of the small space stations in Kurd Lasswitz's *Two Planets* and the film *Moonraker* as "space habitats."

Second, in a discussion of the iconography of the space station which to some extent parallels mine, Nicholls claims that another typical "motif has the space station representing the anthropological observers in the sky, looking down at the primitives below," citing

Patricia McKillip's *Moon-Flash* (1984), Brian W. Aldiss's *Helliconia* trilogy (1982, 1983, 1985), Stanislaw Lem's *Solaris*, and Fritz Leiber's *A Specter Is Haunting Texas* as examples (1137). In a sense, this motif is an implicit aspect of the space station as a transitional point, since one purpose that a vantage point halfway between Earth and space can serve is as a neutral observation point; and I discussed, for example, how a space station resident in Juanita Coulson's *Tomorrow's Heritage* works to mediate a conflict between his terrestrial older brother and his younger sister who lives in a space habitat. Still, to call something an "iconic motif" in science fiction is to imply that it is seen numerous times in the literature; and, based on my own knowledge of the subject (more extensive, I believe, than Nicholls's), I cannot see the evidence for his claim. To be specific, ignoring the dubiously relevant examples of Lem and Leiber, I can think of only a handful of stories that reflect in any meaningful way to the role Nicholls describes: Arthur C. Clarke's "The Lion of Comarre," Robert F. Young's "The Moon of Advanced Learning," and perhaps—stretching a bit—Philip K. Dick's *Dr. Bloodmoney* and the Justice League of America's satellite headquarters observed in innumerable old comic books. In short, while I will grant one point to Nicholls—that McKillip's and Aldiss's novels certainly should have been included in my critical survey—I will stand by my original description of the iconography of the space station.

Were I still poring through bibliographies and bookstores looking for examples, I could surely find hundreds of examples of stories involving space stations in the last decade, but they are rarely prominent; indeed, the obsessive recent interest in colonizing the planet Mars, the subject of numerous novels, implies a new recognition that large-scale habitation of outer space may not represent a realistic prospect in the near future, inspiring a renewed interest in establishing human settlements on the surfaces of other worlds. For the most significant developments in this area during the 1990s, one must turn to television—specifically to the appearance, in 1993, of two major television series—*Babylon 5* and *Star Trek: Deep Space Nine*—taking place on space stations. When they first appeared, still feeling a sense of duty toward space station research, I intently watched the two-hour pilot film for *Babylon 5*, as well as all twenty-two episodes of the first season of *Star Trek: Deep Space Nine*; however, having resolved to end my research in 1994 and move on to other priorities, I rapidly lost interest and paid relatively little attention to later episodes of those series.

In most respects, *Babylon 5* seemingly had the potential to be the more interesting series. Its creator spent one year soliciting advice about his proposed series from science fiction readers, and, no doubt as a result, *Babylon 5* was the first space station film or television program which displayed some awareness of developments in the written literature of the last thirty years. Because the station was shown as a huge cylinder, and because it featured a large, open interior area with beautiful gardens and landscapes, *Babylon 5* arguably represented the first true space habitat ever depicted on film. Also, one scene of the film shows areas of the station with unusual environments for various aliens, including a very cold chamber for methane-breathers—a concept probably borrowed from James White's Sector Twelve stories. The existence of these sections suggested that future episodes might involve imaginative encounters with genuinely inhuman aliens—as opposed to the people-with-funny-makeup aliens that permeate *Star Trek: Deep Space Nine*—though this rarely occurred during the series. Indeed, even in the original pilot film, there were signs that originality and inventiveness would not always be the hallmarks of the series, since it featured only recognizably humanoid aliens, including a crude caricature of a Russian diplomat, and its story line was a routine melodrama: a saboteur wearing a "Changeling Net" impersonates station head John Sinclair and implicates him in the attempted assassination of a visiting alien dignitary. Subsequent episodes, primarily focusing on the convoluted politics of the various alien races interacting at the station and a war with an enigmatic alien race, fascinated loyal fans but had little to offer in the way of innovative depictions of everyday life in a space habitat.

Star Trek: Deep Space Nine first merits one immediate word of praise: with all due respect for the delicate porcelain beauty of the space station in *2001: A Space Odyssey*, Deep Space Nine must be regarded as the most beautiful space station ever seen on film. Based on the classic wheel or doughnut design, the station adds graceful elongated fins—called "pylons"—which extend above and below the wheel. The sequence in the opening credits is also impressive: first, the camera pans through what seems like an endless, empty starry sky; then, in one corner of the screen, a tiny little circle appears, which the camera gradually approaches. This constitutes a powerful depiction of the essential strangeness and loneliness of life in deep space, perhaps the most powerful ever seen on film. The series itself, of course, never evokes that mood, as the station is rather a lively beehive of activity, with life constantly disrupted by an unending stream of visitors from various worlds.

I previously suggested that there is something inherently undramatic about staying in a space station, and in the first season alone there were already several episodes in which characters left the station to primarily present adventures on other planets. To achieve drama in the space station itself, the series emphasized the theme of conflict involving various colorful aliens. First, there was the underlying scenario of the series: after sixty years of occupying Bajor and oppressing its people, the evil Cardassians finally withdrew from the planet and from their orbital space station. The Bajorans then asked the Federation, represented by Commander Benjamin Sisko, Chief O'Brien from *Star Trek: The Next Generation*, and others, to establish a presence on the station and thereby prevent the Cardassians from returning. When a stable wormhole maintained by mysterious aliens was discovered in the Bajoran system, Deep Space Nine was moved nearby, to assume even greater importance as a starting point for expeditions into the mysterious and uncharted Gamma Quadrant. Thus, episodes could be built around two recurring tensions: the Bajorans and the Federation working against the ongoing machinations of the Cardassians, and the newly-independent Bajorans resisting the decisions of the Federation. In addition, the regular cast included four aliens whose relationships with humans and with each other were not always harmonious: Odo, a "shapeshifter"; Quark, a typically duplicitous Ferengi; Dax, a "symbiote" consisting of a young human woman physically and mentally linked to a small immortal alien implanted in her body; and Kira, a Bajoran who is Sisko's second in command. Finally, while other familiar aliens from the *Star Trek* universe like Vulcans and Klingons made appearances, the wormhole provided a convenient way for new and previously unknown aliens to wander into the vicinity of the station.

In its first season, *Star Trek: Deep Space Nine* already managed to employ most of the basic plots—and some of the hoariest clichés—seen in previous space station stories. In "Captive Pursuit," O'Brien and an alien crawl through a ventilator shaft to avoid capture. In the first episode "Emissary," the station is besieged and almost destroyed by Cardassian warships, and the station is also attacked by aliens in "Captive Pursuit." An alien invader who takes over the personality of Dr. Bashir is featured in "The Passenger." In "Emissary," the station moves outward from its planetary orbit to assume its new position near the wormhole; in "Q-Less," the station almost plunges downward into the wormhole. In "The Forsaken," a playful alien computer intelligence, likened to a dog, invades the station computer, making Deep Space Nine something of a "living space station." A recurring subplot involved a school headed by O'Brien's wife, a variation on the common theme of the space station as an ideal place to educate young spacemen. Forms of madness have repeatedly afflicted station residents due to various causes: a strange disease that reduces people to babbling in "Babel"; an alien intelligence that turns people into power-hungry plotters in "Dramatis Personae"; and a wave of Bajoran religious hysteria directed against the station school in "In the Hands of the Prophet." These hasty plot summaries may not do justice to the series; the episodes were usually lively, entertaining, and occasionally intelligent, which is perhaps all one can ask for from a television series.

Another general theme surprisingly emerged during the first season of *Star Trek: Deep Space Nine*: the idea of *games* or *play* that dominated several episodes. In "Captive Pursuit," aliens who love hunting have bred a race of intelligent humanoids to serve as prey that they can chase across space and kill; in "Move Along Home," aliens obsessed with playing games, after being cheated at Quark's roulette table, trap Sisko and other crewpersons in a miniature game world, and Quark must move them to a winning conclusion; in "Battle Lines," two feuding factions on a small planet, infected by a bioengineered virus, are condemned to eternally fight, kill each other, and return to life, essentially making all of their activity a pointless game; in "Dramatis Personae," as the title suggests, the crew of Deep Space Nine is engaged in a form of play-acting, a mock battle for control of the station; and in "If Wishes Were Horses," two of the visiting aliens disguise themselves as Rumpelstiltskin and a twenty-first-century baseball player. This recurring theme of play—which re-emerged later in the most famous episode of the series, "Trials and Tribble-ations," built around footage from the most playful episode of the original *Star Trek* series, "The Trouble with Tribbles"—may indicate that there is something inevitably unimportant or inconsequential about being in a space station. In this respect, the most fascinating feature of *Star Trek: Deep Space Nine* may be that, unlike the first two *Star Trek* series, the opening credits lacked a verbal prologue spoken by the leading character. Indeed, how could Commander Sisko dramatically describe the mission of Deep Space Nine? To send people out to explore strange new worlds? To wait for new life and new civilizations to come and visit us? To boldly sit where no one has sat before?

In later seasons, *Star Trek: Deep Space Nine* increasingly focused on the Bajoran religion, conflicts and conspiracies involving its priests, and the Bajorans' growing conviction that Sisko represented a pivotally important figure in their religion, fortuitously brought by divine intervention to guide Bajor during a period of crisis. At times, this atmosphere of religious piety could make Deep

Space Nine seem like a successor to the unique monastery in Michael Moorcock's *The Fireclown*; and since the setting of a space station proved amenable to an emphasis on a topic usually marginalized in science fiction, this again suggests that the icon of the space station runs counter to many impulses that fuel major works of the genre in epitomizing the themes of inward movement, a key aspect of religious fervor. This might also explain why *Star Trek: Deep Space Nine*, despite consistently respectable ratings, proved by most measures the least popular of the first four *Star Trek* series.

Just as *Babylon 5* and *Star Trek: Deep Space Nine* were establishing themselves in the public consciousness, there appeared a third, and less significant, television series taking place on a space station: Gerry Anderson's *Space Precinct*. While the other two series were based on extensively developed future universes, Anderson was apparently content to transport a modern American metropolis to a space station and decorate it with a few aliens and bits of advanced technology, as was apparent from the early episode that I stumbled upon while channel-surfing, "Protect and Survive." With a cast of normal-looking humans mixed in with colorfully unpersuasive latex-masked aliens, I could deduce that the series took place in a space station of the far future, but the script of the episode seemed to have been transcribed, line by line, from a routine American cop show of the 1960s. A powerful and respected, but secretly corrupt, man has committed a terrible crime; there is only one witness who can identify him as the perpetrator; to protect the witness, policemen take him to a seedy hotel on the poor side of town; the bad guy's henchmen find out where he is and try to kill him; the policemen get the wounded witness into their car, and a furious car chase ensues as they rush him to the hospital; and the witness finally arrives safely, so he can deliver his damning testimony in the nick of time just before the case against the bad guy is dismissed. Although the witness was a blue-skinned alien with a long tongue used for catching flies, and although the furious car chase involved flying cars, that hardly made any of this seem original; and while I have been told that some later episodes of the series were marginally better, it is hardly surprising that such a derivative series failed to make much of an impression and vanished after a single season.

There is one final paradox to explore: despite the failure of *Space Precinct*, both *Babylon 5* and *Star Trek: Deep Space Nine* lasted a long time—five years and seven years respectively—and both series inspired a number of original novels and quantities of fan fiction. Thus, Babylon 5 and Deep Space Nine have undoubtedly become the most famous and familiar space stations in science fiction, suggesting that interest in space stations has risen to an all-time high. On the other hand, the continuing controversies and delays involving the construction of the *actual* space station, and the complete lack of any public concern over this issue, can be said to indicate that public interest in space stations remains at an all-time low.

To those who follow the news, the stories about the international space station long had a depressing familiarity. First, estimates of the cost of the station increased alarmingly; proponents of the station then announced plans to downscale or re-design the station and eliminate some features in order to make it cheaper; in response, former supporters charged that such a stripped-down station would be unable to achieve any original purposes and hence would not be worth building, while opponents screamed that even this reduced expenditure was a wasteful extravagance in an era of soaring budget deficits; the space station was voted on by the House of Representatives; and the project barely survived for another year. (In June, 1993, the station's margin of victory was one vote.) It was only after years of such arguments that opponents, having succeeded in reducing the planned station to a useless but economical construct, finally accepted its inevitability and stopped fighting to eliminate the project.

However, even though it is now basically functional and continuously inhabited, there is no reason for anyone to be optimistic about the future of the international space station. In its present state, the station is little more than an orbiting tin can, not suited to serve as either as a site for meaningful scientific research or a launching pad for further space missions; and any significant upgrades before the station reaches the end of its anticipated lifespan are extremely unlikely, to say the least. Prospects for a newer and better station, perhaps as a prelude to the Moon colony or Mars expedition grandly described in endless commission reports, were dim even before the 2003 *Columbia* disaster, and seem even dimmer now.

I have read stories like Robert Heinlein's "'If This Goes On—'" (1940) and Dean McLaughlin's *The Man Who Wanted Stars* which envision future Americas which embark upon ambitious space programs and then abandon them, but such scenarios always seemed far-fetched to me. Today, such stories sound grimly prophetic. As I have argued, though, it is wrong to blame short-sighted politicians and bureaucrats for this situation; rather, it may be that we have fundamentally misunderstood the human character, that we have over-estimated the human capacity to commit to a project as vast, as expensive, and as lengthy as the exploration and habitation of outer space.

If there is a silver living to this dark cloud, it is this: writers and readers have often complained that advancing scientific knowledge has increasingly limited the imaginative vistas of science fiction. Today, except as alternate history, writers cannot tell the story of the first space flight or the first Moon landing, they cannot describe strange creatures and exotic princesses on an Earth-like Mars, and they cannot depict perilous voyages across the oceans of Venus or people shrinking in size to adventure on microscopic worlds. If the large and productive space stations of science fiction were now becoming part of everyday human existence, the fictional possibilities in the space station theme would similarly diminish, since reports of the actual experience of long-term life in space would explode old myths and establish new realities. But as long as significant space stations remain a feature of the distant future, writers will remain entirely free to consider the vast and, I have argued, largely unexplored possibilities of human life in outer space. Thus, while the coming years may represent a depressing hiatus in the actual establishment of societies in space, they just might become the golden age of space station literature.

14. *The Problems of Space Flying*:
How Science Fiction Inspired the Space Station

In ancient Greece, Aristophanes's comedy *The Birds* described a farcical utopia in the sky called Cloudcuckooland. In 1721, Jonathan Swift's *Gulliver's Travels* visited the flying city of Laputa. In 1869, Edward Everett Hale's "The Brick Moon" depicted an artificial satellite accidentally launched with people on board who adapt to life in orbit. Though these stories have all been cited as humanity's first vision of a "space station," they were arguably only fantasies, reflecting no understanding of conditions in outer space or the problems involved in living there. Hard scientific work would be needed to make dreams of cities in the sky into realistic possibilities.

The first man to offer a blueprint for a functional space station was Russian schoolteacher Konstantin Tsiolkovsky, who designed a cylindrical facility with a greenhouse, laboratory, living quarters, and docking area for spacecraft. His didactic novel *Beyond the Planet Earth* (1920) remarkably anticipated today's international space station by picturing a space station with a crew of six people from Russia, America, France, England, Germany, and Italy, all nations now involved in its construction. In the 1920s, members of the German Rocket Society discussed space stations in nonfictional works: Hermann Oberth's *The Rocket into Interplanetary Space* (1923) introduced the term "space station," while Hermann von Noordung's *The Problems of Space Flying* (1929) went into detail about space station design and construction. More extravagantly, Englishman J. D. Bernal's extended essay *The World, the Flesh, and the Devil* (1929) predicted gigantic spheres in space as future homes for humanity. However, these proposals bore no immediate fruit: in the 1930s and 1940s, Adolf Hitler diverted the activities of the German Rocket Society to war preparations, and except for the lonely experiments of American Robert Goddard, people generally displayed no interest in space travel.

The exceptions were the writers and readers of American science fiction, devoted to garish magazines filled with exciting space adventures. When *The Problems of Space Flying* was republished in the magazine *Science Wonder Stories* in 1929, with a striking cover by Frank R. Paul, they were introduced to space stations, which soon became regular elements in their stories. As stopovers for weary space travelers, one space station was located halfway between Earth and Mars, while another was halfway between the Sun and Alpha Centauri. Murray Leinster's "The Power Planet" (1931) proposed space stations as sources of energy for Earth; Basil E. Wells's "Factory in the Sky" (1941) demonstrated the potential benefits of space factories; and George O. Smith's "Venus Equilateral" stories (1942-1945) featured an inhabited communications satellite. In effect, science fiction writers critically examined the concept of space stations and concluded that they would be practical and helpful in various ways.

After World War II, German rocket scientists immigrated to America and the Soviet Union, where governments coveted their expertise. One German scientist, Wernher von Braun, took a leading role in America's space program, and following the logic of former German Rocket Society colleagues and science fiction writers, he decided that a space station was an essential first step in conquering space. Accordingly, the March 22, 1952 issue of *Collier's* magazine featured several articles by scientists, including von Braun's "Crossing the Last Frontier," that described and advocated the construction of an American space station. Illustrated by space artist Chesley Bonestell and others, this issue first publicized the wheel- or doughnut-shaped design that became the most popular image of the space station, most memorably displayed in the film *2001: A Space Odyssey* (1968).

Impressed by the articles in *Collier's*, science fiction writers enlisted in the cause of promoting the space station as a necessary base for further expeditions into space. Novels like Arthur C. Clarke's *Islands in the Sky* (1952) celebrated the people who built and inhabited space stations, and space stations began to appear in science fiction films like *Project Moonbase* (1953) and *Conquest of Space* (1955). At the height of the Cold War, works of fiction and nonfiction often emphasized the military value of space stations: vigilant Westerners could establish observation posts and prevent Communists from building orbital launching pads for deadly missiles. However, Cold War tensions of a different sort soon canceled von Braun's plans for a space station. In 1961, after Russians launched the first man into space, President John F. Kennedy needed to announce an impressive goal to re-establish American superiority in space, and he chose a landing on the Moon over the construction of a space station.

With official plans for a space station on hold, the dreamers again came to the forefront—literally, in a big way. While science fiction had characteristically featured the smaller space stations favored by Tsiolkovsky and von Noordung, writers had also imagined grander structures. Some described space stations thousands of miles in diameter with millions of inhabitants, perhaps traveling through space as "generation starships" like the one in Robert A. Heinlein's "Universe" (1941). One recurring theme was a literal city in space, resembling a city on Earth, protected by a transparent dome. Engineer Dandridge Cole argued in books like *Beyond Tomorrow: The Next 50 Years in Space* (1965) that huge space colonies might effectively evolve into new organisms, termed "Macro-Life," composed of innumerable living creatures. Such visions of space communities became attractive in the early 1970s, because new evidence indicated that all worlds in our Solar System were barren, lifeless, and ill-suited for human settlements. For that reason, scientist Gerard O'Neill built upon Bernal's and Cole's expansive projections to propose building huge space habitats to house human colonies. A typical design was an enclosed cylinder, rotating to simulate Earth gravity by means of centrifugal force, with landscapes and buildings on the interior surface. People might establish utopian communities inside such cylinders, powered by solar energy and offering unique pleasures like zero-gravity "flying" at the center of the cylinder. Organizations emerged to advocate building a space habitat at one of the five LaGrange points where the gravitational forces of the Earth and Moon are balanced.

Science fiction writers, always seeking new settings for their stories, were soon portraying space habitats in novels like Ben Bova's *Colony* (1978), Mack Reynolds's *Chaos in Lagrangia* (1984), and Isaac Asimov's *Nemesis* (1989). But their tone was often critical. Knowledgeable writers recognized that building a successful space habitat would be far more difficult and expensive than proponents claimed. They noted that these structures would be incredibly vulnerable, since even a tiny breach in the hull could kill every resident. They envisioned insular, frightened communities plunging into madness or civil war. In short, while science fiction writers examined and embraced small space stations, they examined and rejected plans for large space habitats, at least in our immediate future. Correspondingly, space scientists grew less interested in these ambitious proposals and refocused their attention on the international space station and similarly modest initiatives.

Still, while the facility now being constructed may seem unrelated to the spectacular predictions of science fiction, its images retain a powerful hold on the popular imagination. Because *Mission to Mars* (2000) described a Mars expedition only two decades from now, the astronauts logically should have departed from the international space station or an expanded version; instead, the filmmakers created an entirely different World Space Station with a rotating wheel—exactly the sort of doughnut in the sky that Bonestell had painted long ago. To many, such a construct still represents the only true "space station." In the future, then, both space station realities and space station dreams will undoubtedly continue to exert an influence on humanity's factual and fictional journeys into outer space.

15. "The Aim of Astronautics": The "Innovative Technologies in Science Fiction" Report on Space Stations in Science Fiction

Since first appearing in Edward Everett Hale's "The Brick Moon" (1869), space stations and related forms of space habitats have been featured in over one thousand science fiction stories, novels, films, and television programs. Many of these stations are only repeated examples of one familiar pattern—the Earth-orbiting, wheel-shaped space station—but there has also been significant variety in the depictions. Science fiction stories therefore offer some interesting ideas regarding the four basic questions that will confront any potential creators of a human habitation in space:

1. Why should a space station or space colony be built?
2. Where should this space station be placed?
3. What basic structure should be employed?
4. What design features should be incorporated into the station?

In this report, I will summarize some of the ideas in science fiction that might be helpful, in the near or far future, to persons engaged in constructing a space station, citing individual stories as sources.

I. The purposes of space stations. The first and most obvious reason for building habitats in space is to provide new homes for humanity, either as an urgent necessity, as in Thomas N. Scortia's *Earthwreck!* (1974), in which Earth becomes uninhabitable after a nuclear war, or simply as a matter of prudence, as Konstantin Tsiolkovsky maintained in "The Aim of Astronautics" (1929): "Man must at all costs overcome the Earth's gravity and have, in reserve, the space of at least the Solar System. All kinds of danger lie in wait for him on the Earth," such as disastrous floods or an asteroid impact (370). One also encounters the argument that space habitation represents the next logical step in human evolution, comparable to the way that sea creatures evolved to live on the land, and numerous stories like Fritz Leiber's *A Specter Is Haunting Texas* (1968) and Bruce Sterling's *Schismatrix* (1985) have depicted exotic new forms of humanity evolving to better live in the vacuum and zero gravity of space. In the immediate future, space stations have been envisioned as the ideal homes for certain types of people, including those dedicated to internationalism, as in Curt Siodmak's *City in the Sky* (1974); monks and others seeking to live a hermetic existence, as in Michael Moorcock's *The Fireclown* (1965); dangerous criminals who need to be safely incarcerated in space, as in Patricia A. McKillip's *Fool's Run* (1987); the physically handicapped, as in Arthur C. Clarke's *Islands in the Sky* (1952); and the weak and elderly, as in Dean Ing's "Down and Out in Ellfive Prime" (1980).

However, beyond their uses as homes for humanity in the near or distant future, other practical reasons for space stations are given in science fiction stories. First, a facility orbiting the Earth might serve as a space fortress, either to dominate or conquer humans, as in Ben Bova's *Millennium* (1976) and *Peacekeepers* (1988), or to defend humans against possible alien invaders, as is proposed in Theodore Sturgeon's "Unite and Conquer" (1948). Other common plans are to employ an Earth-orbiting station as a launching pad for future space expeditions, as in Murray Leinster's *Space Platform* (1953) and many other stories; as a facility to monitor and regulate traffic in space, as in E. C. Eliott's *Kemlo and the Zones of Silence* (1954); as a logical meeting place for an international organization or world government, as in Arthur C. Clarke's "The Lion of Comarre" (1948); or as the headquarters of a global communications network, as in Juanita Coulson's *Tomorrow's Heritage* (1981). Ben Bova's *The Weathermakers* (1967) suggests that a space station equipped with laser beams and other devices might be able to control Earth's weather by eliminating hurricanes and other dangerous conditions. Science fiction stories also originated the concept of stations that tap solar power and beam it to Earth, as in Isaac Asimov's "Reason" (1941), and space stations are regularly presented as a good place to train young astronauts, as in Richard Elam, Jr.'s "The Iron Moon" (1952).

Science fiction stories have discovered many other purposes for space stations, in Earth orbit or elsewhere. One encounters the notion of setting up a series of manned or unmanned space stations to rescue space travelers, as in Jack Williamson's "Dead Star Station" (1933), or as refuges for space travelers in danger, as in C. E. Fritch's "Many Dreams of Earth" (1954). Science fiction has envisioned large factories in space, obtaining and processing raw materials from the asteroid belt and other sources, as in Basil E. Wells's "Factory in the Sky" (1941) and Jerry Pournelle's "High Justice" (1975). There are stations set up to carry out scientific research, especially in meteorology and astronomy, as in Douglas R. Mason's *Satellite 54-Zero* (1971), and a space station might be a particularly good place for dangerous research, as suggested by Thomas R. Dulski's "My Christmas on New Hanford" (1982), in which research involving potentially explosive antimatter is conducted at a space station. Terry Greenhough's *Thoughtworld* (1977) is one of several stories suggesting that people's psychic powers might be best studied, and might significantly increase, in outer space. In addition, science fiction has long recognized that the environment of space could provide an excellent location for innovative and flexible medical treatment, as most expansively depicted in James White's *Hospital Station* (1962) and its sequels. Space stations might also be used as havens for endangered species, like the biosphere filled with plant life in the film *Silent Running* (1971), or as habitats for newly bioengineered creatures, as in Robert Silverberg's "Our Lady of the Sauropods" (1980), where a large space station becomes a home for recreated dinosaurs that is considerably safer than Jurassic Park.

Finally, science fiction stories depict space stations as ideal facilities for various sorts of entertainment. There are imaginative dreamlike environments available for visitors in the immense "pleasure world" of C. L. Moore's *Judgment Night* (1942); Somtow Suchariktul's *Mallworld* (1980) features a huge cylindrical shopping center with over 20,000 "shops, hotels, department stores, holopalaces, brothels, psychiatric concessions, suicide parlours, and churches" (24); hotels and resorts have been featured in many stories, including Jack Vance's "Abercrombie Station" (1952) and Curt Siodmak's *Skyport* (1959), and there is a satellite casino in Ron Goulart's *Everybody Comes to Cosmo's* (1988); Robert Silverberg's *Regan's Planet* (1964) and *World's Fair 1992* (1970) envision a future World's Fair being held in a space station; Alfred Slote's *Omega Station* (1983) imagines an orbital "summer camp" for youngsters; and there are spectacular space brothels featured in Philip K. Dick's *The Crack in Space* (1965) and Mike Resnick's *Eros Ascending* (1984) and its three sequels. New possibilities for the arts in zero gravity include space dancing, as in Spider and Jeanne Robinson's *Stardance* (1979); new forms of sculpture, as in

Bob Buckley's "The Star Hole" (1972) and Fritz Leiber's "The Beat Cluster" (1961); and new sports, like "flying" with artificial wings through zero gravity, as first suggested in Konstantin Tsiolkovsky's *Beyond the Planet Earth* (1920), and the new game of "SkyBall" mentioned in Chris Claremont's *FirstFlight* (1987).

II. The locations of space stations. Space stations are most often pictured orbiting Earth, either close to the planet or in geosynchronous orbit; other popular locations are the stationary L-4 and L-5 positions between the Earth and the Moon. Stories that posit human colonies on other worlds regularly place space stations in orbit around those worlds, like the Moon-orbiting space station of Robert A. Heinlein's "Space Jockey" (1947), the Mars-orbiting space station of J. M. Walsh's *Vandals of the Void* (1931), the Venus-orbiting space station of Arthur C. Clarke's *The Lost Worlds of 2001* (1972), and the Mercury-orbiting space station of Frederik Pohl and Jack's Williamson's *The Reefs of Space* (1964). In addition, space stations have been placed in orbit around the gas giant planets: Jupiter, as in Eric Vinicoff's "Repairman" (1984); Saturn, as in Joseph P. Martino's "The Iceworm Special" (1981); and Uranus, as in Bruce Sterling's "Spider Rose" (1982). However, a number of other, more innovative locations have also been suggested.

Jack Williamson's "Crucible of Power" (1939) places a space station very close to the Sun to tap a special form of solar energy. George O. Smith's *Venus Equilateral* (1948) features a station in the orbit of Venus, forming an equilateral triangle with Earth and Venus, so that it can be in constant radio contact with both Earth and Venus. In Robert A. Heinlein's "Misfit" (1939), a station is moved halfway between the Earth and Mars to serve as a stopover for space travelers; as a variation on this idea, Manly Wade Wellman's "Space Station No. 1" (1934) places a station in the orbit of Mars, but on the opposite side of the Sun, as a useful stopover when Earth and Mars are in opposition. Space stations are also found in the asteroid belt, as in Basil E. Wells's "Factory in the Sky" (1941) and H. C. Petley's "And Earth So Far Away" (1977); beyond Pluto at the edge of the Solar System, as in Frederik Pohl and Jack Williamson's *Starchild* (1965); and out in interstellar space, as Wilson Tucker's "Interstellar Way-Station" (1941). A space station might also be located near any sort of interesting phenomenon in space, as in William Gibson's "Hinterlands" (1981), where a space station is established to investigate a mysterious space warp.

Finally, science fiction has imagined space colonies with no fixed location that would serve as spaceships, traveling from star to star as "generation starships." H. Thompson Rich's "The Flying City" (1930) tells of an alien race that constructs an immense disk when their home planet was doomed and goes "voyaging through space on their marvelous disc...content to drift on and on in the interstellar void" (264), while Don Wilcox's "The Voyage That Lasted 600 Years" (1940) was the first story to envision humans undertaking a similar journey. Other noteworthy stories that explore this option include Robert A. Heinlein's "Universe" (1941), Clifford D. Simak's "Target Generation" (1953), Brian W. Aldiss's *Starship* (1959), and William R. Forstchen's *Into the Sea of Stars* (1986).

III. The structures of space stations. Science fiction has depicted a number of possible structures for space stations, most famously the doughnut or wheel shape immortalized in the film *2001: A Space Odyssey* (1968) and recently revived in the film *Mission to Mars* (2000). Stories like Steven Gould's "Rory" (1984) also anticipated a shapeless assemblage of various modules, resembling the International Space Station now being constructed. However, other designs have also been advanced.

First, the major advantage of the doughnut shape—rotation allowing for a sort of substitute gravity—can also be achieved with other rounded forms. Konstantin Tsiolkovsky long ago suggested an immense ring encircling an asteroid in "Changes in Relative Weight" (1894); and a year later, he became the first to suggest an enclosed sphere in *Dreams of Earth and Sky* (1895). Another early writer, Otto Gail, proposed a dumbbell shape, two spheres joined by a thin corridor, in *The Stone from the Moon* (1926). A large cylinder was the design for the space station in Robert A. Heinlein's "Delilah and the Space Rigger" (1949), and later became the standard model for the immense space habitats favored by Gerard O'Neill and his followers. Other rounded shapes of space stations encountered in science fiction include the top, as in the film *Star Trek VI: The Undiscovered Country* (1991); the disc, as in the film *Project Moonbase* (1953); the cone, as in Frank Belknap Long's *Space Station #1* (1957); and the helix, as in Arthur Byron Cover's *Stationfall* (1989). Dan Simmons's *The Fall of Hyperion* (1991) offers brief but evocative descriptions of a variety of space structures, including "zero-g globe cities, great irregular spheres of transparent membrane looking like improbable amoebae filled with busy flora and fauna," "ten-klick-long thrust clusters, accreted over centuries, their innermost modules and lifecans and 'cologies looking like something stolen from O'Neill's Boondoggle and the dawn of the space age," "hollowed-out asteroids long since abandoned by their residents, now given over to automated manufacturing and heavy-metal reprocessing," and "immense spherical docking globes" (436-437). A unique sort of space station is the "Dyson tree" in Rachel Pollack's "Tree House" (1984), a gigantic, genetically-altered tree which serves as a home for people in space.

Another form of space habitation frequently encountered is the city in space, naively imagined as a conventional metropolis placed on a flat surface, covered with a transparent dome, and launched into space, as most memorably depicted in James Blish's *Earthman, Come Home* (1958) and his other "Cities in Flight" novels. A variation on the idea is Spaceland in Alfred Bester's *The Demolished Man* (1953), a "flat plate of asteroid rock" with protective domes over various settlements that grew into "an irregular table in space, extending hundreds of miles" (154).

Another common design, already mentioned in the quotation from Simmons, is the roughly spherical station that is constructed by hollowing out an asteroid, as first described in detail in Robert A. Heinlein's "Misfit" (1939). Hugo Gernsback's *Ultimate World* (1975) describes aliens who seize the asteroid Eros, move it into Earth orbit, and hollow it out to serve as their "City in the Sky" (125). A striking example of this design is found in Louis Charbonneau's *Down to Earth* (1967), where hologram projections create the comforting illusions of terrestrial landscapes and city streets for residents inside of a barren, hollowed-out asteroid.

Finally, space stations are always employed as the upper anchor of the massive surface-to-space transportation systems known as "space elevators," most notably featured in Arthur C. Clarke's *The Fountains of Paradise* (1979) and Charles Sheffield's *The Web between the Worlds* (1979). A few stories, like the aforementioned *The Fountains of Paradise* and David Brin's "The Crystal Spheres" (1984), further envision that several of these stations in the same orbit might someday be linked both to Earth and to each other, creating a gigantic inhabited ring around the planet; in Brin's futuristic language, it would be a "gleaming, flexisolid belt of habitindustry around our world" (130).

IV. The design features of space stations. In describing in some detail the construction and habitation of various types of space stations, science fiction stories have offered a number of potentially good suggestions that might be considered by persons designing or planning a space station.

Some of these fall into the category of specific devices to build into or bring to the station. To maintain constant contact between modules during power failures, Hal Clement's "Answer" (1947) envisions a mechanical system of communication with speaking tubes and bells. To reduce overall station weight, Victor Appleton II's *Tom Swift and His Outpost in Space* (1955) suggests an oxygen-helium atmosphere. To simulate Earth gravity, Albert Saari's "Sitting Duck" (1952) proposes that a form of artificial gravity could be achieved on a space station by means of "a continuous fan-drawn suction" (126). Robert A. Heinlein's "Waldo" (1942) describes in some detail a space station without any floors that necessarily employs a system of indirect lighting. Arthur C. Clarke's *Islands in the Sky* (1952) depicts a simple device consisting of a spring in a hollow tube, called a "Broomstick," that astronauts could employ to take short trips around and away from the station. Concerned about prompt treatment of injured astronauts, Elizabeth Moon's "ABCs in Zero G" (1986) proposes spacesuits with limbs that unscrew and a "can-opener" device that could quickly remove spacesuits. Anticipating the danger of onboard fires (as actually occurred on board the Mir space station), Lester del Rey's *Step to the Stars* (1954) suggests the installation of a sprinkler system in a space station. To help maintain the morale of space station residents, J. Lloyd Castle's *Satellite E-One* (1954) proposes the use of bright colors for interior decoration, and Harry Harrison's *Skyfall* (1976) describes the benefits of continuous background music resembling Muzak. And while smoking will probably never be allowed on space stations, two stories—Robert A. Heinlein's "Waldo" (1942) and Murray Leinster's *Space Platform* (1953)—do go to the trouble of designing zero-gravity ashtrays, both featuring a suction tube to draw in the ashes.

A few interesting suggestions involve the projected inhabitants of a space station. Rather than training scientists with Ph.D.'s to build space stations, stories like Lester del Rey's *Step to the Stars* (1954) and Lee Correy's *Space Doctor* (1981) suggest hiring construction workers, who are better prepared for such activity, and sending them into space to do the work. Arthur C. Clarke has twice emphasized the potential benefits of having pets on board space stations: in "The Other Side of the Sky" (1958), a canary that stops singing warns residents about oxygen loss, just as canaries once served the same purpose in coal mines, and "The Haunted Spacesuit" (1958) speaks "Tommy, our recently acquired cat" and notes that "Pets mean a great deal to men thousands of miles from Earth" (62). In Vonda N. McIntyre's *Barbary* (1986), a cat on a space station proves extremely useful in combating an infestation of rats. To deal with another type of vermin—cockroaches—Bruce Sterling's "Spider Rose" (1982) suggests that, since they are almost impossible to exterminate, the cockroaches might be genetically engineered to serve as attractive pets of another kind.

Science fiction writers have expressed great concern about possible threats to a space station, including meteors, collisions, plagues, armed attacks, and sabotage, and they have proposed a few solutions. Douglas Mason's *Satellite 54-Zero* (1971) suggests that, at all times, at least one resident on a space station should be "in space gear, ready to go out and deal with any emergency like major meteorite penetration" (62). Martin Caidin's *Killer Station* (1984) notes the need to install heavy shielding to protect astronauts during solar flares. To protect against missile attacks, Murray Leinster's *Space Tug* (1953) describes a passive defense system that would throw out bits and pieces of junk to deflect incoming missiles; and to deal with troublemakers and saboteurs on board the station, Paul Preuss's *Breaking Strain* (1987) suggests that a simple stun-gun could deal with them without potentially damaging the station hull like other weapons. Finally, since science fiction regularly predicts that space station residents will often go insane, possibly threatening the safety of the station, Martin Caidin's *Killer Station* (1984) proposes that a psychologist should always be on board to watch for signs of mental illness, but it is also acknowledged that the very presence of such an observer might actually increase tensions.

Finally, while science fiction generally maintains that the hazards facing space stations of modest size are surmountable, there is more skepticism about the large space habitats that were championed by Gerard O'Neill in the 1970s and 1980s. Such structures are regularly viewed as susceptible to innumerable problems and vulnerabilities that cannot be adequately addressed, as most vigorously argued in Mack Reynolds and Dean Ing's *Trojan Orbit* (1985). Reynolds and Ing compare attempting to construct a huge space habitat with current technology to asking the Wright brothers in 1903 to build a supersonic jet aircraft; no matter how much money was provided, the Wright brothers would have been unable to achieve such a goal. They conclude that "We do not as yet have the knowledge to build a valid space colony" (232), suggesting that present-day designers should focus on learning how to build and maintain small space stations before undertaking more grandiose projects.

Conclusion. In various stories featuring space stations, science fiction has offered a number of general and specific suggestions that might someday be helpful to policymakers or engineers engaged in the creation of a space station or space colony. Of course, stories are not blueprints, and nothing in science fiction will ever substitute for the many hours of painstaking work and extreme attentiveness to detail that will always be necessary elements in the construction of a space station. Still, it never hurts to receive advice, and since the advice offered by science fiction is usually intelligent and very economical to obtain, it represents a resource worth consulting.

16. *The Fountains of Paradise*: An "Innovative Technologies from Science Fiction" Overview of Space Stations and Space Colonies in Science Fiction

Most space stations in science fiction serve predictably as stopovers for travelers, laboratories, factories, or military bases. But some envisioned facilities offer intriguing ideas for builders and residents of future space stations.

Arthur C. Clarke's "The Lion of Comarre" (1948) proposes a space station as headquarters for a world government, Michael Moorcock's *The Fireclown* (1965) creates an orbiting monastery, Patricia A. McKillip's *Fool's Run* (1987) designs a space prison, and Dean Ing's "Down and Out in Ellfive Prime" (1980) offers a comfortable home for the elderly. Space stations could protect endangered species, as in the film *Silent Running* (1971), or house bioengineered creatures, like the recreated dinosaurs in Robert Silverberg's "Our Lady of the Sauropods" (1980). For tourists, science fiction suggests satellite casinos, World's Fairs, summer camps for youngsters, and brothels for adults. Innovative space activities include zero-gravity dancing, as in Spider and Jeanne Robinson's *Stardance* (1979), exotic sculpture, as in Fritz Leiber's "The Beat Cluster" (1961), and "flying" with artificial wings, as in Konstantin Tsiolkovsky's *Beyond the Planet Earth* (1920).

Moving farther into the future, science fiction imagines space stations as essential homes for humanity should Earth become uninhabitable, as in Thomas N. Scortia's *Earthwreck!* (1974). Arguing that space life represents the next logical step in human evolution, Bruce Sterling's *Schismatrix* (1985) depicts strange new forms of humanity evolving beyond Earth, while Terry Greenhough's *Thoughtworld* (1977) suggests that psychic powers might increase in space. Space stations themselves might evolve to become generation starships traveling to distant stars, as in Don Wilcox's "The Voyage

That Lasted 600 Years" (1940); or series of orbital stations might be connected by cables to Earth and each other to form an immense inhabited ring around the planet, as in Clarke's *The Fountains of Paradise* (1979). Clearly, when writers imagine what humanity might someday do with space stations, the sky is not the limit.

PART SIX

BIBLIOGRAPHY

I. Science Fiction Works Involving Space Stations

The following is a list of the 398 science fiction works involving space stations which were described or mentioned in the main text. For plot summaries and commentaries on virtually all of these works, and for similar information on over five hundred other relevant works which were not cited in this study, please consult *The Other Side of the Sky: An Annotated Bibliography of Space Stations in Science Fiction, 1869-1993.*

Aldiss, Brian W. *Helliconia Spring.* New York: Atheneum, 1982. 361 pp.
—. *Helliconia Summer.* New York: Atheneum, 1983. 398 pp.
—. *Helliconia Winter.* New York: Atheneum, 1985. 281 pp.
—. *Starship.* [also known as *Nonstop*] 1958. New York: Avon Books, 1969. 224 pp.
Allen, Amanda. "Rolling Down the Floor." In *Carmen Miranda's Ghost Is Haunting Space Station Three.* Edited by Don Sakers. New York: Baen Books, 1990, pp. 163-170.
Allen, Roger MacBride. *Farside Cannon.* New York: Baen Books, 1988. 406 pp.
Anderson, Poul. *Hunters of the Sky Cave.* In *Agent of the Terran Empire.* New York: Ace Books, 1980. Originally published in shortened form in *Amazing Stories* (June, 1959). Also published as a novel under the title *We Claim These Stars!* New York: Ace Books, 1960. 125 pp.
Appleton, Victor. [pseud.] *The City in the Stars. A Tom Swift Adventure [#1].* New York: Wanderer Books, 1981. 191 pp.
Appleton, Victor, II. [pseud.] *Tom Swift, Jr., and His Outpost in Space.* [*Tom Swift, Jr. #7*] New York: Grosset & Dunlap, 1955. 210 pp.
—. *Tom Swift and the Cosmic Astronauts.* [*Tom Swift, Jr. #16*] New York: Grosset & Dunlap, 1960. 184 pp.
"The Ark in Space." *Doctor Who.* London: BBC-TV, January 25, 1975, through February 15, 1975 [four episodes].
Ash, Alan. *Conditioned for Space.* London: Ward, Lock & Co., Limited, 1955. 192 pp.
Asimov, Isaac. *The Caves of Steel.* 1954. New York: Pyramid Books, 1962. 189 pp.

—. "For the Birds." *Isaac Asimov's Science Fiction Magazine*, 4 (May, 1980), pp. 82-90.

—. "The Greatest Asset." *Analog Science Fiction/Science Fact*, 88 (January, 1972), pp. 44-50.

—. *Nemesis*. Garden City, New York: Doubleday, 1989. 364 pp.

—. "Reason." In *I, Robot*. By Isaac Asimov. 1950. New York: Signet Books, 1964, pp. 45-63. Story originally published in *Astounding Science-Fiction* in 1941.

"Babel." *Star Trek: Deep Space Nine*. Los Angeles: KCOP, January 26, 1993. [Program episodes were nationally syndicated and shown at different times during the week.]

Babylon 5. [television movie] Los Angeles: KCOP, February 25, 1993.

Ball, Brian N. *Singularity Station*. New York: DAW Books, Inc., 1973. 176 pp.

Barr, Tyrone C. *The Last Fourteen*. [Also known as *Split Worlds*] 1959. New York: Chariot Books, 1960. 156 pp.

"Battle Lines." *Star Trek: Deep Space Nine*. Los Angeles: KCOP, April 27, 1993.

Beliayev, Aleksandr. *The Struggle in Space*. Translated by Albert Parry. Washington: Arfor, 1965. 116 pp. Originally published in Russia in 1928.

Benford, Gregory. "Dark Sanctuary." In *The Endless Frontier, Volume I*. Edited by Jerry Pournelle. New York: Ace Books, 1979, pp. 285-299.

—. *Jupiter Project*. 1975. New York: Berkley Books, 1980. 182 pp. An earlier version appeared in *Amazing Science Fiction* (September-November, 1972).

—. "Redeemer." In *The Endless Frontier, Volume II*. Edited by Jerry Pournelle with John F. Carr. New York: Ace Books, 1982, pp. 405-418.

—. *Tides of Light*. New York: Bantam Books, 1989. 362 pp.

Bernard, Rafe. *The Wheel in the Sky*. London: Ward, Lock, & Co., 1954. 192 pp.

Bester, Alfred. *The Demolished Man*. 1953. New York: Random House, 1996. 243 pp.

Bishop, George. *The Shuttle People*. New York: Bantam Books, 1983. 210 pp.

Bisson, Terry. *Voyage to the Red Planet*. New York: William Morrow, 1990. 224 pp.

The Black Hole. Walt Disney, 1979.

Blish, James. *They Shall Have Stars*. [also published as *Year 2018*] [*Cities in Flight #1*] 1957. New York: Avon Books, 1967. 159 pp.

—. *A Life for the Stars*. [*Cities in Flight #2*] 1963. New York: Avon Books, 1968. 143 pp.

—. *Earthman, Come Home*. [*Cities in Flight #3*] 1958. New York: Avon Books, 1968. 253 pp.

—. *The Triumph of Time*. [*Cities in Flight #4*] 1958. New York: Avon

Books, 1968. 158 pp.

Bova, Ben. *Colony.* New York: Pocket Books, 1978. 470 pp.

—. *Exiled from Earth.* New York: Dutton, 1971. 202 pp.

—. "Isolation Area." In *Battle Station.* By Ben Bova. New York: TOR Books, 1987, pp. 114-145. Story originally published in 1984.

—. *Kinsman.* New York: Dial Press, 1979. 245 pp.

—. *Mars.* New York: Bantam Books, 1992. 502 pp.

—. *Millennium: A Novel about People and Politics in the Year 1999.* 1976. New York: Del Rey/Ballantine Books, 1977. 294 pp.

—. *Peacekeepers.* 1988. New York: TOR Books, 1989. 337 pp.

—. *The Weathermakers.* New York: Holt, Rinehart, and Winston, 1967. 249 pp. A portion of the novel was published as "The Weathermakers."

—. "The Weathermakers." *Analog Science Fiction/Science Fact,* 78 (December, 1966), pp. 52-80.

Brin, David. "The Crystal Spheres." *Analog Science Fiction/Science Fact,* 104 (January, 1984), pp. 128-143.

—. "Tank Farm Dynamo." In *The River of Time.* By David Brin. New York: Bantam Books, 1987, pp. 185-205. Story originally published in 1983.

Brown, Dale. *Silver Tower.* 1988. New York: Berkley Books, 1989. 384 pp.

Brown, Slater. *Spaceward Bound.* New York: Prentice-Hall, Inc., 1955. 213 pp.

Brunner, John. *The Crucible of Time.* New York: Del Rey/ Ballantine Books, 1983. 288 pp. Novel originally published in *Isaac Asimov's Science Fiction Magazine* in 1982 and 1983.

—. *Sanctuary in the Sky.* New York: Ace Books, 1963. 122 pp.

—. *The Shock Wave Rider.* New York: Harper & Row, Publishers, 1975. 246 pp.

Buckley, Bob. "The Star Hole." *Analog Science Fiction/Science Fact,* 90 (October, 1972), pp. 70-93.

Bujold, Lois McMaster. *Falling Free.* New York: Baen Books, 1991, 1988. 307 pp.

Bulmer, Kenneth. [writing as Tully Zetford] *Star City. Hook #3.* 1974. New York: Pinnacle Books, 1975. 154 pp.

Caidin, Martin. *Four Came Back.* New York: D. McKay, 1968. 275 pp.

—. *Killer Station.* New York: Baen Books, 1985, 1984. 370 pp.

Cameron, Berl. *Solar Gravita.* London: Curtis Warren Ltd., 1953. 159 pp.

"Captive Pursuit." *Star Trek: Deep Space Nine.* Los Angeles: KCOP, February 2, 1993.

Carr, John F. "Shapes of Things to Come." In *The Endless Frontier, Volume II.* Edited by Jerry Pournelle with John F. Carr. New York: Ace Books, 1982, pp. 359-373.

Castle, J. [Jeffrey] Lloyd. *Satellite E One.* London: Eyre & Spottiswoode, 1954. 164 pp.

Charbonneau, Louis. *Down to Earth.* [Also known as *Antic Earth*] New

York: Bantam Books, 1967. 221 pp.

Cherryh, C. J. [Carolyn Cherry] *Downbelow Station*. New York: DAW Books, 1981. 432 pp.

Christensen, Kevin. "Bellerophon." In *The Endless Frontier, Volume II*. Edited by Jerry Pournelle with John F. Carr. New York: Ace Books, 1982, pp. 228-275. Story originally published in *Destinies* in 1980.

Claremont, Chris. *FirstFlight*. New York: Ace Books, 1987. 243 pp.

Clarke, Arthur C. *The Fountains of Paradise*. 1979. New York: Ballantine Books, 1980. 297 pp.

—. "The Haunted Spacesuit." [Also known as "Who's There?"] In *Fifty Short Science Fiction Tales*. Edited by Isaac Asimov and Groff Conklin. New York: Collier Books, 1963, pp. 61-66. Story originally published in 1958.

—. *Imperial Earth*. New York: Ballantine Books, 1976. 301 pp.

—. *Islands in the Sky*. 1952. New York: Signet Books, 1960. 157 pp.

—. "The Lion of Comarre." In *The Lion of Comarre and Against the Fall of Night*. By Arthur C. Clarke. New York: Harcourt, Brace & World, 1968, pp. 3-62. Story originally published in *Thrilling Wonder Stories* in 1949.

—. *The Lost Worlds of 2001*. New York: Signet Books, 1972. 240 pp.

—. "The Other Side of the Sky." In *The Other Side of the Sky*. By Arthur C. Clarke. 1958. New York: Signet Books, 1959, pp. 26-44. Story originally published in 1957.

—. *Rendezvous with Rama*. 1973. New York: Ballantine Books, 1974. 274 pp.

—. *Sands of Mars*. 1951. New York: Pocket Books, 1959. 217 pp.

—. *The Songs of Distant Earth*. New York: Ballantine Books, 1986. 253 pp.

—. *2001: A Space Odyssey*. Based on a screenplay by Stanley Kubrick and Arthur C. Clarke. New York: Signet Books, 1968. 221 pp.

—. *2061: Odyssey Three*. New York: Ballantine Books, 1987. 276 pp.

—. "Venture to the Moon." In *The Other Side of the Sky*. By Arthur C. Clarke. 1958. New York: Signet Books, 1959, pp. 70-93. Story originally published in 1956 and 1957.

Clarke, Arthur C., with Gentry Lee. *Rama II*. New York: Bantam Books, 1989. 420 pp.

Clement, Hal. [Harry Clement Stubbs] "Answer." In *The Best of Hal Clement*. Edited by Lester del Rey. New York: Ballantine Books, 1979, pp. 147-171. Story originally published in 1947.

—. "Fireproof." In *Space Lash*. [Also known as *Small Changes*] By Hal Clement. New York: Dell Publishing Company, 1969, pp. 80-95. Story originally published in 1952.

Clough, B. W. [Brenda] "Provisional Solution." In *Carmen Miranda's Ghost Is Haunting Space Station Three*. Edited by Don Sakers. New York: Baen Books, 1990, pp. 1-4.

Cole, Allan, and Chris Bunch. *Sten*. New York: Del Rey/Ballantine Books,

1982. 279 pp.

Conquest of Space. Paramount Pictures, 1956.

Cooper, Edmund. *Seed of Light*. New York: Ballantine Books, 1959. 159 pp.

Cooper, Edmund [as George Kinley]. *Ferry Rocket*. London: Curtis Warren Books, 1954. 158 pp.

Cooper, Tom. *War Moon*. New York: Worldwide Books, 1987. 381 pp.

Correy, Lee. [G. Harry Stine] "Industrial Accident." In *Great Science Fiction Stories by the World's Great Scientists*. Edited by Isaac Asimov with Martin Greenberg and Charles Waugh. New York: Donald I. Fine, Inc., 1985, pp. 170-191. Story originally published in 1980.

—. *Manna*. New York: DAW Books, 1983. 293 pp.

—. *Space Doctor*. 1981. New York: Ballantine Books, 1985. 245 pp.

Coulson, Juanita. *Tomorrow's Heritage*. Book One of the Series Children of the Stars. New York: Del Rey/Ballantine Books, 1981. 372 pp.

Courtney, Robert. "One Thousand Miles Up." *Science Stories*, No. 4 (April, 1954), pp. 88-101.

Cover, Arthur Byron. *Stationfall*. A Byron Preiss Book. An Infocom Book. New York: Avon Books, 1989. 297 pp.

Cowley, Stewart. *Starliners: Commercial Spacetravel in 2200 A.D.* New York: Exeter Books, 1980. 90 pp.

Cross, John Keir. *The Stolen Sphere*. [Also known as *The Flying Fortunes in an Encounter with Rubberface*] 1952. London: F. Muller, 1953. 220 pp.

del Rey, Lester. [Walter Alvarez del Rey] *Mission to the Moon*. New York: Holt, Rinehart and Winston, 1956. 207 pp.

—. *Moon of Mutiny*. New York: Holt, Rinehart and Winston, 1961. 217 pp.

—. *Siege Perilous*. [Actually written by Paul Fairman, based on detailed outlines by del Rey] New York: Lancer Books, 1966. 157 pp.

—. *Step to the Stars*. 1954. New York: Paperback Library, 1966. 160 pp.

Diamond, Graham. "'Outcasts.'" In *Habitats*. Edited by Susan Shwartz. New York: DAW Books, 1984, pp. 100-119.

Dick, Philip K. *The Crack in Space*. New York: Ace Books, 1966. 190 pp. Originally published in shortened form as "Cantata 140" in *The Magazine of Fantasy and Science Fiction* (July, 1964).

—. *Dr. Bloodmoney [or How We Got Along after the Bomb]*. 1965. New York: Carroll & Graf, 1988. 298 pp.

Dicks, Terrance. *Doctor Who and the Revenge of the Cybermen*. 1976. London: W. H. Allen and Co., 1978. 128 pp.

Dickson, Gordon R. *The Pritcher Mass*. 1972. New York: TOR Books, 1983. 251 pp.

—. "Steel Brother." *Astounding Science Fiction*, 48 (February 1952), pp. 103-124.

Dillingham, Peter. "House." [Poem] In *The Endless Frontier, Volume I*. Edited by Jerry Pournelle. New York: Ace Books, 1979, pp. 257-260.

Drake, David. *Fortress*. New York: TOR Books, 1987. 311 pp.

Drake, David, and Bill Fawcett, editors. *Battlestation, Book 1*. New York: Ace Books, 1992. 258 pp.

—, editors. *Battlestation, Book 2: Vanguard*. New York: Ace Books, 1993. 264 pp.

"Dramatis Personae." *Star Trek: Deep Space Nine*. Los Angeles: KCOP, June 1, 1993.

Dulski, Thomas R. "My Christmas on New Hanford." *Analog Science Fiction/Science Fact*, 102 (December, 1982), pp. 64-81.

Duncan, David. *Dark Dominion*. New York: Ballantine Books, 1954. 206 pp.

Earls, William. "Jump." *Analog Science Fiction/Science Fact*, 84 (October, 1969), pp. 126-137.

Earth II. Metro-Goldwyn-Mayer, 1971.

Elam, Richard M., Jr. [Richard Mace] "The Ghost Ship of Space." In *Super Science Stories*. [Original title: *Teen-Age Super Science Stories*] By Richard M. Elam, Jr. 1957. New York: Lantern Press, 1967, pp. 132-206.

—. "The Iron Moon." In *Teen-Age Science Fiction Stories*. By Richard M. Elam, Jr. New York: Lantern Press, 1952, pp. 147-168.

—. "Mercy Flight to Luna." In *Super Science Stories*. [Original title: *Teen-Age Super Science Stories*] By Richard M. Elam, Jr. 1957. New York: Lantern Press, 1967, pp. 82-91.

Eliott, E. C. [Reginald Alec Martin]. *Kemlo and the Sky Horse*. London: Thomas Nelson and Sons Ltd., 1954. 189 pp.

—. *Kemlo and the Zones of Silence*. London: Thomas Nelson and Sons Ltd., 1954. 201 pp.

Ellison, Harlan. "The Discarded." In *Alone against Tomorrow*. By Harlan Ellison. 1971. New York: Collier Books, 1972, pp. 33-48. Story originally published as "The Abnormals" in *Fantastic* (April, 1959).

"Emissary." *Star Trek: Deep Space Nine*. Los Angeles: KCOP, January 5, 1993.

Fish, Leslie. "Bertocci's Proof." In *Carmen Miranda's Ghost Is Haunting Space Station Three*. Edited by Don Sakers. New York: Baen Books, 1990, pp. 193-210.

—. "Carmen Miranda's Ghost." [song] Lyrics and sheet music in *Carmen Miranda's Ghost Is Haunting Space Station Three*. Edited by Don Sakers. New York: Baen Books, 1990, pp. [vii-viii], 306. Song copyrighted 1985.

Flynn, Michael E. "The Washer at the Ford." *Analog Science Fiction/Science Fact*, 109 (June, 1989), pp. 14-70, and (July, 1989), pp. 126-176.

"The Forsaken." *Star Trek: Deep Space Nine*. Los Angeles: KCOP, May 25, 1993.

Forstchen, William R. *Into the Sea of Stars*. New York: Del Rey/Ballantine Books, 1986. 231 pp.

Fritch, C. E. "Many Dreams of Earth." *Orbit Science Fiction*, 1 (November/December, 1954), pp. 98-107. Also published under the title "Space Station 42." In *Space Station 42 and Other Stories*. Sydney, Australia: Jubilee Pub., 1958.

Fyfe, Horace B. "Sinecure 6." *Astounding Science Fiction*, 38 (January, 1947), pp. 55-71.

—. "Thinking Machine." *Astounding Science Fiction*, 48 (October, 1951), pp. 63-82.

Gail, Otto. *The Stone from the Moon*. Translated by Francis Currier. *Science Wonder Quarterly*, 1 (Spring, 1930), pp. 294-359, 418-419. Originally published in Germany in 1926.

Gernsback, Hugo. *Ultimate World*. Edited with an introduction by Sam Moskowitz. 1971. New York: Avon Books, 1975. 187 pp.

Gerritsen, Tess. *Gravity*. New York: Pocket Books, 1999. 342 pp.

Gibson, Edward. *Reach*. Garden City, New York: Doubleday, 1989. 334 pp.

Gibson, William. "Hinterlands." In *Burning Chrome*. By William Gibson. 1986. New York: Ace Books, 1987, pp. 58-79. Story originally published in 1981.

—. *Neuromancer*. New York: Ace Books, 1984. 271 pp.

Gilliland, Alexis A. *Long Shot for Rosinante*. [*Rosinante #2*] New York: Del Rey/Ballantine Books, 1981. 181 pp.

Girard, Dian. "Invisible Encounter." In *The Endless Frontier, Volume II*. Edited by Jerry Pournelle with John F. Carr. New York: Ace Books, 1982, pp. 205-209.

—. "No Home-Like Place." In *The Endless Frontier, Volume I*. Edited by Jerry Pournelle. New York: Ace Books, 1979, pp. 123-128.

Gog. Ivan Tors Productions, 1954.

Goldstein, Stan, and Fred Goldstein. *Star Trek Spaceflight Chronology*. Illustrated by Rick Sternbach. A Wallaby Book. New York: Pocket Books, 1980. 192 pp.

Gorath. [*Yosei Gorasu*] Toho, 1962.

Goulart, Ron. *Everybody Comes to Cosmo's. The Exchameleon Book Three*. New York: St. Martin's Press, 1988. 184 pp.

—. *Star Hawks: Empire 99*. Illustrations by Gil Kane. New York: Playboy Press Paperbacks, 1980. 192 pp.

Gould, Steven. "Rory." *Analog Science Fiction/Science Fact*, 104 (April, 1984), pp. 96-109.

Grant, Lee. "Signal Thirty-Three." *Fantastic Science Fiction*, 4 (October, 1955), pp. 38-63.

Green, Joseph. "Three-Tour Man." *Analog Science Fiction/Science Fact*, 89 (May, 1972), pp. 112-125.

The Green Slime. [*Gamma Sango Uchu Daisakusen*] Toei/Southern Cross Films, 1968.

Greenhough, Terry. *Thoughtworld*. London: New English Library, 1978, 1977. 144 pp.

Groom, Pelham. *The Purple Twilight*. London: T. Werner Laurie, Ltd., 1948. 281 pp.

Gunn, James. *Station in Space*. New York: Bantam Books, 1958. 156 pp.

Haldeman, Jack C., II. *Vector Analysis*. 1978. New York: Berkley Books, 1980. 183 pp. A portion of the novel appeared in *Analog Science Fiction/Science Fact* in 1977.

Haldeman, Joe. "More Than the Sum of His Parts." In *Nebula Awards 21*. Edited by George Zebrowski. New York: Harcourt Brace Jovanovich, 1987, pp. 153-175. Story originally published in *Playboy* (May, 1985).

—. "Tricentennial." In *The Endless Frontier, Volume I*. Edited by Jerry Pournelle. New York: Ace Books, 1979, pp. 96-121. Story originally published in *Analog: Science Fiction/Science Fact* (July, 1976).

—. *Worlds: A Novel of the Near Future*. 1981. New York: Pocket Books, 1982. 239 pp.

—. *Worlds Apart: A Novel of Future Survival*. 1983. New York: Ace Books, 1984. 227 pp.

Haldeman, Joe, and Jack C. Haldeman II. *There Is No Darkness*. New York: Ace Books, 1983. 245 pp. Portions of the book previously published in *Isaac Asimov's Science Fiction Magazine* in 1979.

Hale, Edward Everett. "The Brick Moon." In *His Level Best and Other Stories*. By Edward Everett Hale. 1872. New York: Garrett Press, 1969, pp. 30-124. Story originally published as "The Brick Moon," *Atlantic Monthly*, 24 (October-December, 1869), and "Life on the Brick Moon," *Atlantic Monthly*, 25 (February, 1870).

Hamilton, Edmond. "Space Mirror." *Thrilling Wonder Stories*, 10 (August, 1937), pp. 43-51.

Harness, Charles L. *The Paradox Men*. [*Flight into Yesterday*] 1953. Revised Edition. 1981. New York: Crown Publishers, Inc., 1984. 202 pp. Originally published in a shorter version in *Startling Stories* (May, 1949), as "Flight into Yesterday."

Harrison, Harry. *Skyfall*. 1976. New York: Ace Books, 1978. 378 pp.

Heinlein, Robert A. *Between Planets*. 1951. New York: Ace Books, 1969. 190 pp.

—. "Blowups Happen." In *Expanded Universe: The New Worlds of Robert A. Heinlein*. New York: Ace Books, 1980, pp. 35-90. Story originally published in *Astounding Science-Fiction* (September, 1940).

—. *The Cat Who Walks through Walls*. New York: Putnam, 1985. 382 pp.

—. "Delilah and the Space Rigger." In *The Green Hills of Earth*. By Robert A. Heinlein. 1951. New York: Signet Books, 1952, pp. 13-23. Story originally published in *Blue Book* (December, 1949).

—. *Friday*. New York: Holt, Rinehart, and Winston, 1982. 368 pp.

—. "The Green Hills of Earth." In *The Green Hills of Earth*. By Robert A. Heinlein. 1951. New York: Signet Books, 1952, pp. 125-134. Story originally published in *The Saturday Evening Post* (February 8, 1947).

—. "It's Great to Be Back." *In The Green Hills of Earth*. By Robert A. Heinlein. 1951. New York: Signet Books, 1952, pp. 74-89. Story originally published in *The Saturday Evening Post* (July 26, 1947).

—. "Misfit." In *Revolt in 2100*. By Robert A. Heinlein. New York: Signet Books, 1953, pp. 170-188. Story originally published in *Astounding Science-Fiction* (November, 1939).

—. "Ordeal in Space." In *The Green Hills of Earth*. By Robert A. Heinlein. 1951. New York: Signet Books, 1952, pp. 111-124. Story originally published in *Town and Country* (May, 1948).

—. "Searchlight." In *Expanded Universe: The New Worlds of Robert A. Heinlein*. New York: Ace Books, 1980, pp. 447-451. Story originally published as an advertisement in *Scientific American* (August, 1962) and other magazines.

—. "Sky Lift." In *The Menace from Earth*. By Robert A. Heinlein. 1959. New York: Signet Books, 1962, pp. 115-128. Story originally published in *Imagination* (November, 1953).

—. *Space Cadet*. 1948. New York: Ace Books, 1969. 221 pp.

—. "Space Jockey." In *The Green Hills of Earth*. By Robert A. Heinlein. 1951. New York: Signet Books, 1952, pp. 24-39. Story originally published in *The Saturday Evening Post* (April 26, 1947).

—. *To Sail beyond the Sunset*. 1987. New York: Ace Books, 1988. 434 pp.

—. "Universe." In *Orphans of the Sky*. By Robert A. Heinlein. 1963. New York: Signet Books, 1965, pp. 7-58. Story originally published in *Astounding Science-Fiction* in 1941.

—. "Waldo." In *Waldo and Magic, Inc.* By Robert A. Heinlein. 1950. New York: Pyramid Books, 1963, pp. 9-103. Story first published in *Astounding Science-Fiction* (August, 1942) and published separately as *Waldo: Genius in Orbit*.

Henderson, Gene L. "Tiger by the Tail." In *The Boys' Life Book of Outer Space Stories*. Edited by the Editors of *Boys' Life*. New York: Random House, 1964, pp. 54-66. Story originally published in *Boys' Life*.

Hendrix, Howard V. *Lightpaths*. New York: Ace Books, 1997. 345 pp.

Higgins, Bill, and Barry Gehm. "Home on Lagrange." [Song] In *The Endless Frontier, Volume I*. Edited by Jerry Pournelle. New York: Ace Books, 1979, pp. 264-265.

Hodgman, Ann. *Galaxy High School*. New York: Bantam Skylark Books, 1987. 96 pp.

Hogan, James P. *Endgame Enigma*. 1987. New York: Bantam Books, 1988. 436 pp.

Hoover, H. M. *Away Is a Strange Place to Be*. New York: E. P. Dutton, 1990. 167 pp.

Hunt, Gill. [pseud.] *Station 7*. London: Curtis Warren, Ltd., 1951. 112 pp.

"If Wishes Were Horses." *Star Trek: Deep Space Nine*. Los Angeles: KCOP, May 18, 1993.

Ing, Dean. "Down & Out on Ellfive Prime." In *The Endless Frontier, Volume II*. Edited by Jerry Pournelle with John F. Carr. New York: Ace Books, 1982, pp. 97-123. Story originally published in *Omni* in 1980.

"In the Hands of the Prophets." *Star Trek: Deep Space Nine*. Los Angeles:

KCOP, June 22, 1993.

Jackson, A. A., IV, and Howard Waldrop. "Sun Up." In *Faster Than Light*. Edited by Jack Dann and George Zebrowski. New York: Ace Books, 1976, pp. 24-36.

Janifer, Laurence M. [formerly Larry Mark Harris], and J. L. Treibich. *Target: Terra*. New York: Ace Books, 1968. 149 pp.

Johnson, Bill. "Meet Me at Apogee." *Analog Science Fiction/Science Fact*, 102 (May, 1982), pp. 74-92.

Kato, Ken. *Yamato—A Rage in Heaven, Part Two: The Way of the Warrior*. New York: Questar/Warner Books, 1992. 297 pp.

Kingsbury, Donald. "To Bring in the Steel." In *The Endless Frontier, Volume I*. Edited by Jerry Pournelle. New York: Ace Books, 1979, pp. 197-252. Story originally published in *Analog Science Fiction/Science Fact* (July, 1978).

Knight, Damon. "Stranger Station." In *SF: The Best of the Best*. Edited by Judith Merril. 1967. New York: Dell Books, 1968, pp. 143-168. Story originally published in 1959.

Kornbluth, C. M. *Not This August*. [Also known as *Christmas Eve*] Garden City, New York: Doubleday, 1955. 190 pp.

Kubaska, Theodore. "Univan and the Wheelies." *Galileo,* 1 (July, 1977), pp. 37-43.

Kube-McDowell, Michael P. "Menace." *Analog Science Fiction/Science Fact*, 104 (February, 1984), pp. 84-105.

Kuykendall, Roger. "All Day September." *Astounding Science Fiction*, 62 (January, 1959), pp. 30-43.

Lande, Irving W. "Slingshot." *Astounding Science Fiction*, 56 (November, 1955), pp. 116-126.

Lasswitz, Kurt. *Two Planets*. [*Auf zwei Planeten*; also known as *Twin Planets*] Abridged by Erich Lasswitz. Translated by Hans H. Rudnick. Afterword by Mark Hillegas. Carbondale, Illinois: Southern Illinois University Press, 1971. 405 pp. Novel originally published in 1897.

Leiber, Fritz. "The Beat Cluster." In *The Seventh Galaxy Reader*. Edited by Frederik Pohl. Garden City, New York: Doubleday, 1964, pp. 199-214. Story originally published in *Galaxy* in 1961.

—. "Kindergarten." In *100 Great Science Fiction Short Short Stories*. Edited by Isaac Asimov, Martin Greenberg, and Joseph D. Olander. 1978. New York: Avon Books, 1980, pp. 101-103. Story originally published in *The Magazine of Fantasy and Science Fiction* in 1963.

—. *A Specter Is Haunting Texas*. New York: Walker and Co., 1968. 245 pp.

Leinster, Murray. [Will Jenkins] *City on the Moon*. New York: Avalon Books, 1957. 224 pp.

—. *Men into Space*. New York: Berkley Books, 1960. 142 pp.

—. "The Power Planet." *Amazing Stories*, 6 (June, 1931), pp. 198-217, 227.

—. *Space Platform*. 1953. New York: Belmont Books, 1966. 157 pp.

—. *Space Tug.* 1953. New York: Belmont Books, 1965. 157 pp.

Lem, Stanislaw. *Solaris.* Translated from the French by Joanna Kilmartin and Steve Cox. London: Faber & Faber, 1971. 216 pp. Originally published in 1961.

Long, Frank Belknap. *The Martian Visitors.* New York: Avalon Books, 1964. 192 pp.

—. *Space Station #1.* New York: Ace Books, 1957. 157 pp.

—. *This Strange Tomorrow.* New York: Belmont Books, 1966. 158 pp.

Lupoff, Richard A. *The Forever City.* Illustrated by Bob Eggleton. A Byron Preiss Book. New York: Walker and Company, 1987. 230 pp.

—. "Stomping Down Stroka Prospekt." *Isaac Asimov's Science Fiction Magazine,* 6 (December 21, 1982), pp. 48-70.

—. *Sun's End.* New York: Berkley Books, 1984. 280 pp.

MacGregor, Ellen, and Dora Pantell. *Miss Pickerell and the Weather Satellite.* 1971. New York: Pocket Books, 1980. 165 pp.

MacLean, Katherine. "The Gambling Hell and the Sinful Girl." In *The Endless Frontier, Volume I.* Edited by Jerry Pournelle. New York: Ace Books, 1979, pp. 267-283. Story originally published in *Analog: Science Fiction/Science Fact* (January, 1975).

—. "Incommunicado." *Astounding Science Fiction,* 45 (June, 1950), pp. 6-32.

Maddox, Tom. "Snake-Eyes." In *Mirrorshades: The Cyberpunk Anthology.* Edited by Bruce Sterling. 1986. New York: Ace Books, 1988, pp. 12-33. Story originally published in *Omni* (April, 1986).

"Mark of the Saurian." *Buck Rogers in the Twenty-Fifth Century.* New York: NBC, February 2, 1981.

Marsten, Richard. [Evan Hunter, formerly known as S. A. Lombino] *Rocket to Luna.* New York: Winston, 1952. 211 pp.

Martin, George R. R. "Nor the Many-Colored Fires of a Star Ring." In *Faster Than Light.* Edited by Jack Dann and George Zebrowski. New York: Ace Books, 1976, pp. 199-220.

—. "The Second Kind of Loneliness." in *Isaac Asimov's Science Fiction Treasury.* Edited by Isaac Asimov, Martin Greenberg, and Joseph Olander. New York: Bonanza Books, 1980, pp. 633-649. Story originally published in 1972.

Martino, Joseph P. "The Iceworm Special." *Analog Science Fiction/Science Fact,* 51 (July 20, 1981), pp. 130-137.

—. "Persistence." *Analog Science Fiction/Science Fact,* 83 (May, 1969), pp. 58-95.

Mason, Anne. *The Dancing Meteorite.* New York: Harper & Row, Publishers, 1984. 214 pp.

Mason, Douglas R. *Satellite 54-Zero.* New York: Ballantine Books, 1971. 185 pp.

Maxwell, M. Max. "Prisoner 794." *Analog Science Fiction/Science Fact,* 92 (September, 1973), pp. 78-93.

McCaffrey, Anne, and S. M. Stirling. *The City Who Fought.* New York:

Baen Books, 1993. 436 pp.

McIntosh, J. T. [James Murdoch MacGregor; this story as by J. T. M'Intosh] "Hallucination Orbit." *Galaxy*, 3 (January, 1952), pp. 132-158.

McIntyre, Vonda N. *Barbary*. Boston: Houghton Mifflin Company, 1986. 192 pp.

McKillip, Patricia A. *Fool's Run*. New York: Warner Books, 1987. 221 pp.

—. *Moon-Flash*. New York: Atheneum, 1984. 150 pp.

McLaughlin, Dean. *The Man Who Wanted Stars*. New York: Lancer Books, 1965. 222 pp. Different versions of Parts I and II were published as "The Last Thousand Miles" in *Astounding Science Fiction* (February, 1956), and "Welcome Home" in *Infinity* (October, 1957).

McNeil, Mark. "Scratches in the Dark." *Analog Science Fiction/Science Fact*, 102 (Mid-September, 1982), pp. 110-119.

Men into Space. New York: CBS-TV, 1959-1960.

Merril, Judith. "Survival Ship." In *Tomorrow, The Stars*. Edited by Robert A. Heinlein. 1952. New York: Berkley Books, 1967, pp. 138-146. Story originally published in 1950.

Merwin, Sam, Jr. "Star Tracks." *Astounding Science Fiction*, 49 (March, 1952), pp. 144-152.

Michaels, Melisa. *First Battle*. [*Skyrider #2*] New York: TOR Books, 1985. 253 pp.

Miller, Walter M., Jr. *A Canticle for Leibowitz*. 1959. New York: Bantam Books, 1961. 278 pp. Some parts of the book appeared in different form in *The Magazine of Fantasy and Science Fiction* in 1955 and 1956.

Mission to Mars. Touchstone Pictures, 2000.

Moon, Elizabeth. "ABCs in Zero-G." *Analog Science Fact/Science Fiction*, 106 (August, 1986), pp. 82-107. Story reprinted in *Lunar Activity*. By Elizabeth Moon. New York: Baen Books, 1990.

Moonraker. Eon Productions/Les Productions Artistes Associés, 1979.

Moorcock, Michael. *The Fireclown*. [also known as *The Winds of Limbo*] Compact SF. London: Richmond Hill Publishing Works, Ltd., 1965. 189 pp.

Moore, C. L. *Judgment Night*. In *Judgment Night*. By C. L. Moore. New York: Gnome Press, 1952, pp. 3-156. Story originally published in two parts in *Astounding Science-Fiction* (August, 1943), pp. 9-52, and (September, 1943), pp. 110-161. Also published as *Judgment Night*. New York: Paperback Library, 1965, 1952. 156 pp.

"Move Along Home." *Star Trek: Deep Space Nine*. Los Angeles: KCOP, March 16, 1993.

Mullen, Stanley. "Fool Killer." *Astounding Science Fiction*, 61 (May, 1958), pp. 109-123.

Munro, John. *A Trip to Venus*. London: Jarrold & Sons, 1897. 254 pp.

Murdock, M. S. *Rebellion 2456*. [*Buck Rogers: Martian Wars Trilogy #1*]

New York: TSR, 1989. 281 pp.

Mutiny in Outer Space. [*Ammutinamento nello spazio*; also known as *Invasion from the Moon*] Woolner Brothers/Hugo Grimaldi Productions, 1965.

Neville, Kris. "Cold War." In *Selections from the Astounding Science Fiction Anthology*. Edited by John W. Campbell, Jr. New York: Berkley Books, 1964, pp. 167-178. Story originally published in *Astounding Science-Fiction* in 1949.

—. "Earth Alert!" *Imagination*, 4 (February, 1953), pp. 6-86.

—. "Satellite Secret." *Space Adventures*, No. 13 (Spring, 1971), pp. 74-83, 131. Story originally published in *Amazing Stories* (April, 1950).

Newman, Richard Louis. *Siege of Orbitor*. New York: Leisure Books, 1980. 254 pp.

Nicholson, Sam. [Shirley Nikolaisen] "He Who Fights and Runs Away." *Analog Science Fiction/Science Fact*, 102 (Mid-September, 1982), pp. 18-50.

Niven, Larry [Laurence van Cott Niven], with Stephen Barnes. *The Descent of Anansi*. New York: TOR Books, 1982. 278 pp.

—, and Jerry Pournelle. "Spirals." In *The Endless Frontier, Volume I*. Edited by Jerry Pournelle. New York: Ace Books, 1979, pp. 27-83. Story originally published in *Destinies* (March-April, 1979).

Norment, John. "Space Platform Xz204c Does Not Answer." *Science Fiction Digest*, No. 1 (1954), pp. 88-89. Story originally published in *Ballyhoo* in 1953.

Oliver, Chad. "Ghost Town." In *Cities in Space: The Endless Frontier, Volume III*. Edited by Jerry Pournelle with John F. Carr. New York: Ace Books, 1991, pp. 163-185. Originally published in *Analog Science Fiction/Science Fact* in 1983.

—. "Meanwhile, Back on the Reservation." *Analog: Science Fiction/Science Fact*, 51 (April 27, 1981), pp. 86-101.

Panshin, Alexei. *Rite of Passage*. New York: Ace Books, 1968. 254 pp.

"The Passenger." *Star Trek: Deep Space Nine*. Los Angeles: KCOP, February 23, 1993.

Petley, H. C. "And Earth So Far Away." *Galaxy*, 38 (August, 1977), pp. 9-29.

Pohl, Frederik. *The Annals of the Heechee*. [*Book Four of the Heechee Saga*] 1987. New York: Del Rey/Ballantine Books, 1988. 341 pp.

—. *Beyond the Blue Event Horizon*. [*Book Two of the Heechee Saga*] New York: Del Rey/Ballantine Books, 1980. 309 pp.

—. *Gateway*. [*Book One of the Heechee Saga*] 1977. New York: Del Rey/Ballantine Books, 1978. 313 pp.

—. *Heechee Rendezvous*. [*Book Three of the Heechee Saga*] 1984. New York: Del Rey/Ballantine Books, 1985. 331 pp.

—. *Man Plus*. 1976. New York: Bantam Books, 1977. 246 pp.

Pohl, Frederik, and Jack Williamson. *The Reefs of Space*. [*Starchild #1*] New York: Ballantine Books, 1964. 188 pp. Novel originally published in *Worlds of If Science Fiction* in 1963.

—. *Starchild.* [*Starchild #2*] New York: Ballantine Books, 1965. 191 pp. A shorter version of this novel originally published in *Galaxy Magazine* in 1964.

Pollack, Rachel. "Tree House." In *Habitats.* Edited by Susan Shwartz. New York: DAW Books, 1984, pp. 122-141.

Pournelle, Jerry. "Bind Your Sons to Exile." In *The Endless Frontier, Volume I.* Edited by Jerry Pournelle. New York: Ace Books, 1979, pp. 130-175.

—. "Consort." In *High Justice.* By Jerry Pournelle. 1974. New York: Baen Books, 1986, pp. 195-222. Story originally published in 1975. [Dates as given in 1986 edition.]

—. "High Justice." In *High Justice.* By Jerry Pournelle. 1974. New York: Baen Books, 1986, pp. 100-151. Story originally published in *Analog: Science Fiction/Science Fact* in 1974.

Powers, William F. "Meteor." *Astounding Science Fiction*, 46 (September, 1950), pp. 107-120.

Pratt, Fletcher. "Project Excelsior." [also known as "Asylum Satellite"] In *Double in Space.* By Fletcher Pratt. Garden City, New York: Doubleday, 1951, pp. 9-113.

Preuss, Paul. *Breaking Strain. Arthur C. Clarke's Venus Prime #1.* New York: Avon Books, 1987. 265 pp. Based on "Breaking Strain." By Arthur C. Clarke.

Project Moonbase. Galaxy Pictures, 1953.

"Protect and Survive." *Space Precinct.* Los Angeles: KCBS, October 3, 1994.

"Q-Less." *Star Trek: Deep Space Nine.* Los Angeles: KCOP, February 9, 1993.

Queen of Outer Space. Allied Artists, 1958.

Quick, W. T. "High Hotel*.*" *Analog Science Fiction/Science Fact*, 109 (June, 1989), pp. 150-178.

Raphael, Rick. "The Mailman Cometh." *Analog Science Fact/Science Fiction*, 74 (February, 1965), pp. 17-33.

Resnick, Mike*. Eros Ascending. Tales of the Velvet Comet #1.* New York: Signet Books, 1984. 254 pp.

—. *Eros Descending. Tales of the Velvet Comet #3.* New York: Signet Books, 1985. 250 pp.

Return of the Jedi. Lucasfilm/Fox, 1983.

"Revenge of the Cybermen." *Doctor Who.* London: BBC-TV, April 19, 1975 through May 10, 1975 [4 episodes].

Reynolds, Mack. *Chaos in Lagrangia.* Edited by Dean Ing. New York: TOR Books, 1984. 256 pp.

—. *Satellite City.* New York: Ace Books, 1975. 238 pp.

—, with Dean Ing. *Trojan Orbit.* New York: Baen Books, 1985. 374 pp.

Rich, H. Thompson. "The Flying City." *Astounding Stories of Super-Science*, 3 (August, 1930), pp. 260-278.

Richardson, Robert S. *Second Satellite*. New York: McGraw-Hill Book Co., 1956. 191 pp.

Riders to the Stars. A-Men Productions, 1954.

Robinson, Kim Stanley. *Red Mars*. New York: Bantam, 1993. 572 pp.

Robinson, Spider, and Jeanne Robinson. *Stardance*. 1979. New York: Dell Books, 1980. 278 pp. Based on the story of the same name originally published in *Analog Science Fiction/Science Fact* in 1977.

"Rough Justice." [no author given] In *Space Wars: Fact and Fiction*. [No editor given] London: Octopus Books, 1980, pp. 10-18.

Saari, Oliver. "Sitting Duck." *Astounding Science Fiction*, 48 (January, 1952), pp. 119-130.

Sakers, Don, editor. *Carmen Miranda's Ghost Is Haunting Space Station Three*. New York: Baen Books, 1990. 306 pp.

Savage, Blake. [pseud. of Harold L. Goodwin] *Rip Foster in Ride the Gray Planet*. [This edition published as *Rip Foster Rides the Gray Planet*; also published as *Assignment in Space with Rip Foster*] 1952. New York: Golden Press, 1969. 253 pp.

Science Fiction. [anonymously written by John Silbersack] No-Frills Books. New York: Jove Publications, 1981. 58 pp.

Scortia, Thomas M. *Earthwreck!* New York: Fawcett Gold Medal Books, 1974. 224 pp.

Shaw, Bob. "Small World." In *The Penguin World Omnibus of Science Fiction*. Edited by Brian Aldiss and Sam J. Lundwall. Middlesex, England: Penguin Books, 1986, pp. 63-77. Story originally published in 1978.

Sheckley, Robert. "Paradise II." In *Time to Come*. Edited by August Derleth. 1954. New York: Pyramid Books, 1969, pp. 187-201.

Sheffield, Charles. "All the Colors of the Vacuum." *Analog Science Fiction/Science Fact*, 101 (February 2, 1981), pp. 60-86.

—. *Between the Strokes of Night*. New York: Baen Books, 1985. 346 pp.

—. "Dinsdale Dissents." *Galaxy*, 38 (July, 1977), pp. 112-122.

—. *The Nimrod Hunt*. New York: Baen Books, 1986. 401 pp.

—. "Skystalk." In *Great Science Fiction Stories by the World's Great Scientists*. Edited by Isaac Asimov with Martin Greenberg and Charles Waugh. New York: Donald I. Fine, Inc., 1985, pp. 52-71. Story originally published in 1979.

—. "Transition Team." In *The Endless Frontier, Volume I*. Edited by Jerry Pournelle. New York: Ace Books, 1979, pp. 325-351. Story originally published in *Destinies* (November-December, 1978).

—. *The Web between the Worlds*. New York: Ace Books, 1979. 274 pp.

Silent Running. Universal/Michael Gruskoff Productions/Douglas Trumbull Productions, 1971.

Silverberg, Robert. "Our Lady of the Sauropods." In *The Endless Frontier, Volume II*. Edited by Jerry Pournelle with John F. Carr. New York: Ace Books, 1982, pp. 139-156. Story originally published in *Omni* in 1980.

—. *Regan's Planet*. New York: Pyramid Books, 1964. 141 pp.

—. *World's Fair 1992*. 1970. New York: Ace Books, 1982. 240 pp.
Silverberg, Robert, and Barbara Silverberg. "Deadlock." *Astounding Science Fiction*, 63 (June, 1959), pp. 92-121.
Simak, Clifford D. *Empire*. New York: World Editions, 1951. 160 pp.
—. "Target Generation." In *Strangers in the Universe*. By Clifford D. Simak. New York: Simon and Schuster, 1956, pp. 69-109. Story originally published in 1953.
Simmons, Dan. *The Fall of Hyperion*. Garden City, New York: Doubleday, 1991. 517 pp.
—. *Hyperion*. Garden City, New York: Doubleday, 1989. 482 pp.
Siodmak, Curt. *City in the Sky*. New York: Putnam, 1974. 218 pp.
—. *Skyport*. 1959. New York: Signet Books, 1961. 159 pp.
Slote, Alfred. *Omega Station*. New York: Harper and Row, 1983. 147 pp.
Smith, Everett C., plot, and R. F. Starzl, story. "The Metal Moon." *Wonder Stories Quarterly*, 3 (Winter, 1932), pp. 246-259.
Smith, George O. *The Complete Venus Equilateral*. With an Introduction by Arthur C. Clarke. 1976. New York: Del Rey/Ballantine Books, 1980. 468 pp. Previous published, with fewer stories, as *Venus Equilateral*. New York: Prime Press, 1947.
—. *Venus Equilateral*. With an Introduction by John W. Campbell, Jr. New York: Prime Press, 1947. 455 pp. Originally published in *Astounding Science Fiction* in 1942, 1943, 1944, and 1945.
Smith, Robert. [pseud.] *Riders to the Stars*. Based on the screenplay by Curt Siodmak. New York: Ballantine Books, 1953. 166 pp.
Snodgrass, Melinda M. *Circuit*. New York: Berkley Books, 1986. 232 pp.
Solaris. Mosfilms, 1971.
Space Academy. New York: CBS, September 11, 1977 through September 1, 1979.
Space School. London: BBC-TV, 1956.
"Specimen: Unknown." *The Outer Limits*. New York: ABC-TV, February 24, 1964.
Stabenow, Dana. *A Handful of Stars*. New York: Ace Books, 1991. 215 pp.
—. *Second Star*. New York: Ace Books, 1991. 202 pp.
Starstruck. [unsold television series pilot] New York: CBS-TV, June 9, 1979.
Star Trek: The Motion Picture. Paramount, 1979.
Star Trek II: The Wrath of Khan. Paramount, 1982.
Star Trek III: The Search for Spock. Paramount, 1985.
Star Trek IV: The Voyage Home. Paramount, 1987.
Star Trek V: The Final Frontier. Paramount, 1989.
Star Trek VI: The Undiscovered Country. Paramount, 1991.
Star Wars. Lucasfilm/Fox, 1977.
Steele, Allan. *Clarke County, Space*. New York: Ace Books, 1990. 231 pp.
—. *Orbital Decay*. New York: Ace Books, 1989. 324 pp.
Sterling, Bruce. *Schismatrix*. New York: Arbor House, 1985. 288 pp.

—. "Spider Rose." In *Crystal Express*. By Bruce Sterling. Sauk City, Wisconsin: Arkham House Publishers, 1989, pp. 27-44. Story first published in *The Magazine of Fantasy and Science Fiction* in 1982.

Sterling, Bruce, and William Gibson. "Red Star, Winter Orbit." In *Burning Chrome*. By William Gibson. 1986. New York: Ace Books, 1987, pp. 80-102. Story originally published in 1983.

Stith, John E. *Memory Blank*. New York: Ace Books, 1986. 230 pp.

Stone, Josephine Rector. *Green Is for Galanx*. New York: Atheneum, 1980. 170 pp.

Sturgeon, Theodore. [formerly E. Hunter Waldo] "Unite and Conquer." *Astounding Science Fiction*, 42 (October, 1948), pp. 63-99.

Sucharitkul, Somtow. [now known as S. P. Somtow] *Mallworld*. 1981. Starblaze Editions. New York: TOR Books, 1984. 284 pp. Portions of the novel appeared as stories in 1979, 1980, and 1981.

Swanwick, Michael. "Ginungagap." In *Nebula Award Stories 16*. Edited by Jerry Pournelle. New York: Holt, Rinehart, and Winston, 1982, pp. 45-84. Story originally published in *TriQuarterly* 49 (Fall, 1980).

—. *Vacuum Flowers*. New York: Ace Books, 1988, 1987. 248 pp.

Sykes, S. J. *Red Genesis*. New York: Bantam, 1991. 358 pp.

Tannehill, Jayne. "Last Words." *Analog: Science Fiction/Science Fact*, 51 (May 25, 1981), pp. 60-69.

Taylor, John Alfred. "Grave-11." *Galileo*, 2, No. 13 (July, 1979), pp. 32-37.

Thomas, Theodore L. "Satellite Passage." In *SF: The Best of the Best*. Edited by Judith Merril. 1967. New York: Dell Books, 1968, pp. 169-179. Story originally published in 1958.

Thunderbirds in Outer Space. ITC Entertainment, 1981 [videocassette; date of theatrical release, if any, unknown].

Tiptree, James, Jr. [Alice Sheldon] "And I Awoke and Found Me Here on the Cold Hill's Side." In *Space Odysseys*. Edited by Brian W. Aldiss. 1976. New York: Berkley Books, 1978, pp. 129-137. Story originally published in 1972.

"The Trial of a Time Lord." *Doctor Who*. London: BBC-TV, September 6, 1986 through December 6, 1986 [14 episodes, also known as four separate adventures under the titles "The Mysterious Planet" (4 episodes), "Mindwarp" (4 episodes), "Terror of the Vervoids" (4 episodes), and "The Ultimate Foe" (2 episodes)].

"Trials and Tribble-ations." *Star Trek: Deep Space Nine*. Los Angeles: KCOP, November 2, 1996.

"The Trouble with Tribbles." *Star Trek*. New York: NBC-TV, December 29, 1967.

Tsiolkovsky, Konstantin. "The Aim of Astronautics." Translated by X. Danko. In *The Call of the Cosmos*. By Konstantin Tsiolkovsky. Edited by V. Dutt. Moscow: Foreign Languages Publishing House, [1960], pp. 333-372. Originally published in 1929.

—. *Beyond the Planet Earth*. [*Outside the Earth*] Translated by V. Talmy.

In *The Call of the Cosmos*. By Konstantin Tsiolkovsky. Edited by V. Dutt. Moscow: Foreign Languages Publishing House, [1960], pp. 161-332. Originally published in 1920.

—. "Changes in Relative Weight." [excerpt] Translated by A. Shkarovsky. In *The Call of the Cosmos*, by Konstantin Tsiolkovsky. Edited by V. Dutt. Moscow: Foreign Languages Publishing House, [1960], pp. 373-399. Story originally written in 1894.

—. *Dreams of Earth and Sky [and the Effects of Universal Gravitation]*. [excerpt] Translated by D. Myshne. In *The Call of the Cosmos*. By Konstantin Tsiolkovsky. Edited by V. Dutt. Moscow: Foreign Languages Publishing House, [1960], pp. 52-154. Originally published in 1895.

Tucker, Wilson. [Arthur W. Tucker, writing as Bob Tucker] "Interstellar Way-Station." *Super Science Stories* (May, 1941), pp. 94-101.

2001: A Space Odyssey. Metro-Goldwyn-Mayer, 1968.

Vance, Jack. "Abercrombie Station." *Thrilling Wonder Stories*, 39, 3 (February, 1952), pp. 10-47

Vinge, Vernor. "Long Shot." *Analog Science Fiction/Science Fact*, 89 (May, 1972), pp. 159-170.

Vinicoff, Eric. "Repairman." *Analog Science Fiction/Science Fact*, 104 (September, 1984), pp. 150-168.

Walsh, J. M. *Vandals of the Void*. *Wonder Stories Quarterly*, 2 (Summer, 1931), pp. 458-513.

Walters, Hugh. [Walter Hughes] *Terror by Satellite*. New York: Criterion Books, 1964. 159 pp.

War of the Planets. [*I Diafanoidi Portano la Morte*; also known as *I Diafandoidi Vergono da Morte*] Mercury Films International/Southern Cross Productions, 1965.

Watkins, William John. *The Centrifugal Rickshaw Dancer*. New York: Popular Library, 1985. 233 pp.

—. "Coming of Age in Henson's Tube." *In Isaac Asimov's Science Fiction Stories #1*. [No editor given] New York: Bonomo Publications, 1979, pp. 34-45. Originally published in *Isaac Asimov's Science Fiction Magazine* in 1977.

—. *Going to See the End of the Sky*. New York: Warner Books, 1986. 230 pp.

Webb, Sharon. "Itch on the Bull Run." In *Isaac Asimov's Science Fiction Treasury*. Edited by Isaac Asimov, Martin Greenberg, and Joseph Olander. New York: Bonanza Books, 1980, pp. 441-451. Story originally published in *Isaac Asimov's Science Fiction Magazine* (August, 1979).

Wellman, Manly Wade. "Space Station No. 1." *Famous Fantastic Mysteries* (September-October, 1939), pp. 27-36. Story originally published in *Argosy* in 1936.

Wells, Basil E. "Factory in the Sky." *Astonishing Stories*, 3 (September, 1941), pp. 68-74.

"The Wheel in Space." *Doctor Who*. London: BBC-TV, April 17, 1968 through June 1, 1968 [six episodes].

White, James. *Hospital Station*. 1962. New York: Ballantine Books, 1985. 191 pp.

—. *Sector General*. New York: Del Rey/Ballantine Books, 1983. 196 pp.

—. *Star Healer*. New York: Del Rey/Ballantine Books, 1984. 217 pp.

White, Ted. *Secret of the Marauder Satellite*. With an "Introduction to This Edition" by the author. New York: Berkley Books, 1978, 1968. 160 pp.

Wilcox, Don. "The Voyage That Lasted 600 Years." In *Skylife: Space Habitats in Story and Science*. Edited by Gregory Benford and George Zebrowski. New York: Harcourt, Inc., 2000, pp. 153-85. Story originally published in *Amazing Stories* in 1940.

The Wild, Wild Planet. [*I Criminali della Galassia*] Mercury Films International/Southern Cross Productions, 1965.

Williams, Ralph. "Bertha." *Astounding Science Fiction*, 52 (January, 1954), pp. 121-142.

Williams, Walter Jon. *Voice of the Whirlwind*. New York: TOR Books, 1987. 278 pp.

Williamson, Jack. *Beachhead*. New York: TOR Books, 1992. 368 pp.

—. "Born of the Sun." In *Before the Golden Age: A Science Fiction Anthology of the 1930s*. Edited by Isaac Asimov. Garden City, New York: Doubleday, 1974, pp. 461-495. Story originally published in 1934.

—. "Crucible of Power." *Astounding Science-Fiction*, 22 (February, 1939), pp. 9-32.

—. "Dead Star Station." In *The Early Williamson*. Garden City, New York: Doubleday, 1975, pp. 178-199. Story originally published in *Astounding Stories* (November, 1933).

—. "The Prince of Space." *Amazing Stories*, 6 (January, 1931), pp. 870-895.

Wylde, Thomas. "The Nanny." *Isaac Asimov's Science Fiction Magazine*, 7 (July, 1983), pp. 138-163.

—. "Space Shuttle Crashes!" In *Far Frontiers*. Fall 1985 Edition. Editors in Chief, Jerry Pournelle and Jim Baen. New York: Baen Books, 1985, pp. 244-266.

Wyndham, John, and Lucas Parkes. [Both pseuds. for John Beynon Harris] *The Outward Urge*. 1959. Middlesex, England: Penguin Books, 1962. 187 pp.

Yamin, Michael. "The Dreamers." *Astounding Science Fiction*, 40 (December, 1947), pp. 67-82.

Yates, W. R. *Diasporah*. New York: Baen Books, 1985. 307 pp.

Young, Robert F. "The Moon of Advanced Learning." *Isaac Asimov's Science Fiction Magazine*, 6 (September 28, 1982), pp. 111-122.

Zebrowski, George. *Macrolife*. New York: Avon Books, 1979. 281 pp.

II. Other Works Cited

Alexander, Kent. *The Space Station*. New York: Gallery Books, 1988. 136 pp.

"Another Shuttle? Not Now." Editorial in *The Los Angeles Times*, August 12, 1986, II, p. 4.

Asimov, Isaac, Charles G. Waugh, and Martin H. Greenberg, editors. *Isaac Asimov Presents the Best Science Fiction Firsts*. New York: Beaufort Books, 1984. 249 pp.

Benford, Gregory. *Across the Sea of Suns*. Timescape Books. New York: Simon and Schuster, 1984. 249 pp.

Bernal, J. D. *The World, the Flesh, and the Devil*. New York: E. P. Dutton & Co., 1929. 96 pp.

Blish, James. "Solar Plexus." *Astonishing Stories*, 3 (September, 1941), pp. 84-89.

Bova, Ben. *The High Road*. 1981. New York: Pocket Books, 1983. 277 pp.

Brand, Jonathan. "Encounter with a Hick." In *Dangerous Visions #3*. Edited by Harlan Ellison. 1967. New York: Berkley Books, 1969, pp. 102-107.

Brin, David. *The River of Time*. New York: Bantam Books, 1987. 295 pp.

Campbell, John W., Jr. "The Place of Science Fiction." In *Modern Science Fiction: Its Meaning and Its Future*. Edited by Reginald Bretnor. 1953. Chicago: Advent Press, 1979, pp. 4-22.

—. "The Science of Science-Fiction." *Space Magazine*, 1 (Winter, 1949), pp. 4-7, 21. Essay originally published in *Atlantic Monthly* (May, 1948).

Carr, Terry. "The Dance of the Changer and the Three." In *World's Best Science Fiction 1969*. Edited by Donald A. Wollheim and Terry Carr. New York: Ace Books, 1969, pp. 259-274. Story originally published in 1968.

Clarke, Arthur C. "Expedition to Earth." In *Expedition to Earth*. By Arthur C. Clarke. 1953. New York: Ballantine Books, 1976, pp. 125-137. Story originally published in 1953 as "Encounter in the Dawn."

—. "I Remember Babylon." In *Tales of Ten Worlds*. By Arthur C. Clarke. New York: Harcourt Brace Jovanovich, 1962, pp. 2-14. Article originally published in 1960.

—. "The Sentinel." In *Expedition to Earth*. By Arthur C. Clarke. 1953.

New York: Ballantine Books, 1976, pp. 155-165. Story originally published in 1951.

Cole, Dandridge M. *Beyond Tomorrow: The Next 50 Years in Space*. Amherst, Wisconsin: Amherst Press, 1965.

Franklin, H. Bruce. *Future Perfect: American Science Fiction of the Nineteenth Century*. 1966. Revised Edition. New York: Oxford University Press, 1978. 405 pp.

Froehlich, Walter. *Space Station: The Next Logical Step*. Washington, D.C.: Government Printing Office, 1984. 52 pp.

Gernsback, Hugo. "Imagination and Reality." *Amazing Stories*, 1 (October, 1926), p. 579.

—. *Ralph 124C 41+: A Romance of the Year 2660*. New York: Frederick Fell, Inc., 1950, 1925. 207 pp. Originally published in *Modern Electrics* in 1911 and 1912.

—. "Stations in Space." In *Air Wonder Stories,* 1 (April, 1930), p. 869.

Gibson, William. "The Gernsback Continuum." In *Burning Chrome*. By William Gibson. 1986. New York: Ace Books, 1987, pp. 23-35. Story originally published in *Universe II*, edited by Terry Carr, in 1981.

Gould, Stephen Jay. "Opus 100." In *The Flamingo's Smile: Reflections on Natural History*. By Stephen Jay Gould. New York: W. W. Norton & Co., 1987, pp. 167-184.

Hardy, Phil. *The Encyclopedia of Science Fiction Movies*. 1984. Minneapolis, Minnesota: Woodbury Press, 1986. 403 pp.

Heppenheimer, T. A. *Colonies in Space*. New York: Warner Books, 1977. 313 pp.

McCollum, Michael. "A Greater Infinity." *Analog Science Fiction/Science Fact*, 100 (November, 1980), pp. 10-54.

Moskowitz, Sam. *Explorers of the Infinite*. Cleveland, Ohio: World Publishing Co., 1963. 350 pp.

Nicholls, Peter. "Space Habitats." In *The Encyclopedia of Science Fiction.* Edited by John Clute and Peter Nicholls. New York: St. Martin's Press, 1993, pp. 1136-1137.

Niven, Larry. [Laurence van Cott Niven] *Ringworld.* New York: Ballantine Books, 1970. 342 pp.

O'Neill, Gerard. *The High Frontier: Human Colonies in Space*. 1977. New York: Bantam Books, 1978. 344 pp.

Pournelle, Jerry, with John F. Carr, editors. *Cities in Space: The Endless Frontier, Volume III*. New York: Ace Books, 1991. 259 pp.

Pournelle, Jerry, editor. *The Endless Frontier, Volume I*. New York: Ace Books, 1979. 376 pp.

—, with John F. Carr, editors. *The Endless Frontier, Volume II*. New York: Ace Books, 1982. 429 pp.

Shaw, Bob. *Orbitsville*. New York: Ace Books, 1975. 243 pp.

Sheckley, Robert. *Dimension of Miracles*. New York: Dell Books, 1968. 190 pp.

Sobchack, Vivian. *Screening Space: The American Science Fiction Film*.

Second, Enlarged Edition. New York: Ungar Publishing Co., 1987. 336 pp. Originally published as *The Winds of Infinity: The American Science Fiction Film, 1950-1975* in 1976.

Stapledon, Olaf. *Star Maker*. 1937. In *Last and First Men and Star Maker*. New York: Dover Books, 1968, pp. 247-438.

Stine, G. Harry. *The Space Enterprise*. New York: Ace Books, 1980. 226 pp.

Suvin, Darko. *Metamorphoses of Science Fiction: On the Poetics and History of a Literary Genre*. New Haven and London: Yale University Press, 1979. 309 pp.

—. "The Open-Ended Parables of Stanislaw Lem and *Solaris*." In *Solaris*. By Stanislaw Lem. Translated from the French by Joanna Kilmartin and Steve Cox. London: Faber & Faber, 1971, pp. 205-216. Novel originally published in 1961.

Swenson, Loyd S., Jr., James M. Grimwood, and Charles C. Alexander. *This New Ocean: A History of Project Mercury*. NASA SP-4201. Washington, D. C., 1966. 681 pp.

Varley, John. *Titan*. 1979. New York: Berkley Books, 1980. 309 pp.

von Braun, Wernher. "Crossing the Last Frontier." *Collier's*, 129 (March 22, 1952), pp. 24-30.

von Noordung, Hermann. *The Problems of Space Flying*. Translated from the German by Francis M. Currier. *Science Wonder Stories*, 1 (July, 1929), pp. 170-180; (August, 1929), pp. 264-272; and (September, 1929), pp. 361-368. Originally published in Germany as *Das Problem der Befahrung des Weltraums*. Berlin: R. C. Schmidt & Co., 1929. 188 pp.

Westfahl, Gary. "Inspired by Science Fiction." NOVA Online website, first posted April 21, 2000.
    At http://www.pbs.org/wgbh/nova/station/inspired.html.

—. "Islands in the Sky: Space Stations in the Universe of Science Fiction." In *Mindscapes: The Geographies of Imagined Worlds*. Edited by George Slusser and Eric S. Rabkin. Carbondale, Illinois: Southern Illinois University Press, 1988, pp. 211-225.

—. "'Man against Man, Brain against Brain': The Transformation of Melodrama in Science Fiction." In *Themes in Drama, Volume XIV: Melodrama*. Edited by James Redmond. Cambridge, England: Cambridge University Press, 1992, pp. 193-211.

—. *The Other Side of the Sky: An Annotated Bibliography of Space Stations in Science Fiction, 1869-1993*. Rockville, MD: Wildside Press, forthcoming.

—. "Small Worlds and Strange Tomorrows: The Icon of the Space Station in Science Fiction." In *Foundation: The Review of Science Fiction*, No. 51 (Spring, 1991), pp. 38-63.

—. "Space Stations and Space Habitats: A Selective Bibliography." In *Skylife: Space Habitats in Story and Science*. Edited by Gregory Benford and George Zebrowski. New York: Harcourt, Inc., 2000, pp. 333-

342.
Wolfe, Gary K. *The Known and the Unknown: The Iconography of Science Fiction*. Kent, Ohio: Kent State University Press, 1979. 250 pp.

Wollheim, Donald A. *The Universe Makers: Science Fiction Today.* New York: Harper Books, 1971. 122 pp.

Index

About the Author

GARY WESTFAHL received a B.A. in Mathematics and English from Carleton College and a Ph.D. in English from Claremont Graduate University. Recipient of the Science Fiction Research Association's Pilgrim Award for lifetime contributions to science fiction scholarship, he has to date written, edited, or co-edited twenty-two books on science fiction and fantasy, including the Hugo Award nominated *Science Fiction Quotations: From the Inner Mind to the Outer Limits* (2005) and the three-volume *The Greenwood Encyclopedia of Science Fiction and Fantasy: Themes, Works, and Wonders* (2005). He has also contributed over two hundred articles and reviews on science fiction and fantasy to scholarly journals and anthologies, the British science fiction magazine *Interzone*, the Locus Online and Internet Review of Science Fiction websites, and numerous reference works, including *The Oxford Companion to the History of Modern Science* and *The Cambridge Companion to Science Fiction*. He now lives in Claremont, California, with his wife Lynne and son Jeremy, and he teaches at the Learning Center of the University of California, Riverside, and for the University of La Verne's Educational Programs in Corrections.

www.ingramcontent.com/pod-product-compliance
Lightning Source LLC
Chambersburg PA
CBHW030919090426
42737CB00007B/242